IN THE EYE OF THE STORM

Herbert Strauss, Berlin, c. 1940

IN THE EYE
OF THE STORM

Growing Up Jewish in Germany,
1918–1943

A MEMOIR

HERBERT A. STRAUSS

FORDHAM UNIVERSITY PRESS
New York • 1999

41606204   1-21-03

Library of Congress Cataloging-in-Publication Data

Strauss, Herbert Arthur.
   In the eye of the storm : growing up Jewish in Germany, 1918–1943
: a memoir / Herbert A. Strauss.
      p.   cm.
   Includes bibliographical references and index.
   ISBN 0-8232-1916-X
   1. Strauss, Herbert Arthur.   2. Jews—Germany—Würzburg
Biography.
   3. Jews—Germany—Berlin Biography.   4. Holocaust, Jewish
(1939–1945)—Germany—Berlin Personal narratives.   5. Würzburg
(Germany) Biography.   6. Berlin (Germany) Biography.   I. Title.
943'.155004924'0092—dc21
   [B]   99-16618
                                                        CIP

Printed in the United States of America

אִם אֵין אֲנִי לִי מִי לִי.
וּכְשֶׁאֲנִי לְעַצְמִי מָה אֲנִי.
וְאִם לֹא עַכְשָׁיו אֵימָתַי.

If I am not for myself—
Who am I?
And if I am for myself alone—
What am I?
And if not now—
When?

From Mishna Nezikin, 4, Avot,
included in daily morning prayers in Pirke Avot.
Ascribed to Hillel Hazaken,
30 B.C.E.–10 C.E.

CONTENTS

ACKNOWLEDGMENTS

These memoirs attempt to recreate the last fifteen years of German Jewry seen through the eyes of a member of the Jewish community born into the "long-armistice period," 1919–39. They record the peak and the destruction of its late, sophisticated culture, and the murder of those who failed to escape in time. the threads that link their discontinuities together are my thoughts and feelings as I remember them from the perspective of eighty years of an intensely lived life. What understanding I have of the several planes of history intersecting in my story I owe to forty years of teaching and writing at the City College of New York and the Technical University of several fields of ancient and modern history. They influenced and enriched my work. I have tried to pass on and expand what I gratefully acknowledge as my debt to teachers, students, and colleagues in New York, Bern, and Berlin, to foundations, libraries archives, government agencies and their officials on two continents. Their civility helped me to restore the human capital that was destroyed in the Third Reich.

I am unable to single out more than a few individuals and organizations whose financial assistance made the publication and translation of this book possible: Research Foundation for Jewish Immigration, New York and its president, Dr. Curt C. Silberman; Grundkredit Bank Berlin; Eberhard Mayntz, Berlin; Michael Höbich, Berlin.

Aside from my personal collection of documents, letters, lecture notes, and transcripts, I was able to draw upon documents from the Attorney General of the State of New York; Bayerisches Staatsarchiv, Würzburg; Central Archives for the History of the Jewish People, Jerusalem; Eidgenössisches Bundesarchiv, Bern; Gedenkstätte Deutscher Widerstand, Berlin; International Tracing Center, Arolsen/Hanover; Jewish Historical Institute, Riga; Landesarchiv Berlin; Research Foundation for Jewish Immigration, Oral History Collection, New York; Schwurgericht Moabit, Berlin; Stauffenberg Gedenkstätte, Berlin; Universitätsarchiv, Würzburg; Wiener Library, London; Zentrum für Antisemitismusforschung, Berlin. I owe special thanks to my late teacher Ernst Grumach, Berlin, for removing lecture transcripts and documents from my unfurnished room in Berlin, Schlüterstrasse 53, in 1942, after the Gestapo had sealed it following my flight into hiding, and storing them in his Berlin apartment until his widow returned them to me in the mid-1980s. I thank the late Ulla von Hielmcrone for taking some of these documents through Nazi customs to Switzerland. I thank Irene Shiroun, Jerusalem, for giving me access to the papers left behind by her late father, Ernst Grumach. They relate to his years at the Hochschule für die Wissenschaft des Judentums, Berlin, 1936–1942. I thank Ilse Schöneberg, Lotte's aunt, for giving me the papers of Ludwig Schöneberg, Lotte's uncle. They concern the activities of Jean Friedrich, wartime delegate of the International Red Cross in Berlin, and Ludwig's links with Swiss military intelligence in wartime; I thank my mother Magdalena Strauss, Würzburg-New York, for saving her family photographs and documents from destruction in wartime Würzburg. I am also indebted to the following men and women for important information: Christiane Balogh-Keller, Berlin; Hildegard Bodländer-Berney, Haifa; Roland Flade, the author of the standard work on Jews in Würzburg; Renate Grumach, Berlin; Norbert Haase, Berlin; Christopher Hamann, Berlin; Ludwig von Hammerstein, Berlin; Vera Ipczynski, Berlin; Tilmann Krach, Mainz; Klaus Mayer, Berlin.

Very personal thanks belong to Daphne Dennis for her unfailing patience with the writing and correction of the manuscript and her empathy into the subject matter. The English original also profited from the publication of a German translation by Campus Verlag, Frankfurt am Main, Frank Schwerer, Publisher, Benedikt Burkard, editor, Bettina Abrabanell, translator—Frank's untimely passing ended a friendship of many years.

This English text owes its publication to the deep commitment of our friends Maria and Norman Marcus, New York, to seeing the memory of our generational experiences transmitted to our children, a token of our growing interfaith understanding. With great sensitivity Dr. Mary Beatrice Schulte and her colleagues at Fordham University Press helped to prepare the manuscript and to smooth out rough edges. Shortcomings, of course, remain the author's responsibility as does his gratitutde for the warmth and friendship that made it lighter to deal with the story of survival amidst destruction.

PREFACE

Between the end of the First and the Second World War, Jewish life in Germany achieved its greatest triumphs and suffered the greatest tragedy of Jewish, indeed of European, history. A differentiated culture and a vital society, for the first time in German history, had used the exciting civic freedom and the cultural dynamics of the Weimar Republic for fifteen short years, only to end in total annihilation. About one-third of the 550,000 Jews living in Germany when Hitler was intrigued into power in 1933 did not survive the mass murder the Nazi government perpetrated. The other two-thirds, excepting those who had died a natural death, fled abroad. In spite of the less than warm reception they often met with in their countries of refuge during those Depression years, they became one of the most creative international migration movements we know.

The first twenty-five years of my life in Germany spanned this world-historic epoch in philogenetic miniature, as it were. It had begun as an idyll and a dream, the protected youth of a middling South German town in a self-assured community and its religious life, the *juste milieu* family of a prosperous businessman and his young wife, life and death from God's hand, traditional Judaism more orthoprax than orthodox, Jewish village culture dating back centuries hesitantly entering the modern world. For a while, Nazism presented a manageable challenge. In the end, it called up a hectic struggle for survival. Coming out of this cauldron changed my personal life and my professional interests. That I fled Germany turned me into a refugee in Switzerland, an immigrant in the United States. Modern European history superseded my involvement in classical Judaism and ancient Greek thought. The last fifty years I have taught, researched, and written about the causes and consequences of what my generation had experienced. I understood survival as an obligation: "There but for the grace of God goes John Bradford." Yet, I did not become one of the Holocaust scholars whom I met in my work, at international conferences, among faculty. An early research experience at the New School for Social Research in New York had already brought me face to face in 1948–1951 with former inmates of Nazi concentration camps, and pointed my own research projects toward social history—it seemed too easy to dig into the masses of documents available on the perpetrators after the War and concentrate attention on the torturers and the killers.

I let fifty years go by before I would write this autobiographical account: I had been exposed to enough discontinuities to avoid the self-stylizations that are almost unavoidable in personalized history, and I had worked long enough in German and Jewish contemporary history Zeitgeschichte) to understand that what had happened to families and individuals had to be linked to the course of Nazi persecution and to the Jewish community's responses to it. The accident of my birth date and culture, and the incredible luck of my escape, had made me a small particle in a momentous historic drama, the flowering, and the fall, the destruction, of my civilization, German Jewish society and civilization, inflicted by a chaotic government enamored with death, in the end with its own death. The autobiographical form would contrast the surreal absurdity of being persecuted by criminals gone mad with the feelings and thoughts that were giving my own growth to maturity its inner meaning. I am proud that I did not buy my survival by compromising my convictions. Those who helped me survive—Christians and Jews—did not suffer damage or were not murdered because the enemy detected what they had done for me. Surviving was not because of my merit. My story should give those who perished a shadow of their unlived lives that would be cast deeper than their names on a thousand monuments. I would not abuse them for purposes alien to their lives and deaths. They would become me; our story would become a template in this fall and destruction of our community.

I had been involved in organized Jewish affairs in school and youth movement, and it determined the course of my life in Nazi Germany. I was in the eye of the storm. Community with others, in all its forms, was the prime condition of my ultimate survival in a swirl of lucky accidents. The help of good people that saved us assigns all collective guilt speculation to the garbage bins of historical explanations.

This book is dedicated to my wife of fifty years; I would not have survived and escaped without her.

1

German Jewish Piety: Würzburg, 1918–1929

THE JEWISH CEMETERY in Würzburg lies outside the limits of the city and the suburbs that used to define its urban space before World War II, on the road to Dettelbach or Rottendorf. It was set up as late as 1881. Before that, Jews used to bury their dead in villages like Höchberg, an old Jewish center of learning even though a village. We used to pass through it on our hikes. That cemeteries lay outside villages and places of settlement, or served more than one Jewish settlement, was customary, dictated by Christian intolerance or (in part) Jewish penury. The Würzburg cemetery has become the resting place of three generations of Strausses, grandparents Leopold and Ernestine, father Benno and mother Magdalena, brother Walther. Not precisely, though. Benno probably died in Treblinka gas chambers in June 1942. Magdalena died in New York in 1981. I had a memorial stone erected for my father, on my brother's grave, noting that he was murdered by the Nazis, and I buried the ashes of my mother with the silent acquiescence of the president of the Würzburg congregation, David Schuster, in the 1980s, on the site of my brother's grave.

My father's name is inscribed on a small and tasteful memorial that Kibbutz Chulatha erected in the 1980s on its ground for the parents of kibbutz members—my sister—killed in the Holocaust. My dissertation of 1946[1] is dedicated to the memory of my father and of my wife's parents, Louis Schloss and Johanna Bildesheim-Schloss, who were murdered in the Holocaust. The names of our parents appear several times in dedications of books or articles I have published, and in a large biographical compilation I directed. It records all Würzburg Jews, 1900–1945, including those deported

---

[1] Herbert A. Strauss, *Staat, Bürger, Mensch: Die Debatten der deutschen National-versammlung zu Frankfurt 1848–1849 über die Grundrechte* (Aarau: H. R. Sauer-länder Verlag, 1947), p. 5.

or killed by the Third Reich.[2] I said Kaddish after our dead in the small synagogue in Würzburg built after the war by the Würzburg congregation on the grounds of the (former Jewish) hospital, now defunct or destroyed, and the old age home attached to it since the 1920s. Their deaths were so senseless and abysmal a destruction of their lives and the order they lived in that this offers little relief for our grim memories. Still, they might have believed in a symbolic immortality such as granted by stone or printer's ink.

The Strauss ancestors lived in that relatively small region of minuscule Southern states that dotted the map of the German ancien régime before the first decade of the nineteenth century. They were ruled by a variety of petty jurisdictions and petty sovereignties before the Napoleonic period consolidated them into Bavaria, Baden, Württemberg, and some small leftover countries, duchies, or enclaves. But they had for centuries shared a common German Jewish religious culture, used a similar German Jewish dialect of German mixed with Hebrew and survivals of their medieval *Judendeutsch*, later identified as West-Yiddish. Their customs and their mentality, religious observances and holy calendar, had made them into one, unified communal culture. I was shaped by it and outgrew its forms, but salvaged its rich harvest of antiquity and sensitivity as I matured away from it, as if repeating the pattern of European and Jewish modernization philogenetically.

Our region stretched from the Rhein and Neckar area to beyond the Main. Its economy was rural in a fertile and lovely area of hills, small river valleys, open fields, and woods. The first Strausses my father traced for us in the 1930s, when ancestoring was the rage, were located in the "Jews-villages [*Judendörfer*] of Württemberg" in the eighteenth century, the earliest birth date entered being 1742. Like most of their fellow village Jews, they traded cattle and produce. At the time, the civilian register was kept by the village priest; there was no public registry as yet. My wife, Lotte, and I once visited the vicarage in Massenbachhausen, a village near Heilbronn, that had our oldest family documents. During the Third Reich, they were removed, like all other Jewish records of this kind, and "concentrated" in a castle, where they became inaccessible. A

---

[2] *Biographisches Handbuch Würzburger Juden, 1900–1945*, ed. Rainer Strätz, 2 vols. (Würzburg: F. Schöningh, 1989), 2:610–11.

Munich cousin, now an archivist in Bavaria, failed in tracing further back what my father had unearthed in the 1930s.

My grandfather was born in Heilbronn in 1826, the first step in our urbanization. He traded in skins and leather, a step up from cattle trading, became successful, moved to Würzburg in 1880 (my father was born in Heilbronn in 1876), and sired sixteen children in his long life, by two wives. All the women in the family except my mother were Jewish girls from the same rural area. Fertility declined from sixteen to three to one child to two children over four generations: from premodern economic and social conditions in a small-town setting to the effect of urbanization after a single generation; to ourselves oppressed by the poverty of immigration; to Jane's reaction to being the only child. I wish we had acted differently.

This was my paternal line of descent. My mother's line was Upper Bavarian Catholic. It had remained unexplored until recently when second cousin Stephan Janker, now a Bavarian archivist, traced his ancestors to a sixteenth-century municipal dignitary in the city of Regensburg. His ancestors may have helped to expel my father's ancestors or their relatives from Regensburg in 1519 when the city expelled its Jewish population for good. The surname of my Jewish great-grandmother, Judith Regensburger, born in Eppingen, a "free Imperial City," in 1792, suggests that her forebears were identified as "coming from Regensburg." The *terminus ad quem*—the last date—for Jewish residence in that city was 1519. Mother was one of five children, both her parents of small-town handicrafts background. I loved this grandmother, a beloved presence in our house, her gentleness honed by a lifetime of care and suffering.

All my mother's sisters were seared by the brutish social and political conditions of the twentieth century. One aunt, Kathi, lost her husband early to tuberculosis and spent the rest of her life around her church and a monastery. So did sister Theres (*sic*), whose husband also died early. A third sister, Louis (*sic*), saw her husband turned into a cripple. He had one leg amputated in World War I after being wounded on the Western front. The youngest sibling, a brother and a latecomer, whom the sisters considered a somewhat slow learner, became an optician.

Mother's family was the most supportive and helpful we had

throughout the Nazi period. It was not only that father had assisted them in many ways when he was still able to, or that they were guests in our home in Würzburg, that created this closeness. They acted not for the nation or for martyrdom in blazing acts of resistance that hide more than reveal civic courage: their humanism comprised religion, family loyalty, revulsion against the flashy brutality of the Nazi regime strutting across Munich in theatrical military gestures. You don't lose husbands to tuberculosis or a leg to the blood-soaked quarrels of the privileged to fall for phony glitter of this kind: you live subpolitically, as you have always lived, as most people had always lived and been controlled by the powerful. It creates a human closeness, the warmth of the home, women's cares, as their men are powerless to act against the forces outside. And I was included in the matter-of-fact loyalty and care in those small row houses—garden apartments in U.S. realtors' parlance—that still had space for refugees from remote politics. Many years later, in Berlin in the 1980s, some students wanted to discover a link between hiding Jews and the sense of victimization, whatever its origin or quality, among potential helpers.

Father and mother met in the Bavarian Alps, where our family would spend part of their summer vacation until the late 1920s. My mother, the photographs reveal, was a beautiful young woman at the time, dark-haired, bright-eyed, slim, olive-complexioned, as she would be until old age took its toll. She was eighteen years old then and eager to see the world beyond the narrow confines of her family. This was her first summer job right out of school. Father, fourteen years her senior, had returned four years earlier from "getting business experience" abroad; and when grandfather Strauss died shortly thereafter, father joined a machine-tool business in Frankfurt am Main, Kassewitz and Company (he was the company), reaching the goal of all commercial employees: "being independent," *selbständig*, being one's own boss. I presume he invested his inheritance, and used his foreign experience to import French and Swiss machinery for German factories.

As I picture him from the few photographs I remember from that period in my mother's treasure trove, from the record collection I perused *ad nauseam* as a very young child in Würzburg, and from my mother's occasional hints about their courtship, he was an energetic, warm-hearted thirty-two-year-old man, good-looking in a portly fashion with a ruddy, outdoor complexion, and he loved the good life of those prewar years, went to operas and operettas with her, visited the Würzburg and Munich theater, loved to travel, and appreciated the good wine whose harvest each year on the slopes rising around Würzburg occasioned good fellowship and good merrymaking. He had grown up a local boy, and retained numerous friendships with his Christian and Jewish fellow pupils in elementary and high school, the Oberrealschule, that prepared him for the "modern," nonhumanistic world of business and engineering. Many of these friendships would withstand the antisemitism of the Third Reich in the male bonding of the *Stammtisch*—the equivalent of the after-work Broadway bar of the Irish and would-be Irish of contemporaneous New York.

Although my father's war service at age thirty-nine (!)—January 1915 to December 1916, in the Bavarian Pioneer Corps, the *Train*—ended prematurely when he fell from a horse, the automobile accident of those days, he was able to serve his country by using his Swiss connections to import machinery for the German war effort.

My parents' romance must have deepened during his army service, but his family opposed a permanent union between Jew and Catholic. Mother spoke later of stormy family councils urging the separation of the lovers. My parents had a strong advocate in one of my uncles, whose name, Arthur, I was given as my first name on my birth certificate. (It turned into my initial from early on, when they called me by my middle name instead.) The union was finally accepted on condition that my mother agree to be instructed in the Jewish religion and be formally received into the Jewish community.

My father was an observant Jew in the manner of South German orthodoxy. The rest of his family—he had three brothers and three sisters by his father's second wife—had moved away from Würzburg and had settled in larger and less traditional towns. None had retained the religious observances of their father's house and of Würzburg orthodoxy. I was never able to ask my father about the background of his decision to conform to Würzburg norms.

My father's family divided geographically and socially into city uncles and country cousins. Five uncles and aunts had established families in cities on the periphery of our region like Nuremberg,

Frankfurt, Mannheim, Wiesbaden, and Karlsruhe. Our cousins lived
in our rural neighborhood in villages with names like Heidingsfeld,
Reichenberg, Mainbernheim, or Külsheim, slurred in daily speech
into diminutives and ellipses outsiders would not recognize. As far
as I know, no member of the clan ever moved permanently north
across the age-old political-cultural divide, the so-called *Mainlinie*.
Some may have emigrated to the United States of America to escape the repressive legislation of nineteenth-century Bavaria that
limited the number of marriages Jews could conclude and the number of houses they could own or live in in any village or town. I
found only faint and uncertain traces of such Strausses in immigrant letters of the nineteenth century preserved in archives. Both
branches of the family would meet only on rare occasions like wed-
dings, funerals, or *bar mitzvoth*. Long residence in a village or
town meant rooted identity. Migration was for the birds, not the
Strausses.

The extended family came alive on visits they paid us when they
were in town—they would be wined and dined in country tradition—and on our Sunday excursions into the neighboring forests
that would end at their homes, with similar honors done to us in
return. Like their ancestors, they still made their—often hard—
living by trading cattle and produce. They usually occupied a farm-
house in the village that was indistinguishable from the middling
farmsteads of their peasant neighbors: house and barn fronting the
street, a big wooden gate opening to the courtyard created by sta-
bles, haylofts, and chicken coops, giving access to the vegetable gardens beyond, past the water pump and trough and the heap of
manure where chickens scratched and roosters ruled. At times, before I was twelve years old and had become too snobbish for such
pleasures, I would spend the summer vacations with a relative, riding overland in his one-horse buggy, and witness his give-and-take
bartering with a peasant, and the handshake and schnapps that
would make the buggy driver drowsy on the way home, the horse
finding its stable door unaided. They would make me help in house,
garden, and stable, a first introduction to a life gone by, as their
children heeded the lure of education and glamour beckoning beyond their gates. Even without Nazi persecution, their way of life
was coming to an end, the German *Judendorf* equivalent of the East
European *shtetl*.

Relations with our city aunts and uncles offered different excitements and were rarer but no less warm and "family." Two of our families were headed by professionals, an apothecary, my protector Arthur, and a professor of business management at a Graduate School of Commerce, the *Handelshochschule* in Nuremberg, the Hungarian-born, Rosenfeld, husband of Aunt Else. The three other families were headed by a jute manufacturer, a traveling salesman whom others used to tease benevolently for his lack of defenses, the shlemiel of the family, and a machine-tool dealer of substantial wealth. They were the kind of successful and civilized families the Nazis loved to hate. Compared to home, Judaism had become marginal in the intellectually and socially grounded liberal style of Southern German politics and taste. They trusted the European traditions of South German liberal Christians, their peers. This trust would render them totally unable to defend themselves against the abysmally mean scum who would ultimately murder them.

Visiting and staying with these aunts and uncles for shorter or longer periods during vacations generally did not create strong emotional bonds, because my cousins, their children, belonged to an "older generation": their parents had married a decade before my parents. The exception was cousin Ilse, for whom I took several bicycle trips through the Odenwald to Mannheim. The most cherished and possibly most influential emotional memory of these pre-adolescent years is linked with brown-haired, dark-eyed, warmhearted Babette Uhlfelder, the mother of a cousin of my age, who would die tragically early in New York in the 1970s. Babette and my mother would shape my ideas of humanity and feminine beauty into complementary and compatible images.

The several family strains I was living in did, of course, represent differences in thought and style as symbolized by these two women, but I felt them, like their images, as complementary, and experienced being German, orthodox, liberal, Jewish, as elements of my life and environment. The differences were individual, not ethnic.

My mother had a deep sense of the emotional significance of religion, although she was reared in the liberal mold of big-city Catholicism in Munich. I always felt her religious temperament more direct, closer to the core of the religious experience, more questioning about the place of religion in the popular enlightenment that dominated public culture when she was growing up. She was instructed for at least a year by the gentle and humane Würzburg rabbi, Dr. Sigmund Hanover, who had been called to the Würzburg pulpit from his Rhineland congregation of Cologne. At the end, the traditional three-men rabbinical college found her prepared enough in Hebrew, the Jewish calendar, and customs to head a ritually proper—kosher—household, in the use of the prayer-books, and in bringing up Jewish children, to be accepted into the community. She became a woman *ger zedek*, a just stranger, who accepts what tradition calls the "yoke of the law" in full measure. She would take on the brunt of persecution, murder of her husband, family destruction, ruin of her life's work, uprooting at an advanced age, and, finally and ironically, the loss of all her possessions during the devastating Royal Air Force air raid on Würzburg on March 16, 1945. She was one of the many heroines among converted Christians whose untold stories would add up to a saga of deep loyalty to the quickly fading memory of Jewish life in Germany. I myself was very conscious of her life when I was called upon later on, during my studies in Bern, Switzerland, to serve as a member of the three-man gremium of experts admitting Swiss Christian brides to Judaism under the guidance of my late friend Rabbi Eugen Messinger.

Rabbi Hanover succeeded with mother beyond what could have been expected had she and father not taken their religious duties meticulously. As a result, I grew up in a kosher, orthodox-conservative household, South German style. My mother (and the household aides then called *Dienstmädchen*, service girls) kept two sets of dishes for meat- and milk-based food, and two different sets for the Passover period, when unleavened bread was prescribed. She gave us all the Sabbaths and holiday ceremonies, and kept a huge coal-burning stove, informally called a *Grude*, in the kitchen beside the gas range, in which precooked food for the Sabbath could be kept hot (or warm) since the law forbids lighting a fire—any fire—on the Sabbath.

I remember my mother's attitude toward Judaism as in some ways more respectful, more concentrated, than my father's and probably my own. Some modern Jewish attitudes differ significantly from Christian usages. Originally, Jews preserved the medieval tradition of opening houses of worship to some everyday activities. Numerous Italian and Dutch church paintings reflect this. The synagogue was the meeting house, the educational center (*shul*), a place for donating funds for charitable or communal purposes, even a place where travelers or migrants, whatever their condition in life, could expect to be invited for a Friday evening or a Sabbath meal, even for a bed to sleep in. When the congregation offered them a more professionalized social service through its aid to migrants (*Wanderfürsorge*), only the very pious would still invite poor travelers to their houses; it was considered a religious duty, a *mitzvah*, to offer hospitality to wayfarers (*hakhnasat orhim*). Part of the service consisted of the cantor's reading Scripture, which, over the years, a good Jew would be fairly familiar with. During part of the Scripture reading (the *haftarah*, excerpts from prophetic books) a person might leave the building; in short, the community aspect of being Jewish would assert itself frequently in the course of the ritual year. Mother understood that being Jewish was being part of the community and interacting with it, even at worship, but she remained a model of pious concentration with her prayerbook while we children would do less proper things like whispering or being unruly.

Even with such offenses against strict discipline, our German Jewish services differed from the services held by our immigrant community from Eastern Europe. In the 1920s, we had a relatively small congregation of Jewish immigrants from Eastern Europe. They wished to continue the religious services they were accustomed to at home—the deep-seated emotions linked to "sacred ethnicity"—and the established congregation, the *Gemeinde*, acceded to their wishes. They voted for Gemeinde representation, and elected a member of their own party in the later 1920s. In summer, with all the windows open, we could hear their services across the courtyard from the synagogue the Gemeinde built for them in a remodeled large room in the schoolhouse. Friendships with their children and comradeships in school helped to overcome the reservations our parents' generation had about the differences in language, customs, and vitality between the "German" and the "Eastern" Jew.

As it was, the Jewish style of religious services differed from the more rigid formalisms we were able to observe in Catholic churches when the Dienstmädchen would take us along—against parental prescription, of course. To my delight, I discovered much later in a New York dissertation[3] that the forces of law and order in German

---

[3] Herman Pollack, *Jewish Folkways in Germanic Lands, 1648–1806*, Studies in Aspects of Daily Life (Cambridge, Mass.: The MIT Press, 1971), pp. 146–56.

Jewish congregations had complained since the sixteenth century about the indecorous behavior of our forebears when Judaism was still folksy and congregations assertive—a tradition preserved to some extent by our immigrant community.

The three children who issued from my parents' love affair were thus brought up in our father's traditional orthopraxy and his continuous involvement in the two worlds that formed the German and the Jewish culture of his hometown, inextricably intertwined, and in my mother's respect for the commitment she had taken upon herself without reservation. She was probably the more enduring influence on us: father would commute between our home in Würzburg and the seat of his business in Frankfurt, about a hundred miles away by an easy train ride, so that for four or five days of the week she controlled our lives with a firm, if benevolent, hand. My brother was easier and more lovable as children go, from their parents' perspective, or so I remember. He was a gentle boy, not very athletic or physical, a cuddly child of a quiet temperament, a nature lover, and a homebody. Because my mother was quite preoccupied with nursing my father's mother, Grandmother Uhlfelder, during her last prolonged bed-ridden debility, I grew up gloriously untrammeled by too-minute supervision. Our house was built on a relatively steep hill overlooking fields, gardens, and the railroad tracks Würzburg/Nuremberg or /Munich, at the edge of a town that managed to become a *Grosstadt* (100,000 inhabitants and over) only by incorporating a nearby village, in about 1930. Mass automobile traffic was still over the horizon. Thus, from age four to seven, until school began, about half-a-dozen enterprising boys from our (well-educated and well-to-do) neighborhood found each other in common curiosity and lived in that nostalgically remembered fantasy land of cops and robbers, Apaches and trappers, or lizards and beetles—especially during the month of May when the competition was on for the championship of shaking the largest number of *Maikäfers* off the trees on top of the hill. About thirty minutes away, as six-year-old feet carry you, was an airfield where small propeller-driven planes and gliders took off from grassy runways you still walked across untrammeled. It fell to me to protect my brother against whatever taunts would come his way when he did not come up to boyish standards or failed to fight back. I did the fighting for him, and it set the tone of our relationship. I half-admired him for walking to the tune of a different drummer, a shortcoming compensated for by my bodyguard function, and at times I remember envying him for the attention my mother gave him, especially after he began to suffer from rheumatoid joints. He died of peritonitis following an appendix operation at age eleven. He was two years my elder, and I had at the time what I recognize today as ambivalent feelings about him.

As a result of such glorious freedom, the boy who started school at age seven thus carried the marks of a German Jewish cultural fusion—if the word "culture" is appropriate—in a most idiosyncratic way. Given the loose if intermittently emphatic parental supervision of these preschool years, I must have been something of an antidisciplinarian. To my enduring annoyance, as a preschooler, I was forced earlier to go to a Jewish kindergarten for a short time whose lady teachers made their charges lie down and sleep after lunch, something I had hardly ever managed in my life thus far. I hated their bunkbeds and their soups and gruels—it was superinflation when I was forced to go there—and food and money were expensive or scarce. I remember the good kindergarten teachers as repressive, although they followed what, in retrospect, I recognize as progressive educational doctrine in caring for us at the time. I may well have been a hyperactive child.

By then, I had acquired a second language, as it were, the softly lilting Lower Franconian vocabulary and pronunciation of my semirural environment. Our maid contributed to this local timbre. Regina, one of the sturdy daughters of a Helmstadt well-to-do peasant, who had not found a husband in her village or in the neighborhood, had taken a position with us that gave her a respected and independent life and a veto-like co-direction in the upbringing of the children. She loved to frighten us with indeterminate objects from her large, dark kitchen that looked like animal innards, or other distasteful objects, and I left beetles in appropriate places for her in exchange. Her room was on the top floor of the house beside our children's room. She went to church regularly and was, no doubt, a pious soul. At one point in the late twenties or early thirties, she married our "*Gasmann*," who came by regularly to read the utilities meters in the cellar. He joined the Nazi Party and, consequently, Regina broke off relations with us to appease her new master. At least she did not try to convert us to Catholicism as her successor would until found out and fired. At regular intervals, a washerwoman would appear, to do the laundry in the laundry room in the cellar in enormous cast-iron vats that had to be heated by coal fire from a grate below. Twice a year our gardener—Hammelbacher—would come to prune roses, plant flowers, and trim hedges and trees. A corner of the garden was turned over to me to plant my cactuses, an early love, and to try to bring them over the snowy season covered with pine twigs. Our German shepherd dog, Wotan (*sic*), had his own doghouse built into the cellar wall. The garden yielded small quantities of fruit and vegetables and large amounts of delicious plums.

If there were tensions and social snobbery built into this half-suburban, half-rural playground, I would not have noticed. Until kindergarten and school I did not have Jewish playmates in the neighborhood, even if I became acquainted with my peers in the congregation during our regular weekly and holiday attendance at the synagogue services. My memory retains childhood frights and childhood triumphs, temporary fears and phobias, the soothing tenderness of a mother, the comradeship of a father who was forty-two years old at my birth and compensated well for it in time spent with the children. Those postwar years, oscillating between the self-inflicted German inflation and the equally self-inflicted deflationary policies that followed, could not have been easy years for the family, although it prospered until the Great Depression destroyed my father's business. These may well have been their last happy years, the afterglow of Benno's love for Magdalena and the emotional security that may have come to us from such fulfillment. In 1923, when my sister was born, and father's wish for a daughter was belatedly granted, I entered school and gained a new circle of friends.

I arrived at school a year later than the usual entering age of six, because my birthday occurred a few weeks after the cutoff date, May 1. I am eternally grateful to the educational bureaucrat who refused to make an exception for me and to set the date aside—what mother would not try to gain time in the race for education and success? My school was a peculiar German/Jewish hybrid, a government-administered parochial school offering both Jewish religious education and Hebrew language instruction and the full curriculum of a public school. Originally a private school offering religious instruction only, it added a full curriculum, and in 1921 it was incorporated into the Bavarian state school system, a combination not unusual in German education aimed at weaning Jews away from their "inferior habits" before granting them full civic equality.

The school was part of a group of buildings forming a walled-in compound. At its center was the synagogue—built in 1838–41 as a rather tasteful and straightforward rectangular building in the local yellow limestone. It had the clean, simple functionalism of the stripped-down government buildings of Munich's Ludwigstrasse. The government building commission of the time had specified that it be built in the "Egyptian style," but the building I remember (renovated in 1926) suggested this only in a few decorative motifs sparingly used. My school was housed on the third floor of a plain building behind the synagogue and separated from it by a courtyard that served us for recess. The building also housed the Gemeinde administration and its social services, a ritual bath, and the prayer room for our immigrants from Eastern Europe. It also had apartments for Fräulein Blum and her helper, the caretakers of the bath, and an apartment for a teacher.

When my mother arrived with me at the school in May 1925, armed with a colorful papier-mâché cone filled with chocolate and candies, I received the usual intelligence test: Herr Direktor Mandelbaum asked me to identify a rooster on a prewar advertising poster which I found rather strange: did he not know it was a *Gockel* (colloquial for rooster)? The school did not attract enough pupils, and had collapsed the first four grades into two, one-room–schoolhouse fashion. I do not remember much of the three Rs we were taught, well enough, it seems, to pass the entrance examination to the *Gymnasium* after four years. My teacher for the first two grades, Fräulein Ottensoser, had discipline problems with me: I was an active, maybe hyperactive, child and soon found myself bored in the classroom, and I would stare out of the window at the pigeons on the roof of the synagogue. It may have been an attention deficiency, an as yet unidentified problem. I also developed a habit of interrupting conversations, because I understood what the speaker wanted to say after his or her first few words and answered before he or she could finish speaking. There were no classes for fast learners, and my mind was on sports.

Moritz Hellmann, the teacher in grades three and four, remains more strongly etched in my memory. He taught me the rudiments of Hebrew grammar so well that I developed a liking for grammatical analysis that was most helpful in studying several other languages later on. He was also the choir director and music teacher, and during the nearly six years I sang in the synagogue choir, I found real pleasure in choral music and in his rudimentary formal analysis of the scores. I remember also his sympathy for some of my childish religious experiences, confined as they were by the framework of the sacred calendar subdividing the year. He had served in the Bavarian army and been discharged after four years of combat duty as a noncommissioned and decorated officer—his decorations were of a higher order than Hitler's Iron Cross Second Class. His army service may have made him into the stern disciplinarian he appeared to us; he may have been the last Jewish parochial school teacher in Germany who used the rod, in two degrees, to punish serious or grave transgressions, like kicking in windows with a soccer ball or defending oneself too vigorously against imagined slights. Like all schoolboys, we, of course, had effective, ironic defenses against the shame such public "humiliations" were supposed to produce, but Herr Hellmann did not know how ineffective his system really was.

The Jewish religious instruction given at the school was part of the traditional *Lebenswelt* (milieu) that had been created by the local pattern of religious observances, baked into a cake of custom. A child would be integrated into several significant spaces. Every week and on all religious holidays, the family gathered around a festive table for blessings and benedictions. Children were blessed by their father and received wine and bread; mother prepared and served the meal, lighted candles, and said her prayers. Passover would unite the family in a more extended commemoration of the Exodus from Egypt. The entire evening was built around children, who were to learn the meaning of symbolic food and didactic and moralistic poetry, and taught to ask the right questions on religious customs. On Sukkot, the Feast of Tabernacles, children had a hand in decorating the *sukka*, the wooden hut in the garden each fall. For an entire week, the family would take all its daily meals in it. Children were properly admired for whatever artwork they had contributed, and partook in the holiday blessings. Children also shared in the services celebrating the inheritance of our Bible (Torah), the feast of Chanukkah (home gaming and gift-giving), the Feast of

Purim (amateur theatricals, masquerades, carrying alms to the poor, general merrymaking).

The synagogue was the "official" space for communal service, and had come to resemble Protestant churches in its stress on decorum, orderliness, and choir singing; in Reform synagogues there was also organ or other instrumental music. Würzburg services had assimilated all these features except instrumental music. The Gemeinde also employed a law-and-order beadle attired in a semimilitary uniform to keep unruly children in check. (Choir boys were unsupervised between performances.) Still, our services retained traces of older functions of what used to be known as *"beth haknesset"*—meeting house—the original meaning of the Greek word "synagogue": the courtyard surrounding the building hummed with worshipers allowed to absent themselves from certain readings to obey calls of nature. During routine recitations, some would whisper with their neighbors; in principle, anybody who felt aggrieved by an unredeemed offense could step up and ask that the service be stopped and communal attention paid to the issue. (It never happened—this was order, after all.) Assisting in the reading of the Torah section due in weekly or holiday sequences allowed for benedictions bestowed on friends or relatives and for announcing pledges to charities or the Gemeinde. Bar mitzvah—coming of age at thirteen—combined public and private celebrations, with the community of worshipers drawn into visiting and gift-giving: the candidate was expected to recite the Scripture portion at hand that day in correct Hebrew—Torah scrolls did not include vowels in their handwritten text—and the correct chanting (*Sprechstimme*) set to ancient notations. Women did not take an active part in the services; they prayed segregated from men (and boys) in the women's compartment, a balcony running around three sides of the room, and were separated by wire-mesh shutters that I never once saw closed. Choir singing gave me ample time to greet mother and scan the rows for schoolmates and acquaintances. Women's formal roles were, of course, inherited from a patriarchal liturgical past, but the lower status articulated in the morning prayers for everyday was long overruled by the secular development toward equality of bourgeois society in nineteenth- and twentieth-century Germany.

Finally, my father took me along to communal services outside the synagogue such as marriages, or services in houses where

mourners were required to stay at home for seven days and symbolize their mourning in several traditional ways. During this time,
pious men (over thirteen years of age) would visit for morning and
evening services. I have distinct memories of laymen reading from
the oral tradition and weaving warm-hearted and naïve-sounding
commentaries into their textual interpretations. I remember pas-
sages they read and interpreted that were meant to help the
mourner overcome his grief and reconcile himself to God's provi-
dence which, no doubt, helped prevent a terrible fate that may have
been in store for the deceased. Theirs was a perfectly cohesive
world, the "world in its proper order," the helping hand of folk
wisdom stretched out by the community and taking the loneliness
away from the mourner who returned to its embrace. I believe that
memories of this experience—the dark rooms, the earnest men, the
mourners, the thought of the dead, the sense of loss overlaid with
homey wisdom, the moral lessons reaching the listener with the
warmth of an effortless certainty—tended to linger on into later
years with the silent moods of a childhood remembered and lost,
the security of a world explained, life "in order."

Much as my memory has stored these images alive in my feelings,
more than the often contentious or petty realities of communal life,
I spent most of my time in the several sports to which I became
addicted during my school years. It probably started with my preschool paradise, tolerated or encouraged by a mother who had her
hands full nursing our ailing grandmother. The grade school (*Israelitische Volksschule*) had no gym. I remember no physical exercise
classes except frequent trips to points of educational value in town.
After I had learned to swim in a swimming pool (*Schwimmbad*) in
the Main River, swimming became a major pleasure through the
years. An island upstream housed a *Naturheilverein*, and after my
father presented me with a bicycle, junior-size, and had one of his
workers give me a few lessons in a quiet street along the *Glacis* park,
I spent much carefree time on the island and in the water, in loose
contacts with boys my age. The new toy became indispensable, a
transportation revolution probably incomprehensible to the auto-
motive late twentieth century. It cut the time to reach school from
home into a fraction of its previous time and made me an express
messenger and shopper for the family; you could give friends, boys,
then girls, a ride on its crossbar, a *verboten* pleasure; it created a new

sociability as we took trips to distant cities in groups of two or three. In 1934 or 1935, I took my first "love trip" to visit a cousin, Ilse, in Mannheim, about a hundred miles away, a day's trip across often hilly terrain. There were as yet few automobiles on the road, and on overnight trips we would stay with family and Jewish friends to avoid possible unpleasantness. Some of the friendships that brought us together on these trips would last a lifetime.

The major passion of those years would develop when I entered high school (the *Gymnasium*). Its curriculum prescribed gymnastics and team sports. The gym (*Turnhalle*) was stocked with the traditional equipment; we marched in formation and ran the distances. The prescribed game was a variant of stickball, probably without any historic connection with baseball and without its cerebral decision-making tensions. The primary interest was, of course, soccer in all its forms, from boys kicking balls around the street to watching the two rival Würzburg clubs playing in one of the leagues. Because we lived close to the field of one of the soccer clubs (the *Kickers*), I would spend many a Sunday afternoon at their games in the company of other boys from the neighborhood. I also collected cards, distributed by cigarette manufacturers, I believe, depicting the international football heroes of the day.

This entire sports culture played an important role in forming my attitudes and values and fed into the habit of *Gemeinschaft* (communality) I absorbed when I entered a youth organization after 1933. Except for school, I was free of any links with organized sports until a year or two into the Third Reich, when I was drawn into the effort to organize a Jewish sports club.

Except for some external restraints in time and space of play, sports offered freedom from supervision, camaraderie under accepted and internalized rules, close touch with nature and the seasons. I fell into these activities quite spontaneously, I believe, but was probably guided by my parents because I had not been expected to live when I was born. (The midwife, on meeting mother and me on the street when I was about six years old, asked: "Was that the kid we did not think we could get through?") I also had been dogged by poor wartime and postwar medical practices during my first year or two (contaminated inoculation serum or equipment in 1918–19 Würzburg). It would have struck me as outlandish to see anything political or ideological in such activities. But with 1933 they both intruded: a Jewish businessman who had cofounded and sponsored a local soccer club befriended me and told me that the Nazis had forced the club to expel him. It had been his life. In 1934 or 1935, I was made to join a training cell preparing potential competitors for a spot on the German Olympic team of 1936: the International Committee had pressured Berlin to offer Jews an equal chance to compete, and Berlin complied to escape unwanted publicity as Germany rearmed and needed foreign currency. It was a farce, of course: Jews had been booted out of all clubs in 1933–34, and all Germany fell on its face obeying the "*Arierparagraph*." My alibi function did not last long, because I refused to give up swimming and boating as required for the field-and-track training I received a few times a week in the idyllic amateurism about to be buried by Nazis and Soviets alike. Politics also brought about Jewish sports clubs in the 1920s when self-defense and virility were considered, by Zionists and non-Zionists alike, elements of Jewish assertion against antisemitism. Most Jewish youngsters belonged to one or another of the Würzburg gymnastics, fencing, ski, athletics, Alpine soccer, etc. clubs, and were considered publicity assets against Nazism by the Jewish community. In fact, probably the best Würzburg soccer player, Walter Hersch, was Jewish, and duly noted as such by friends and foes. After all these clubs were dissolved in 1933, the government permitted a "nonpolitical" Jewish sports association in Bavaria, probably thinking that it would foster emigration. I knew nothing of these calculations, of course, and helped build a sports arena and soccer field north of the town in the Main valley as a communal duty. The dedication proved my nemesis, as I was allowed to start in two middle-distance races in the adult division (I won both) and promptly came down sick with an attack of pleurisy six weeks later. I learned or believed I had learned the limits of physical endurance and, in another way, had enough school free time to begin reading histories of philosophy, a major break in my education. I still kept playing soccer with our team and took part in regional or statewide competition among Jewish gymnastics and sports clubs, as they had to be called by government fiat. I would miss the friendships and the camaraderie of my teammates and of men like Alfred Günzburger, who knew so much about the human aspects of sports. When I left town in 1936, I was ready to rely on physical agility to see me through whatever came.

In this respect, at least, I remember my childhood and adolescence as private and happy, a sense of movement and growth, more Thomas Mann's Hans Hansen than his Tonio Kroeger.

Similarly, there was no conflict in our house between our ex-Catholic mother and our Jewish father. Neither was an intellectual, if the word means habitually dealing with abstract ideas, art, or theoretical issues of religion and morality. Father may have had more years of formal schooling for his business career at the Würzburg *Realschule*, and he certainly had seen more of Germany, Europe, maybe the world overseas than my mother had. Our record collection suggested that they both enjoyed opera and operetta during the years of their courtship and the short years of prosperity of the Weimar Republic when they had moved to our villa—it was sold in 1932, at the height of the Depression in Germany, after my bar mitzvah in June 1931. My mother retained her ability to learn and absorb quickly all through her life. In this country, she learned English in night courses given in New York schools when she was well over sixty years of age, fighting sleep and taking notes in her clean handwriting, and she passed the "examination" for U.S. citizenship for proficiency in English and the American Constitution before a smiling judge in New York in the 1950s. He saw a Jewish mother looking back at a life of troubles and still not giving up. It was, in fact, a charming occasion. Lotte and I were witnesses and towers of calm, while a lifetime of panic in dealing with officialdom and its life-threatening authority confused all mother had learned about the Constitution. We had agreed that mother would answer all questions with "yes" unless I would tug at her sleeves when she was supposed to say "no." Well, she managed to the point where she got overconfident and enunciated her consent before she had even heard the question. Mother did confess, on that occasion, that she indeed wanted "to overthrow the government by force and violence." As the judge looked smilingly over his glasses, and I nudged her, mother quite composedly corrected herself with several hasty "No-noes," and saved the day.

In Würzburg, she would regularly visit the lectures given in one of the hospitals close to where Roentgen had discovered x-rays in the nineteenth century. But because she was allergic to the smell of ether, then used in giving anesthesia, she would at times faint and be sent home by ambulance. I sympathized, because I had such an-

esthesias several times in my own life, including after a sports accident, and hated the smell, too.

I do think that my mother was ambitious not only for us but also
for herself, and that she had the more acute observation and the
faster mind, even if life had confined her to smaller worlds than
would be usual today. My father was an avid newspaper reader and
Stammtisch debater, and he loved adventure and detective stories,
but by the time I was able to understand what his values were I had
left Würzburg for Berlin. He was then sixty years old, I was eighteen. He was born and bred in town, possessed of the Dickensian
stolidity his rather portly figure suggested. As a matter of habit, he
would take his glass of wine (or beer) with a mostly non-Jewish
round of friends, like him natives of the town, and school chums, of
middling wealth and unshakable self-righteousness and respectability. I think that most of his friends stuck with him during the Nazi
years. He also had broad respect in the Jewish community. We had
a kosher household, but I tend to think we did not all that strictly
subordinate ourselves to the fine points of the code. We exchanged
flatware and dishes for Passover to avoid contamination with leav-
ened bread or non-*pessachdige* (Judendeutsch for Passover-exclusive
and -worthy) utensils. We bought only kosher meat and ate neither
pork nor eel, examples of forbidden dishes, and my mother properly
immersed the meat in water for hours, after salting it thoroughly to
obey the injunction against consuming blood. We did not travel or
ride a bike or public conveyances on the Sabbath, and, during all
my six years at the Neue Gymnasium Würzburg, the three Jewish
members of my class, including me, were excused every Sabbath of
the school year from writing or taking examinations. Writing was
forbidden as well for its suggestion of working, and the Sabbath
was the most tyrannically dominant cause for injunctions that active
children like me found often quite limiting. Yet, only my sister, not
I, dared to break the rule against riding a bicycle on Sabbath and
she brought a firestorm upon herself in consequence.

My father was not learned in Jewish matters. His piety was dictated by the milieu that had shaped him since his youth and that
gave his life meaning and form—or at least during the later years of
his life when I was growing up. Culture had created this German
Jew in the image of the habits of his hometown. He was a businessman all his life, dealing with machine tools new and used, and dur-

ing World War I was used by the Bavarian army command to help procure Swiss machine tools for German/Bavarian industry. Since Nazi ideologues cast aspersions on such activity as profiteering later on, it is clear that the fatherland behaved dastardly toward him, in spite of the fact that he had served at the front. It must have been a significant experience for him. I used to play with his cavalry dress sword and the loaded six-shooter he kept in our dining-room cupboard, a room used only for formal occasions. In about 1928, I discovered the gun, played with it, and nearly shot myself in the head when I accidentally discharged a bullet. It lodged in the wall above a staircase leading to the second floor. A narrow escape, and a great fright for my parents.

Well, then, my parents' values at the time must have been quite conventionally Franconian small-town. My mother was apolitical and carried images of the Bavarian royal house, the Wittelsbacher, in her head. She spoke of Ludwig II, the king who was murdered, so she believed, by his physician and a cabal of his enemies in the palace. That long remained Bavarian folklore. During the 1920s, my father used to attend reunions of his military regiment in a Würzburg beer garden, and we were supposed to cheer for a man with a white flowing beard—Bavarian royalty. My parents were not serious monarchists; they had no very deep political convictions except against Nazism and Hitler and his ilk. I cannot judge whether they understood the danger of Nazism in time. For years after Hitler seized power, father would predict that for "good economic reasons," and because "the Allies" would not tolerate him, Hitler would fall within six weeks of the date. Father had voted Social Democratic after the Revolution of 1918 and the establishment of the Weimar Republic, and although his wide newspaper reading also included the Communist press his friend the newspaperman would pass on to him, together with the liberal-business *Frankfurter Zeitung*, his intellectual makeup precluded unconventional political ideas or attitudes.

Whatever the emotional strains may have been that accompanied my growing up, or the frustrations and tensions that beset my idyll when the economic depression destroyed my father's business independence, they were contained within the religious culture of family and community and the space I was able to carve out for myself, probably from early on. I remember enough hard facts and situations to support my recollection of the *feeling tone* of physical growth, school, sports, camaraderie, the wonders of an expanding horizon of those years. Both my parents, no doubt, were old-style authoritarians. Father was softer and more friendly but given to outbursts of quick temper and dressings-down. On the whole, I loved but also respected him. We were not infrequently together when we went swimming in a *Schwimmbad*, had outings when mother and sister were traveling on visits to the Munich branch of the family, when I fetched him from his Stammtisch in the Raths-keller or the Franziskaner-Weinstube, or when we ate river fish together in a fish-fry restaurant in an old quarter of the town across the river. We regularly went to synagogue together every Friday and Saturday, although afterward we children would want to be with other children rather than stay at home—television had not yet infantilized parents and children alike. We shared the religious ceremonies held in the house, built a *sukka* for the eight days of the Sukkoth festival, and had our meals in it after saying the short pray-ers (*kiddush*) required, as long as we had a garden and our house in Edelstrasse 6. We also held the Passover seder, a series of prayers said on two evenings in the family circle at home. It was festive, mother lit candles, and we were supposed to lean back on our chairs to stress that we ceased being slaves in Egypt and had been free ever since. We left a table setting and a chair free for the prophet Elijah, who, we were told, was expected to share our meal. A piece of unleavened bread, the *Aphikomen*,[4] a matzoh, was broken off early from one of the three matzoth on the ritual plate decorated with the foods symbolic of the exodus from Egypt. Later, children were supposed to find it where the head of the household, his dignity enhanced by ceremonial aura, had hidden it.

The Jewish family in this stable and unvarying pattern—the Jew-ish community in its weekly religious gathering, its public spaces for socialization, its regular routines; the regularized institutional behavior that included school and leisure, youth movements, and amateur theatricals—provided a strong and intense framework for me as a boy, even if I tired later of its routine character and the repetitiveness of it all. We no longer mix mild force, shame, guilt,

---

[4] 'Επικῶμον—epikomon–Greek: festive or exuberant conclusion of meal; in Jewish usage, dessert, symbolized by the hidden and found matzoh.

fright, altercations, or admonitions in educating our children as my parents and their peers did at the time. My parents may well have been undemonstrative in expressing their love for us; there may well have been an element of cruelty in the signals we internalized in these early days as part of our dealings with others. We lived in a culture of scarcity, where wasting food or breaking or losing things was linked with guilt feelings and scoldings. And we engaged in a good deal of one-upmanship and people-bashing, small-town gossip, putting the other down. This may well have been reinforced by the Jew's need to intellectualize his environment, to anticipate and neutralize the surprises it may hold for him and endanger him. But on the most intimate level it also provided the warmth of the nest, and innumerable incidents of care, of love, of security and joy, that would make any one-dimensional sequence of remembered facts a serial pedagogical fallacy. I suspect that from the early 1930s on, when the Depression imposed real hardship on the family, and father could not work his way out of our economic decline after some disastrous schemes had failed for their sheer adventurousness, the sense of defeat sapped his strength. We would rent rooms to students in our large Johannitergasse apartment, and the turmoils of my teen years would break the bonds, even if the home provided a safe haven for me as I now entered upon a phase of delicate emotional separation. There must have been elements of character that were inherited and now shaped me and molded me for life. My recollection is that I was both assertive and sensitive and afraid of many things at the time, man- or nature-made. Memory, intellect, and quick reasoning were, no doubt, inherited. Physical agility, probably also physical energy, were inherited all these, of course, shaped by education and experience. I felt secure in the authoritarian love of my parents, intimidating at times as was the respect that was thus inculcated in me with possibly mixed emotional consequences for my later life. I was probably more of a street urchin then, with little concern for girls and for what were considered girlish ways. It may have given me an adolescent sense of worth when I began to face Nazism. But that knowledge of our superiority, and our ironic contempt for the Nazis, may have been a Jewish cultural defense mechanism as well as a teenage conceit, denying the realities of the threat. It had deep roots in Jewish religious, cultural, and communal traditions that became permanent in my attitudes, infinitely reinforced by the quiet spite the Third Reich was to create.

Yet, the fear I just mentioned does not emerge in my recall as the dominant tone of the relationship between my parents and me. The incidents I remember were highly dramatic but not traumatic, even if they replaced the secure emotional bond with a moment of threat. The fact was that, as for other children, such authoritarian streaks were part of an expected way of behaving that included the entire range of relations and presupposed unbreakable security.

Growing up separated me at some time, or in slow stages I cannot reconstruct, from the adult world. The latest stage arrived when I entered puberty; I followed a pattern that was probably universal, but was at least quite characteristic for the family situations I knew of: you enter a world of thought, emotions, preoccupations, yearnings, nature, or, in my case, music, that reflects your tentative and new sense of life—*Lebensgefühl*—but would make you vulnerable if you shared it with the very surroundings out of whose negation it was emerging in the process of self-finding or -definition. I don't presume these forms of adolescent psychology are unique: in fact, in my early teens I started reading books on *Jugendpsychologie* in search of learning what was happening to me and why it was confused and painful. But it occurred to me later that these aspects of my growing up had several social consequences that shaped these years and, maybe, my reactions to living under a murderous and persecutory system. First, you gravitate toward activities that create communities with your peers—the peer group, youth culture, by whatever name, an internal outlet that saves you from ever having "nothing to do or nowhere to go." But you also cherish forms of activity that cater to your need for dropping out of the pressures you yourself create or the changes in your life created from within.

Within the family, my younger sister was more company and friendship than I realized or was ready to concede at that time of primitive masculine self-assertion. I do remember developing closer relations with my older brother, who was happy to be protected against taunts and brawls by his combative younger sibling. I don't believe the semi-streetwise urchins I had been hanging out with, before I started school, touched deeper layers of emotions one way or the other. In grade school I remember friendly feelings for quite a few of my fellow pupils in Fräulein Ottensoser's and Herr Hellmann's class, including girls I got along well with. In the *Gymnasium* I felt at home with most of my fellow students, with the exception of a few, mostly Protestant, stuck-ups who reflected the reservations their parental homes harbored toward "the Jews." Because in a class of (initially) about thirty students only three or four appeared to provoke hostile reactions in me, they were the more negligible, as I had a secure position in the *Gymnasium*, on two counts important for adolescent values: I excelled in practically all the sports we engaged in, and I was a fair and easygoing student and a good team player. I also was nonchalant about learning to the point where at least twice in my *Gymnasium* years well-meaning professors lectured me in front of the class on my squandering my gifts: I was not familiar with the New Testament, they understood, but I did not put my talents to proper use (Matthew 25:14–29). Because at times I borrowed other people's homework before class began and copied it quickly, and because I was quite active in inventing inconveniences for unpopular teachers and still ranked persistently one step below the class *Primus* in class standing, my position was secure, and, with the exceptions noted, relations were quite close and cordial.

My best friends in the class, though, were my two Jewish fellow students. They were not athletic; one of them, in fact, was overweight and unhandy in physical matters. Our relationship developed first, I believe, when, two or three times a week, the Catholic and Protestant classmates had their separate religious instructions, and we gained a free hour which we often spent in a house nearby, the Neuberger or the Reis apartment. For a while, the three of us belonged to Jewish youth groups that became active after 1933–34. Our relationships ripened at that time into a philosophical and disputatious committee for solving the riddles of the universe. I do not remember very clearly which riddles of God, world, or religion we were solving and resolving at which time in our youth. But I remember the emotional elation I used to feel when, at night, we took our walks up the hill and through a park landscape, passing an eighteenth-century jewel of a rococo chapel built into the western hillside across the river, the *Käppele*. In 1964, when I once again visited the town that had filled me earlier with disgust about man's opportunistic capacity to live with evil and exploit it, I managed to slip away and puff up its steep stairs, passing pavilions where stone actors in baroque-Roman theater costumes pathetically reenact the stations of the cross. You climb past the church and its overloaded interior—in a side room you find wax replicas of legs, arms, and other organs, or small *ex voto* paintings commemorating miraculous interventions of the Virgin Mary of the *Käppele* in the catastrophes of life. Then, past the church you follow a road that allows a view of the town below, and get enveloped by the park for a rendezvous with those hours lost in time and death.

I do not remember when I became the involved reader I would be for much of my future life. Father bought me at least twenty volumes of juvenile adventure stories written by Karl May about Indians and trappers, Old Shatterhand and Winnetou, Bedouins and Christians, exotic lands and noble suffering. I read about thirty or forty of the remaining volumes, fast, with the world completely shut out. I remember reading *Leatherstocking* in a single one-day orgy in the sun until I got a nosebleed—memory places the incident still in our house, before I turned thirteen years of age. (I remember how concerned mother and Regina were with me, a foolish boy.) But when did I start reading Saint-Exupéry, Hermann Hesse, Erich Kästner, Ernst Wiechert, Rilke's *Cornet* and *Book of Hours*, juvenilia like *Das neue Universum* (it mixed literature with serious teaching on science and geography)? When did I discover *Die jüdische Kiste*, a collection of Jewish jokes in my father's bookcase (glass-encased for status), and when did I begin to entertain adults with material whose self-deprecating meaning I did not grasp? When did I discover risqué (French) comics in the secondhand bookstore? On my thirteenth birthday I was showered by well-meaning friends of the family with educational literature like Brehm's *Tierleben*, or books the donors had received as premiums from their book club. It included the more than mildly antisemitic novel *Soll und Haben* (*Debitor and Creditor*) by Gustav Freytag, which, I presume, was read as a reminder of a past overcome—the antagonist was a greedy and crooked young businessman whom Freytag had speak *Jargon* (Juden-deutsch), although he had him matriculate from a *Gymnasium* and go to a university, where *Jargon* was not recognized as a language. Other favorite hand-me-downs from book club premiums were realistic novels like Gottfried Keller's *Der grüne Heinrich*, a lengthy *Bildungsroman*, or his short stories, Montaigne's *Essays*, the collected works of Heinrich Kleist, the eighteenth-century *honnête homme*'s

Matthias Claudius's *Der Wandsbecker Bote*, his bourgeois patina speaking to the feeling hearts of a weepy time, and so on. Somebody also gave me Ninon de Lanclos's *Dangerous Liaisons*, which the donor probably had read as little as I would, finding it boring after a few pages—who cared? I presume serious reading started after age fifteen or sixteen. It must have been preceded by years of indiscriminate curiosity for the worlds enclosed between two covers. There was no technical or scientific literature among the books available to me or given to me. Nobody guided my obvious passion for reading into channels, systematic or not. I do not remember books with Jewish contents or translations from Yiddish or Hebrew literature until after the coming of the Third Reich. Only then did Jewish or Zionist replace German literature. The Schocken Verlag (a publisher), Chemnitz, offspring of a well-known Zionist department store, brought out several attractively bound series at reasonable prices. One series resembled the popular *Inselbücher*. I do not remember when I started buying them in some numbers. When the Gestapo seized my books in 1942, they stole my small collection of these books, too.

I do not remember when the Würzburg theater turned me into an enthusiastic, at times deeply smitten lover of the stage. My parents considered it educational to see "classical plays" from the always terribly hot top rung of the small Würzburg house. My experience with a Habimah play in 1928, which I will touch upon later, occasioned my first visit to the theater. I remember two Schiller plays (*Kabale und Liebe* [Love and intrigue]; *The Robbers*) and two Kleist plays (*Minna von Barnhelm*; *Der zerbrochene Krug* [The broken jug]), but presume there were quite a few others. My first opera was Wagner's *Parsifal*; I remember having uncritically enjoyed it and being overwhelmed by its lengthy score.

The religious experiences of this preteen period are equally hard to locate precisely. I do remember moments of unusual intensity but do not know how composite of several occurrences the moment was I see now as one. When I entered school I was already quite at home in the rituals that identified the holy days during the sacred year. It set markers as the secular year did. Because they were associated with activity involving the family, they meant comfortable assurances of normality. Nothing was done in haste or excess in this measured ritualism. Although it was becoming routine, it allowed for moments of unexpected intensity. The prayers, easily read in German translation printed alongside the Hebrew, the cantor's chant, and the congregation's responses—grave men, silence, serious demeanor created the mood—especially when the service turned to sin, repentance, forgiveness, God's grant of life or death in the year to come. From the choir balcony you would see the congregation prostrate themselves following the cues of prayerbook and local custom, dressed in the white shrouds that would cover them at their burials. The lachrymose mood would go through several stages in daylong prayer, especially on the Day of Atonement, when abstaining from food for twenty-four hours heightened your awareness as it dizzied your body. And it was modified on numerous occasions celebrating long-gone agricultural custom in biblical Judea, or historic miracles, deliverance, joy in having been entrusted with the Torah, the Law, the prophetic books kept alive through interpretation and ritual. The services passed through highs and lows, from jubilation to desperation in the course of a year. They gave me a firmly grounded sense of time, once I was taught to see the whole. And at rare moments, light and shadow playing through the windows and the slightly stained-glass bull's eye in the east wall atop the Torah shrine might link the natural with the divine being addressed inside.

Our service, of course, did not enact a central mystic event like the Mass whose meaning was beyond my understanding as a child, even if Regina, against strict orders from mother, occasionally took us to church with her and explained it all in her uninstructed way. The very formal movements of priest and choir boys, the glittering monstrance, the bells ringing—above all, the art-filled interiors of the churches bursting with gilded ornaments, the altars and the darkened paintings made more realistic by being linked with statuary—contrasted infinitely with the naked simplicity of our architecture in synagogue or study room. Even if at my age I felt this more than I was able to articulate, or than I could place into any context of faith and history, the visual impressions of these early years would be integrated into art history and aesthetic pleasure later on.

For the family and its members, these last years of the Weimar Republic were peaceful and filled with real mutuality, but in 1927, my brother's death threw the family into mourning. Sister Edith, only four years old at the time, would slowly fill the emotional void in my parents' lives. In 1930, the beginning worldwide Depression would ruin father's business, a defeat from which he never recovered. Around this time also, my beloved Grandmother Hinterneder died, a few weeks before my bar mitzvah in 1931. I don't believe many acquaintances and friends of the family expected the brutal ways that would strain Jewish life with Hitler's appointment to the chancellorship. Father never believed that it could happen.

2

High School, Apprenticeship: Würzburg, 1929–1936

IN 1929, shortly before my eleventh birthday, I was admitted to the high school Neues Gymnasium in Würzburg. It seemed a natural decision to enroll, given our family's then still-undented prosperity and middle-class status, and my being a "gifted child." I had been most comfortable in the Jewish parochial school Israelitische Volksschule Würzburg, and had liked my teacher during the last two years, Moritz Hellmann, disciplinarian though he was. The entrance examination to the Gymnasium I passed easily. I do not remember what the subjects were, but I was pleased that the three pupils from Moritz Hellmann's class had passed without difficulties. It seemed to confirm him as a teacher in his own and his colleagues' eyes. My four years in the Jewish parochial school also coincided with the most peaceful four years of the Weimar Republic. The Jewish community's sense of security about its links with Christians was at its peak, and old hostilities seemed buried or near-buried in the easygoing atmosphere of the town. Each group was busy with its religious and social life. Being sent to this parochial school had not amounted to a statement against public education. It reaffirmed a half-century of Würzburg community tradition. I remember nothing of these four years that would have stressed the negative in our self-awareness—our identity was not gained at the expense of invidious comparisons. If I should have felt disadvantaged by the school, it would have resulted from its character: two grades (one and two, three and four) met together in one classroom and had one teacher each, like a one-room schoolhouse, because enrollment there was insufficient.

The Gymnasium I entered in the spring of 1929 was—is—a dignified two-story red-sandstone building equipped rather sparsely with Spartan classrooms, a gym, a dirt court for recreation, sports, and recess, and some breakfront closets exhibiting physics instruments of somewhat dated vintage even then. A large auditorium, the Aula, served for school convocations and school orchestra practice. Mine was one of two Humanistische Gymnasiums in town. Its curriculum was based on a foundation of Latin and Greek language teaching over nine and six years, respectively. A third language, French, was added in the fifth form. This curriculum originated in the revival of antiquity at the end of the eighteenth century as a post-Christian *Bildungsreligion* (religion of culture). "Humanism" dominated artistic and intellectual ideals. The Humanistische Gymnasium was the mainspring of the German *Bildungsbürgertum*— the mostly professional middle class based on university education. This type of school had broadened its social function in the course of the nineteenth century to satisfy the need for bureaucrats, clergymen, and managers, while retaining its sense of elitism. New types of schools more attuned to modern languages, technology, and science had been added.

At the time I did not know this, of course, but it helps to explain my experiences. Education in the sciences was generally deemphasized, at least during the six years I attended the school. Training in Latin and Greek was thorough and at least during the first few years predominantly philological. Historical or philosophical exegesis of the classical texts we read in the original was rather neglected. Instructions in German were based on readers and, at one point, on a translated Scandinavian epic (the *Edda!*), presumably an innovation demanded by the Third Reich. We also were taught geography, geometry, algebra, chemistry, botany, and zoology (taxonomy), and probably other subjects. There was no modern and, during the first six years, only limited medieval history, as far as I remember. Instead, we went over Greek and Roman history twice in succession. In 1933 or 1934, incongruously and without links to our curriculum, the teachers, apparently on orders, had to switch for some weeks to German history in the twentieth century. We had to buy a paperback, the *Aufbruch der Nation* (The awakening of the nation) by Stoll and Hoffmann, as represented by the rise of National Socialism to power, which included some antisemitic disquisitions on the deleterious Jewish role in Germany's misfortunes since 1917, now gloriously ended by Adolf Hitler. The teacher excused us three Jews from some lessons in this propaganda history, I suspect to spare himself and us embarrassment. Until the spring of 1935, when

I left the school, I did not notice any effort to teach "racial science" (*Rassenkunde*). I don't know what happened afterward at the school. In 1936, at a *Fortbildungs-Schule* (continuation school, the eleventh school year being mandated by law), I was required to attend a class of this kind, with rather hilarious results.

That I am not entirely sure of many of the details I have just related may indicate that I was not too impressed by what I was learning except for the languages and their grammar based on the old scholastic categorizations. I do not know what was taught after 1935 and in the three highest forms. I was taken out of school by my parents after I had reached the "middle maturity" upon completing the sixth (tenth) form. The final matriculation examination would have occurred at the end of the ninth (thirteenth) form, and it was only much later, in the middle of the war, in 1941–42, that I reentered the last remaining Jewish high school in Berlin as an "adjunct" pupil and made up the *Abitur*, the final matriculation examination, with the very last class of Jewish pupils. It was administered in full compliance with state regulations under the most unusual circumstances.

The Neue Gymnasium I entered thus represented a classical tradition that understood itself as providing a humanistic, universal, education—*Bildung* based on Greek and Latin/Roman civilization. This by itself set it apart from the mixture of barbarism and technological hubris at the core of National Socialism. During twelve years of Nazi rule, the nazification of classical philology, ancient history, and the study of classical philosophy no doubt made advances on several levels of Gymnasium and university research and writing and, I presume, classroom practice. I do not need to review the literature on this subject. When I left the Gymnasium in April 1935, the only self-proclaimed Nazi I detected among my teachers was a substitute German literature teacher who had mentioned to our class that he had done service (*Dienst*) in the SS and in a concentration camp. Ironically, I was the only one among his pupils who had done some amateurish readings in Nietzsche's works, and had heard about the then fashionable historic decadentist Oswald Spengler, and some other names (as yet with little contents) I had picked up, in my bedridden desperation, from my histories of philosophy. During the last class I had in school before leaving, at the end of the fall/winter term of 1934–35, he lectured us with some emotion on national values and expressed sympathy for me, because I had to leave under circumstances beyond my control. I was the only Jewish pupil of the original three remaining, and felt helpless and stared in embarrassment in front of me, hard put to avoid blushing. Knowing nothing about SS behavior in concentration camps, I did not understand that he was demonstrating a tiny independence against whatever had made him join.

The fact was that the Neue Gymnasium, perhaps unlike the Alte Gymnasium, our sister school, was saturated with Catholic teachers and students who had been active in Bavarian political Catholicism, the Bavarian People's Party, which was dissolved in 1933. Some pupils belonged to the several Catholic youth groups that had predominated in town before 1933. Most of our teachers were at an advanced stage of their teaching careers, some visibly close to retirement. We heard rumors that some of them—the biologist, for example—had been sent to Würzburg by the education authorities in Munich as a demotion for anti-Nazi political activism in another city. As far as I know, only one of the teachers, the professor of music, was dismissed from his position after the war for having been a member of the Nazi Party, but he never let on during the six years I spent in his classes and played in the second violin section of the school orchestra after years of violin lessons under his guidance. My favorite gymnastics teacher was a German conservative who gave no indication that he favored Nazism—if anything, he may have been an old-style monarchist. During my six years, with the exception mentioned earlier, none ever alluded to Nazism in class in any form I could detect. The students in the two sections of my form belonged in the vast majority to the Catholic Church. The class spirit, it seemed to me, was shaped by a solid contingent of students preparing for the priesthood. They were housed in a priest-supervised dormitory, the Kilianeum, and had come primarily from villages. Typically, they were of a less-than-affluent peasant background. Studying for the priesthood was not considered on a par with owning a farm or marrying a farmer's daughter. Typically, they had been tutored at home by their village priests who had identified them as suitable candidates for a clerical vocation. Each morning, they would walk to school in a loose formation that snaked through the formal rococo garden of the former palace of the Würzburg prince-bishop, the Residenz. After school they walked back in smaller units as classes were dismissed in the afternoon. The rest of the class was also predominantly Catholic. Among these two groups, there were few traces of National Socialist sympathy, even if their parents could have been expected to find virtue in the economic and law-and-order promises of Nazi propaganda directed at the middle-class and the upper-workingclass segments of the population. More openly identified with Nazism were a few students whom I remember as being housed in a secular (or Protestant?) dormitory for better-off out-of-towners, the Julianeum, and some Protestant pupils from professional or well-to-do homes. I remember only one of them, the son of a high school teacher, coming to school in the uniform of the Hitler Youth music band: he was a good violinist. I understand that the more forward ones later served in the SS or the Luftwaffe, suffering high casualties during the war. The Hitler Youth violinist survived—he became a physician—but suffered a nervous breakdown or psychosis. When I met him again in the 1980s, he seemed rather unreconstructed in his stereotyped nationalist attitudes.

The antisemitic nationalism that had prepared Nazism, or the anti-Judaism of the several religious or folk traditions that had transmitted anti-Jewish invectives, stereotypes, or hatred from time immemorial to the twentieth century, appeared only a few times in the experiences of us three Jewish students in that class. The families of my two Jewish fellow students had left Würzburg by then. My friends were not very gifted for gymnastics and sports, the status symbols of boys' schools, and suffered occasional ribbings by some of our fellow students. Because they were close friends of mine I stayed clear of the usual banter, even though with a sense of patronizing and protecting them. I don't remember if Christian students were in the same predicament at the time. They would not have been teased differently or less benevolently.

My own six years in the Neue Gymnasium Würzburg divided about evenly into the late Weimar and the early Nazi period, and brought me from childhood into adolescence. I had entered the Gymnasium ready to like the new experiences, large and small, I would face. My Jewish communal background, my anchors in the day-to-day folk traditions of Würzburg neo-orthodox Judaism, the ease of being with others in a group, did not clash with the mentality of boys who had been formed by their own religious and church roots in community and family. There was nothing in my new activities that would make me question or leave me unduly self-conscious about who I was and what I believed and did in my religion. New friendships formed, some lasting over the entire span of my Gymnasium years, even if our joint activities as friends brought us into each other's houses only when we crammed for examinations. Besides school, it was hikes and soccer or other forms of sports that created friendships between about half a dozen other boys and me. The only fight I remember with one of my fellow students took place during the usual fifteen-minute recess. One morning I flew into one of my then not uncommon rages in response to an anti-Jewish epithet he had used in a friendly altercation with me, and I hit him rather wildly and bloodied his nose, which soiled whatever he wore that morning. When the teacher supervising the recess pushed his way through the circle of boys watching the scene, it was all over. This remained an isolated incident. We became friends afterward.

My memory of the Gymnasium has remained warm and friendly. I see no reason why it should have tricked me into euphoric delusions, since I remember several incidents on the street or on group hikes in which I reacted to antisemitic taunts by boys or groups of Hitler Youth in similar fashion and with similar good results. (Friends now living in New York and Seattle confirm this recollection. I do not like seeing myself as a quick-tempered street fighter, or as the fool I must have been to take on a contingent of Hitler Youth during a hike with "my" youth group on the hilly Rottendorf plateau north of the city.) Violent incidents were few and far between during the three years of the Third Reich I stayed in town. I did not feel like a victim or that I was being singled out for personal persecution.

Comparing my later experiences as a student (in Berlin and Bern) and as a college teacher (in New York and again in Berlin) to those in Würzburg, I do not believe that my Gymnasium teachers welcomed personal contacts with their pupils outside the classroom, except for the regular *Schulausflug* (hiking day). Once a month, we took to the woods on the hills adjoining the town under the guidance of one of the teachers. We usually ended up near a country inn or beer garden to take some refreshments—I do not remember if we were allowed to drink beer and at what age. We Jews were excused from writing on Saturdays—*Shabbes* in the local dialect for *Shabbat*—and were excused for the important Jewish holidays, a total of about fourteen schooldays during the year. During such days, teachers did not schedule written examinations, and because we three were good-to-excellent students, we had no scholastic problems with the examinations. I easily assimilated bodies of facts: I would cram the afternoon before history examinations, following weeks of classroom absorption of facts and contexts, and do well. Facts took their places in a chronological and spatial gestalt in my memory, and could thus be called up if needed. I also "saw" the pages when I tried to remember. I then forgot the *Stoff* (material) in detail while retaining a context on which to build. I did well with German composition and the languages, especially Greek and Latin with their perspicuous grammatical structures. In mathematics, which was taught by professors who did not arouse my interest, I oscillated between successes and failures in examinations for a mediocre passing grade. I also developed an interest in natural science during visits to the small Würzburg museum of natural history, then located at the top floor of the Residenz. This interest died in the Gymnasium, although I took two years' additional voluntary afternoon classes in chemistry. Jewish students were given religious instruction two afternoons a week by an academic teacher of religion, Dr. Hammelburger, with good results from the point of view of his prescribed curriculum, but less effective for what religion could have meant for an adolescent beginning to question literal verities. I left the Gymnasium well trained in the humanities, especially Greek and Latin, and several sports, but without guidance about what really preoccupied my mind during those years.

All in all, I worked a minimum, but it sufficed to keep me in good standing at home, and frequently one rung below the class *Primus*, a talented country boy whom I viewed then as a future cardinal in Rome. I believe he had to serve in the German army in World War II and in the 1980s ministered to a country parish near town. He had been in Rome to study at the prestigious Collegium Germanicum.

Thus, my memory suggests that even if school did not challenge me enough, it opened up a new world of history and languages, and conveyed a limited and often frustrating basis for my budding interests in the ancient world, in Jewish history, the Hebrew language, and the Old Testament. They would fill many hours of my life with joys of recognition and discovery.

Still, at the time, the safe retreat to what we were taught as grammatical absolutes had already oriented us toward "the truth." I remember one episode with a substitute teacher who did try to teach the *humanistic* values of the Humanistische Gymnasium. He had chosen the contrast between Kleon and Perikles in Thucydides's history to hint at the vulgarities of populist demagoguery, but I missed his point and his veiled parallels to the contemporary Kleon in Berlin. I did not want to be bothered with more than the "Pensum," the daily quota of routine memory work, the concrete "truth" in which I have seen so many minds in so many disciplines seek refuge and atrophy before their time. I had long forgotten the episode until I included Thucydides (in translation) in a text-oriented survey course of "great historians," "historiography," at the City College of New York in the 1960s. By then it was too late for apologies to the Würzburg professor. The college, in its own nineteenth-century ways, imposed just retribution on my unpedagogical disrespect for "the truth" later on: I was assigned to teach survey courses in European history to freshmen entering college from the deteriorating New York City school system. They, too, believed we taught "the truth."

The Gymnasium was probably as nonpolitical in its dedication to the curriculum before as it was after Hitler's appointment to power in January 1933. Its teaching staff was solidly middle-of-the-road and probably addicted to the pleasures of opinionating with regular cronies the way solid citizens were expected to contribute to world affairs. The Catholic atmosphere of the Gymnasium during those first three years of the Third Reich, it appears in retrospect, probably reflected the attitudes of the town's Catholic churchgoing middle classes, craftsmen, and retailers. The clergy, led by a much respected bishop, Dr. Matthias Ehrenfried, a local country boy, had already been in an energetic clinch with Nazi racism and anti-Catholicism before 1933, but was cowed by violence in town. The outspoken editor of the local Bavarian People's Party newspaper had been arrested and his paper *verboten* as early as 1933. Like their Berlin party center, they had sold their political freedom of action for a mess of job security for Catholic civil servants, and, like the other Weimar parties, dissolved their party in the threatening atmosphere emanating from Hitler. The conclusion of the Concordat between the Vatican and the Reich government in June 1933 represented a diplomatic and church gain: the Vatican had long sought to add a Reich agreement to its older concordats with states like Bavaria and Prussia. It was the first international treaty of political significance concluded by the Third Reich—as compared to trade treaties with the Soviet Union earlier in 1933, for example—and meant a diplomatic triumph for Hitler's government. Vatican Secretary of State Eugenio Pacelli's *Realpolitik* (he and Franz von Papen initialed the treaty in Rome) foreshadowed his papal policies during the Second World War after he was elected pope (Pius XII). In 1937, a papal bull (*Mit brennender Sorge*) issued by Pius XI was already publicly accusing the Reich government of violating the Concordat, while Nazi propaganda chided the German church and its leaders for political activities they had allegedly agreed to end.

This conflict may have taken many institutional political forms in Würzburg of which I was oblivious. I suspect that was true also of most Jews not linked professionally with the numerous bureaucrats in city and country offices, or with professional colleagues in law or medicine. At home, father spoke a good deal about events and newspaper reports, mostly at the dinner table. I don't remember talk on how antisemitism touched him personally; by then his small business, like his small job with the Gemeinde's membership department, was conducted mostly with fellow Jews. He did talk with us about the violent intrusion of Storm Troopers (SA) into the bishop's palace and the destruction they wrought. The year was probably 1935. And there was a good deal of anxious and concerned talk during the first year of the Third Reich about members of the Gemeinde being taken into "protective custody," arbitrary arrest without cause but under a legal pretext, about searches in Jewish homes, about the persecution of individual Jews whom the Nazis hated for one reason or another. They included the owner of the most popular cabaret, "Central-Café," the most prestigious antique furniture and art dealer, in whose apartment house we lived after we were forced to sell our house, and others less known. There were rumors and reports of bloody attacks on village Jews who for one reason or another were singled out for vendettas. In an adjoining county—Protestant Middle Franconia—some Jews had even been killed by a sadistic local SA gang, even if the courts were still functioning well enough in this case of murder "without orders from above" to lead to trial and convictions. I don't remember the ludicrously mild sentences imposed by the court (Gunzenhausen, ca. 1934–35).

In this developing atmosphere of persecution, the Gymnasium, students and professors, had no part. I have read numerous autobiographical reports on how difficult life was becoming for Jewish pupils in non-Jewish schools after 1933. We were at best barely touched by broken friendships or refused contacts, and no teacher in our years as Jewish pupils together, and in the last year or two during which I was the only Jewish pupil, uttered an anti-Jewish or antisemitic word to our faces. That this silence did not exclude prejudice came to light with our art teacher. I had never been able to draw a straight line, to say nothing of drawing the objects he put before the class to be reproduced in pencil or charcoal on paper. The professor lived on our street, and one day he confided to my mother that I had a fine head but obviously Jewish hands—I just could not draw. Because I was among a band of obstreperous boys who did all sorts of things to frustrate Herr Müller, I may well have provoked him into voicing his aggressive stereotype. If he had been alive to the town and its exquisite public art—a living museum in its original setting—he would not have wasted years on teaching us to draw vases and wooden blocks, but would have made us aware of and taught us to appreciate the unique world we lived in. He may, of course, have had to follow the prescribed curriculum designed by wise educationists in the ministry in Munich. Thus, I never had a course in art appreciation or art history.

This was one of the lasting shortcomings of the tough-minded but ultimately pedestrian humanistic curriculum that had been prescribed by the probably church-influenced education authorities in Munich, the Bavarian state capital: they failed to appreciate the value of the visual component of classical culture. There was an unsophisticated nationalist component, the "dulc' et decorum'st pro patria mori,' but the *Iliad*'s Helen was drowned in philology rather than plastically made alive through all world literature and art. I began to fill the gap by haphazard voyages of discovery into literature, the theater, museums, modern art: the only store specializing in modern art objects and fine reproductions for the young or the impecunious was Laredo's, on Bahnhofstrasse, owned by probably the only Jew of Sephardic (Spanish North-African) origin in town. His son Günther went to school with me, they were our neighbors, and I spent quite a few happy hours in their house in Keesburgstrasse, the first flat-roof building in town and an object of wonderment to the conventionally roofed-over citizenry. Laredo's had the first fully Bauhaus interior I encountered. Beautiful, warm-hearted Mrs. Laredo—she had come from Giessen to Würzburg—and her (Würzburg-born) husband, Oscar, the major, maybe the only, modernist in our neoromantic art world, may well have become unconsciously associated in my life with my feeling of being at home in New Functionalism ever since.

In addition, what I did become aware of in my environment was creating a lifelong interest in visual art, preferences for some periods and styles, intellectual and political contexts for religious art, for cultural history. I probably was not yet twenty years old when I discovered Jacob Burckhardt and Johan Huizinga; subsequently I learned a great deal from Heinrich Wölfflin, and general histories of art, and gained, and am still gaining, untold hours of pleasure from their worlds. Maybe Müller would have spoiled it all had he tried to teach his kind of art history.

I ascribe my unruffled schoolyears to the fact that it took time to nazify institutions, to penetrate the youth culture that had been one pillar of the Catholic educational system. The virulent Catholic rejection of modern culture and economics as "Jewish" did not come up in class. Catholic anti-Judaism, more subtle and more spiritual, only occasionally broke through the daily routine, most clearly during the week before the Easter recess. Then, the teacher of religion (twice weekly), a monsignor (Klett?), must have portrayed the story of Jesus's trial, death, and resurrection with enough charismatic passion to imprison his class in a past made present through polemical texts such as the synoptic gospels. It would take the class some half-hour to return to reality, and although his teaching never led to any anti-Jewish words, it did create a momentary barrier between us. Similarly bleary eyes and excited passions of remembered mythological history we Jewish students did not experience. During their hours of religious instruction we used to play soccer on a nearby large empty lot called the "parade ground"— *Paradeplaz*—or spend time in one another's homes. Only the Jewish Teachers Seminary, which had given the town its institutional distinction in the world of Jewish education, was known to have engaged an emotional and charismatic rabbi of mystic leanings (Samson Raphael Weiss) in the 1930s, who left his students similarly affected on Sabbath afternoons. The seminary leaders may have felt, I venture without source or personal experience, that their measured and reasonable orthoprax teacher training needed to connect with the revival of mysticism then emerging among the more thoughtful of orthodox rabbis.

I trust that the Easter passion texts projected a biblicism that had cost many an ancestor's life in the not-too-distant past. I know now what I did not know then: that the local Nazi press had tried to construe a ritual-murder story around the murder of a country boy in the 1920s at a nearby village, Manau, and that religious art in churches still depicted medieval or early modern fairy tales of hosts desecrated by Jews, affirming the mystery of the spiritual presence through very unspiritual materialistic miracles. If pious minds believed such stories to be true, that belief did not translate into political or social or economic behavior which, until 1933, had been controlled by the reality principle of *do ut des*, on both sides.

I do not know how much Nazism subsequently penetrated this Humanistische Gymnasium. Nothing is known about resistance to Nazism among teachers or students. It did not have an effect I could perceive during the first three years of the Third Reich. The simple fact was that Catholic culture rested on a rich and deeply anchored or newly revived folklore, and disposed of comfort systems and functional group structures for all conceivable human crisis situations. It had turned them into ritual, custom, faith, externalized daily routine, and the unquestioned presence of hierarchies of saints, from the Virgin Mary down. The Nazi revolution could offer nothing remotely equal in rootedness, and provided no similar life-giving myth to the faithful. The Germanic tribalism they tried to introduce at some spots in 1933–34 turned into a ludicrous flop. The Judaism we practiced was just as unshakable in its certainties and just as rooted in folklore's man-centered views of nature and of divine intervention in human affairs. Maybe this essential difference between the classical religious and the racist myth makes it better understandable that in 1945 so many Germans found it humanly possible to see themselves as victims of the regime they had followed so faithfully and with such a split consciousness, and to overlook so many features of their folk beliefs that in the end facilitated their acceptance of the racist mythology. Folkloristic traditions transmitted a highly physical concept of who outsiders would be— the hunchback, the cripple, the deformed and handicapped, the gypsy, the physically stained homosexual. It included the stereotype of the physically weak and militarily unhandy Jew who did not conform to the beauty ideals of the majority long before the Nazis idolized the blue-eyed, blond Nordic.

After I left the Gymnasium, relations with my fellow pupils petered out, although I did not leave town for another eighteen months, in 1935–36. They must have stood for the final matriculation examination in 1937 or 1938, since the Education Ministry had cut one year from the required nine. The last time I was touched by the *Kulturkampf* spirit among my Catholic fellow pupils was when I stood by myself, unrecognized, before the open gate to our synagogue courtyard on November 10, 1938, and observed the embers of the bonfire the Storm Troopers had lighted that night. They had desecrated and burned what was combustible of the synagogue interior, including some Torah scrolls. At one point in this vigil, the familiar queue of seminarians came up Domerschulgasse and squeezed by me on the narrow sidewalk. They were on their way from the student dormitories, the "Old University" of the sixteenth century, to the "New University" of the nineteenth, where most disciplines offered lectures and conducted seminars. While they passed by without word or greeting, just eye contact, one of them stepped out of line and said, "Today it's you, Herbert, tomorrow it'll be us" in the inimitable dialectic inflection of his Lower Franconian village of Wasserlosen, near Hammelburg. The student, a small cheerful redhead—it had earned him the nickname "the red Gössmann"—retook his place in the snake without waiting for an answer or greeting. We had often played soccer together. His brother Alois wrote me from Wasserlosen in June 1994 that Josef was killed in action near Smolensk in October 1943. Two of his five brothers also died in World War II. His study of theology and philosophy at the University of Würzburg had been cut short by service in the Labor Services and the German army in 1939–40. Advancing to lieutenant after attending officers' training school, he had been wounded at the beginning of the German invasion of the Soviet Union in 1941, but was assigned to frontline duty again in

1943. He was commanding an infantry company when he died on October 22 of that year. I never learned if he maintained his anti-Nazi stance to the end.

Thus, the culture that had shaped me, the Jewish at first dominating then balancing the German in content and attitude, had blended almost seamlessly into this German-Christian school, whose traditional Catholic contents I could understand as a regrettable dilution of the correctly abstract and, on the surface, nonmythological rigor of ancient Judaism. We had been here for a few thousand years; they came from our world; we shared a basic outlook on the divinely controlled worlds of man and nature. Judaism was giving me a sense of personal integrity over the at first negligible then obtrusive, then menacing, then rapacious images I was forming of the Nazi Party before and after Hitler was made chancellor by the conservative club-heads around Hindenburg. What happened north of the Main River divided the good from the bad in my nativist geography. In 1933, I was fully preoccupied with the self-created turmoils that go with maturation at that age, emotionally as well as intellectually and, in Jewish terms, politically. What I was able to observe and understand of Nazism is probably impossible to reconstruct. When I added contemporary history to my self-education in New York, and ten years afterward began to teach courses on the Weimar Republic and the Third Reich, I had bridged this intellectual and professional gap in my life and education. Even studying European history in Bern with a teacher I revered, Werner Naef, did not introduce me to the essays and the scholarly analysis that had been devoted to Nazism in the Western world since 1933, primarily by émigrés from Germany and, most incisively, by scholars of leftist persuasion or under Marxist influence.

The first encounter with avant-garde culture I remember occurred as early as November 19, 1928—the date is anchored in the literature on the incident. On the evening of that day, the Würzburg Municipal Theater offered as a *Gastspiel*—guest performance—a Yiddish play, *The Dybbuk*, by Anski, put on by the Yiddish Theater Company Habimah. It speaks for the artistic sense of the theater director that he offered a show in the then avant-garde expressionist and surrealistic style made famous by Habimah. My parents permitted me to accept a free ticket from a Jewish member of the Würzburg Voluntary Fire Brigade, Jakob Sichel, a neighbor of ours and one of the first men I had met until then who not only was smart or clever but projected serenity and intellectual reserve, wisdom, if the term were not so shopworn.

He was detached to man a fire station in the theater that evening, and, attired in his fireman's uniform and shining brass helmet, he took me downtown to Theaterstrasse (*sic*) where the Stadttheater was located. I was deeply engrossed in the mysterious events happening on stage, but because the performance was given in Yiddish (or Hebrew?) and my ten-year-old mind was hardly attuned to Jewish mysticism or Eastern European culture, my memories remain quite vividly visual. (Habimah, I learned much later, was then just about to relocate from its home in Moscow to Tel Aviv.) When I met Mr. Sichel after the performance, the streets around the theater were filled with police and a crowd shouting anti-Jewish and anti-Communist slogans—expressionism was *Kulturbolschewismus* to the Nazis. Nazi juveniles were using the occasion to show their anti-semitism as a respectable defense of traditional culture, and were rioting against the audience as they left the theater. I took Mr. Sichel's hand and, protected by his shining helmet, he being unrecognizable as a Jewish fireman, we went the accustomed way home, past the Residenz and its formal gardens.

Some rioters were sentenced to mild prison terms and released on probation.

Except for the small incidents and brawls I mentioned earlier, nothing of remotely similar significance involved me while I lived in Würzburg, from 1933 to 1936, three years into the Nazi rule. I missed noticing the violence and brutality the Storm Troopers unleashed for months following the Nazi takeover, even though father discussed the multiple steps of discrimination and persecution directed against individual businessmen. The word "Dachau" (a concentration camp near Munich) acquired an ominous, threatening overtone. The family of a friend of my father's was the only one among family intimates touched by Nazi political murder at that time. On August 7, 1933, Felix Fechenbach, a fellow Jewish Würzburger, was shot, gangster style, by four Nazi thugs near Detmold, where he edited a Social Democratic Party newspaper. He was taken "for a ride" while he was being transferred from one prison to another, and shot in cold blood, probably on Reinhard Heydrich's orders. He had been on the Nazi hit list for allegedly treasonable behavior since serving as private secretary to Kurt Eisner, the revolutionary anarchist and head of a left-wing government in Munich after 1918.

After 1933, there were also a number of demonstrations against Jewish department stores. Retail stores affixed labels to their windows declaring themselves "German business." Early in 1933, the Nazis burned the files of the Social Democratic Trade Union headquarters after raiding the union hall (*Gewerkschaftshaus*) in Augustinerstrasse. In May, students burned the books of Jewish writers and scholars whom they considered symbols of Weimar culture, or political enemies. I saw none of these ludicrous gestures or demonstrations, but heard of them in concrete detail when they affected persons in our circle of acquaintances, or prominent persons. That most of my father's and mother's friends in the Christian community remained loyal to them, and father's reduced business and work were almost completely limited to fellow Jews, may now have supported his often-expressed view that Hitler "can't last long, his economy is *kaputt*," the "Allies won't tolerate him," and similar powerless incantations to the ruler of the universe, and to law and order or reason. After the first violent phase of the takeover had passed by mid-1933, normality appeared to return to the Jewish community, but on quite a different level from pre-Nazi coexistence. Würzburg Jews began to leave town for larger cities to prepare their emigration, or emigrated to European destinations, Palestine, or the United States. The Gemeinde offered advisory services, functioning as the local representative of such central Berlin agencies as the Hilfsverein der Juden in Deutschland or Palästina-Amt. Lawyers and law school graduates opened offices to advise prospective émigrés on the numerous legal chicaneries involved in the flood of forms and papers required for persons and property to be transferred. The Palestine Office and the orthodox Zionist Labor Party Bachad (*Brith Chalutzim Dati'im*—Association of Religious Pioneers) organized agricultural training centers, or placed young people on farms near Würzburg, mainly those operated by fellow Jews where they would be assured a supply of ritually acceptable (kosher) food and imported kosher meat.[1]

---

[1] The orthodox rabbi Dr. Esra Munk, Berlin, had negotiated an agreement with the Nazi government that "allowed" relatives of German Jews abroad to "donate" foreign currency that would pay for meat imports. The Reich needed all foreign

The revival of synagogue attendance observed in other cities did not apply to Würzburg: I did not see the "liberals," who had been less observant than the rest of us, show up at services more than was their wont. But their children, and youth in general, began to reorient themselves as careers and work in Germany appeared less certain.

Of course, I became quite aware of the charged atmosphere ushered in by the arrival of the Third Reich in town. On some glorious spring day in 1933, I was excused from attending school and sent home. As I rode my bicycle through the town center, I had to ride through a sea of red swastika flags, the town hall had its ancient tower (*Grafeneckartsturm*) decorated with long swastika banners, and there were crowds in the streets. I had the anticipatory feeling of change, a mix of getting ready for a new situation and a heightening of my defenses, that I would experience several times later on when great changes imposed themselves on my life—but I had no fear and no sense of personal danger. There was none. I was fifteen years of age then, involved in the inner dialogues of adolescence, and immune to looking beyond the personal, unable to estimate the dangers ahead.

I have puzzled about this experience, which recurred on several occasions later on. I presume it compares to the complex feelings of soldiers going into combat. I ascribed it to the pubescent's sense of invincibility which makes him accept risks a more mature person would shy away from. I also presume that the prolonged tensions of living in a hostile environment foster such attitudes, or that getting out of numerous threats unscathed either inured me to reality or prolonged puberty. I have ascribed my sense of self to the intensive influence of the Jewish religious and folk culture that shaped my youth. It had continued in the Zionist belief system we wrestled with at the time, and provided political and ethnic rationales for the self-assurance we needed to disregard the barrage of invective that surrounded us in Germany. That I wrote "we" without thinking points up, too, that adolescent turmoil, the concentration on the

---

currency for its trade balance and rearmament. See Michael Munk, "Austrittsbewegung und Berliner Adrass Yisroel Gemeinde, 1869–1939," in *Gegenwart im Rückblick: Festgabe für die Jüdische Gemeinde zu Berlin 25 Jahre nach dem Neubeginn*, ed. Herbert A. Strauss and Kurt R. Grossman (Heidelberg: Lothar Stiehm Verlag, 1970), pp. 146–47.

self, occurred in the almost collective atmosphere of our group life. Our old Jewish and new Zionist commitments, the community under stress, lowered barriers between people. We were closely attached to our peers in informal sociability; age and status barriers between teachers and students diminished as the sense of threat increased—all these probably contributed to warding off a feeling of personal victimization.

The changed atmosphere in town after 1933, to return to the point, showed up most visibly in externals like flags, uniformed men marching, Hitler Youth rushing through the streets or being met on hikes, the ubiquitous Hitler salute and the raised right fascist arm copied from Italy. Until I left town for Berlin in 1936, it failed to inspire fear. It was too pompous, too make-believe, to see rotund men playing at becoming soldiers on Sunday mornings at the large square before the Residenz, their beer bellies belying their martialism. Nazi culture did show up in some new holidays the Nazis introduced from their own calendar, such as November 9, commemorating the failed beerhall putsch in Munich in 1923, or in such holidays as May Day they appropriated from the Socialist International or Memorial Day for men killed in action (Heroes Remembrance Day, People's Mourning Day) they took over from the Weimar Republic. But the fact was that their creed had no roots in folk traditions, even if they undertook to appropriate as many as possible, and they had no rituals to equal the grooves of acceptance that years or centuries of repetition had carved into religious consciousness. It may have been more than just a brawl when my Catholic classmates told me about the attacks they had to weather when Hitler Youth in 1935 or 1936 attacked them during a public Corpus Christi procession and tried to strip them of their Catholic boy scouts' uniforms. In strange contrast, Zionist boy scouts were permitted by police ordinance to wear their uniforms, *at least indoors*. This was meant to advance emigration to Palestine, then the professed goal of Nazi antisemitic policies. Jewish institutions experienced the transition from their established reliance on local, state, or national laws and constitutional safeguards to Nazi discrimination as a discontinuous process. Its "dual state" quality, noted by Ernst Fränkel[2] especially for the Jewish sector, set the period dis-

---

[2] Ernst Fränkel, *The Dual State: A Contribution to the Theory of Dictatorship* (New York: Oxford University Press, 1941).

tinctly apart from the Holocaust, with 1938–41 forming the transition. I believe the low level of alarm I felt about the Nazis in Würzburg was justified by the historic perspectives we learned from embracing Zionism and its larger time frame. That same level of alarm was woefully counterproductive when the threats to life and limb paced the assurance we derived from misreading the intentions of an ultimately deadly enemy.

It was not during my Gymnasium time, however, that I witnessed the abysmal depth to which Nazi cynicism had lowered human decency, but during the subsequent eighteen months of post-Gymnasium apprenticeship in a mail-order company for hardware and machine tools. There, the senior office manager, named Meyer, a member of the SA, and one of the workers, "SS-man Jobst," secretly informed the Gestapo in about 1936–37 that the Jewish owner was filling orders from armed forces or NSDAP procurement agencies, a business activity not formally forbidden, even if the buyers requested "neutral labels" to conceal their buying from a reliable, if Jewish, source. It implied an awareness that it was politically incorrect economic behavior, although it was not uncommon in business relations between Jews and Christians during those years. Contrary to Nazi economic policy, as directed by Hjalmar Greeley Schacht, Heydrich's secret police imprisoned the Jewish owner I worked for. Afterward he agreed to turn over his business to an "Aryan." He died of a heart attack after he had founded a retail bakery store in New York following his emigration, unable to stand the physical strain involved. His son, Walter Reis, one of my best friends in Würzburg, has been practicing psychiatry in Pittsburgh for many years now after serving in the U.S. army in World War II. I knew, of course, many decent Christians during those years, but I cannot recall more than a few Nazi Party members among them, even if after 1933 greed (*Habgier*), not ideology, had become the major motive for joining the Party.

My father was fifty-seven years old in 1933, fourteen years older than my mother and forty-two older than I. He, too, took steps to leave Germany and tried to locate members of the Strauss family who had emigrated to the United States in the nineteenth century. Jews from Bavaria and South Germany had found opportunities in America in some numbers during the first half of the century, when the law that liberated them politically restricted them severely in economic and social activities. His search brought no results. Still, he registered me (and possibly my sister, Edith) for immigration visas at the U.S. Consulate in Stuttgart, although the waiting list for immigrants from Germany (quota 25,000) had grown hopelessly long by 1938. We paid little heed to this until after November 1938, when every Jew sought escape hatches wherever they led. Though our chances of being called to the consulate were slim to begin with, they had evaporated completely by mid-1938: a (German) employee of the visa division had sold advance placement on the waiting list to applicants, and we were left behind. My sister and I expected to migrate to Palestine.

By the judgment of the 1930s, my father was not suitable for emigration because of his age, and would not have found a country that would have admitted him, having little capital and an undesirable occupation—merchant. If asked, he might have cited many reasons for staying put: his age, his occupation, the restrictions imposed by immigration countries, the rigors of starting anew. He might have mentioned his roots in the life of a town where the family had lived about half a century before 1933, and his optimistic inability to fathom the depth of criminality to which obedience to authority would lead the children of his generation of *honnêtes hommes*. He did not feel alarmed enough to leave town.

The decisions and perceptions that controlled his attitudes and rendered him passive during the Third Reich were thus the stuff human character is made of. Emigration was a personal decision. His feeble attempts to flee floundered on obstacles like age and lack of relatives or connections abroad, and, of course, lack of funds to buy his way out of Germany and into a country of refuge or temporary settlement. But this not only was linked to his personality and character. It also sprang from the culture that had shaped him. He had been living in a perfectly satisfactory local network of business and friendships, his society (*Gesellschaft*) was community (*Gemeinschaft*), the face-to-face community of a town that had preserved many features from before industrialization, in both the smaller Jewish and the larger Christian sectors. His life was built on trust and shared values, even on shared mentalities. Across the barriers of theology and ritual, Jews and Christians in Würzburg understood each other's unarticulated, almost instinctual humanity, as they shared the bourgeois virtues of work and thrift, solidity and family, decency and decorum, as they coped with aging, sickness, and death. Prayers and ritual, practiced daily and in the cycles of human life and communal time, defined my father's splendid connectedness with a tradition he found meaningful and was able to live and thus make it truth. Yet, generations of this same bourgeois culture had blunted the existential edge, the watchfulness that is much of the written or spoken lore of Judaism conveyed even in translations. Since emancipation began, Jewish social history had imprisoned communal attitudes in a popular enlightenment that was bleached of the sense of danger the grandfather generation still remembered from ghetto times, poverty, marginal trades like peddling, or isolation. German provincial and Jewish provincial cultures stemming from the same epochal and social roots, and decaying into the same Pickwickian *Gemütlichleit*, had turned into a comfort system that reached existential depths and became religion only at rare moments of deep personal crisis.

That his connectedness had not promoted larger perspectives produced my father's decision to take me out of the Gymnasium after I had completed six years of the nine-year course. That gave me *Mittlere Reife*, a junior degree compared to the final Abitur, the matura. This six-year high school diploma was an educational relic from before World War I, when it was also called *Einjähriges*, the one-year degree, because it entitled graduates to serve one year instead of two in the draft army of their respective state—armies had been left under the sovereignty of the states making up the Reich in 1871. It may have been invented as a boon to business and industry which required, not refined classicists, but middle-management personnel, or as a concession to rising status needs among classes that demanded to be integrated into the widening white-collar sector of the economy. With the shift to the professional, long-service army of the Weimar Republic, the term, if not the social context, lost its meaning. The Abitur remained the main dividing line in the social structure. Graduates were entitled to study at a university and follow professional careers. The higher ranks or the well-connected or well-born joined several establishments, but even routine professionals, for example in law or medicine, saw themselves as apart from businessmen who lacked academic degrees and were expected to pay their respect to status.

As far as I can reconstruct my father's thinking at that time from remembered conversations, reversing his appraisal of the Jewish and the German situation in the mid-1930s, he was unable "to see a future for me" in completing high school and obtaining the Abitur—Jews were barred by Nazi law from entering universities or obtaining university degrees. By then times were not easy financially for the Strauss family, and an additional income might help. On the presumption that "they" would not last very long in government, as he kept insisting for perfectly logical and perfectly unrealistic reasons, I should be directed into the occupation he knew best and had practiced all his life, business, and learn it as he had, "from the ground up" by becoming an "apprentice."

At the time, in 1935, the Nazi government was priming the pump of its economy by creating jobs in public employment and creating paper credits (*MEFO Wechsel*) to finance its rearmament while imposing universal wage and price controls to hide the resulting inflationary pressures. The recovery from the Depression—its lowest depth had already been left behind in 1933—created an incipient boom for business and lowered unemployment, all of which was gaining Hitler solid support. Some Jewish business, in spite of the slew of discriminatory restrictions on its activities, was also helped along by this turn, while Jewish employees, Jewish labor, and the lower-income groups were losing ground. On the Würzburg level, Jewish retail stores were harassed and put under pressure to sell out or close, but Christian customers continued to patronize them because they offered better merchandise or services, or cheaper goods to lower-income groups, young households, or the numerous low- and middle-level civil servants in this city of civil servants (*Beamtenstadt*). This socially beneficial function of modernized merchandising methods may have helped to maintain customer loyalty against the increasingly ubiquitous intimidations, fed as they were by the "National-Socialist" retail trade association (NSHAGO). This may have supported my father's rosy view of a Jewish future in Germany. He may also have been guided by a peculiar contradiction in the directives and advisories sent by the Jewish center in Berlin, the Reichsvertretung, to local Gemeinden. Around this time, I discovered much later when I researched Jewish policies in Nazi Germany, the policymaking central agency representing Jews in Germany, the Reichsvertretung der Juden in Deutschland, advised Jewish labor exchanges to channel properly prepared Jewish youngsters into commercial careers and provide Jewish business with the apprentices it needed, that is, very cheap labor. In the 1980s when I looked through the available sources, I could not locate the rationale connected with this directive as printed in the advisory bulletin. It flatly contradicted officially sanctioned policies to retrain youngsters for emigration. Commercial occupations were in oversupply and usually disqualified a Jew from Germany for admission as an immigrant unless he was supported by family ties abroad or his own independent means.

Objectively, of course, it made no practical sense to qualify for admission to a university if the Nazis barred you from entering. This prevailed even against the urging of Religionslehrer Dr. Hammelburger (a prestigious figure) and some of my teachers at the Gymnasium. I know of no attempt to change my father's mind that would have been made by the youth leader I worked with in the Gemeinde, Dr. Kurt Freudenthal. I do not know why he failed to draw my father's attention to preparation for emigration as the most productive goal for a Jewish boy of seventeen in 1935, or for completing high school abroad (for example, in England, then a working program), or to emigration to Palestine and the occupational training in the crafts or in agriculture that went with it. Emigration to the United States my father considered practical only in 1938 when the waiting list at the U.S. consulate was already many times larger than the available number of visas under the (restrictive) application of the quota law.

That I did not feel strongly about leaving school prematurely says something about my state of mind at the time. I was seventeen years old and preoccupied with finding my "identity," a term befitting the stereotyping of a core self that has its place in the development of an adolescent. I had no sense of class or status; leaving the Gymnasium barred the usual avenue to professional status and a university degree. "Advancing" from a business family to a university degree—a doctorate and a professional career as an *Akademiker*—reflected an ingrained Jewish preference for intellectual values and a traditional conditioning for study or for human relations based on healing and justice, as in medicine or law, law at the time still being perceived as part of the service professions that were worth spending a life with. Socially and economically, the middle-class quality of Jewish life had been acquired through hard labor and against odds. Jews had been "parvenus," meaning, without pejorative overtones, that they saw themselves for at least one or two generations as needing recognition and acceptance, and equal access to careers and occupations symbolizing them. They moved from lower-middle-class retailer or employee and traveling salesman to business independence, from the eastern parts of North Germany that had been part of Poland until 1815 to the large centers of Jewish life in Breslau, Leipzig, Cologne, or Berlin, and from the numerous pockets of rural traditionalism to towns and metropolises. Immigrants from Eastern Europe paralleled the process, as they migrated from an intense communal folk culture to the large urban concentrations of German Jews. In this multifaceted social dynamic, Jews had anticipated a general social process toward services and better training that would ultimately become recognizable in industrial societies, but they had the additional memory of centuries of oppression and quasi-pariah existence, and were reminded of it constantly by the coexistence and intermingling of populations that represented earlier stages of Jewish modernization.

That I did not realize that the Gymnasium was the entrance ticket to being an *Akademiker* and to higher status has puzzled me in retrospect for some time. My family simply did not articulate its judgment on others in such terms. They did, of course, live within the status system of Gemeinde and town, and had clear ideas about groups higher or lower in income or respectability. But they had their own multifaceted snobberies; they did respect differences in wealth or influence but linked evaluation with the personal or moral qualities of a person and with his standing in the Jewish community—learning, religiosity, service, standing in the non-Jewish community, and wealth if it impressed them as large and secure, and honestly acquired. I was taught, not to become something but to become someone, and earning a fortune was not a goal they impressed on me. It may well have been my mother's values that social climbing and making a secure and comfortable living were not primary goals in life. I discovered these dimensions of living in the modern world only when I was thrown back entirely on my own nonexistent financial resources upon arriving in New York City in 1946, the proverbial penniless immigrant with wife and (soon-to-be-born) child. Until then, I had been a student in two academic institutions, living on students' stipends or meager allowances.

Around the time I left the Gymnasium I was in the painful throes of orienting myself to a new world—Palestine, Zionism, socialism, the kibbutz. The ideological nature of this dimly perceived new world effectively screened out the bitter realities that would face an immigrant to Palestine at that time. In Würzburg, and then in Berlin, it took the form of radical verbal rejections of what appeared as the declining form of life of the liberal middle class.

In spite of the turmoils that accompany adolescence I remember this particular juncture as a uniquely happy period. A youth group comradeship was developing into my first love. Anne Ehrenbacher was entering our group of closer friends, joined our youth group, went with us on our weekly hikes and our holiday encampments; she had a beautiful clean face, a lovely voice, a confident mind. Her mother, born Else Selig, was a sister-in-law of Hugo Sinzheimer's, a prominent Social-Democratic law professor and legislator. She had returned from Nuremberg to Würzburg, where she was born, after her husband, a Social Democratic lawyer, died there soon after the Nazis came to power. Apparently, she had not found the companionship that would equal her artistic and intellectual style of life. The three children—Anne was the oldest—and the young mother had no links with our community and lived apart from its religious culture. Anne remembers today that I appeared to her as a difficult boy, moody, tense, impatient, intent on making sense of the numerous new impulses that crowded in. She was the first person—we were just barely seventeen years old when we met—who concentrated my feelings on herself, a girl becoming a young woman who would accept me as I would accept her, unconditionally and without making demands as the significant others in our lives had done so far. We shared a first love, shared interests, shared happy hours, shared aesthetic experiences, as we lived by the code our cultures provided, and lived through the seasons that orchestrated feelings fresh as day.

We drifted apart when I left Würzburg, and by 1938 we were pressed into other molds. Anne reached England and the United States and married our mutual best friend Walter Reis, while he served in the U.S. army. She worked while he studied and received a Ph.D. in psychology and an M.D. They have three lovely children, all either physicians or studying medicine, and have made a personal and professional success of lives dogged by health problems. Walter has specialized in psychiatry and is a most respected and widely known pillar of the University of Pittsburgh psychiatry department. Our friendship has endured to this day.

By about 1934–35, when I dropped out of the Gymnasium and Nazism was beginning to make ugly inroads into morality and everyday life among Würzburg opportunists, a new energy appeared among Gemeinde youth that would shape my life and thought until 1943.

This new energy was the Jewish version of an intrinsically German innovation, the youth movement. The forms to which we were introduced in Würzburg in some ways reinforced our cocoon, but in other ways broke down the walls that separated us from political and social realities—as far as we would be capable of grasping them.

Our Würzburg version, the last such "movement" in German Jewish history, was a far cry from its original, the youth culture and protest groups known, since the turn of the century, as *Wandervogel* (literally, migratory birds, but figuratively, roamers). Elements of their original style had survived in some romantic and primitivist ideas and activities by the time it arrived in town. But Jewish youth organizations had turned to political and socioeconomic realities—the 1920s had suggested to German as well as to Jewish political parties that political education began with youth and early indoctrination. Quite early also, even before the First World War, Jews had been repelled by the sticky racism and nationalism of the Germanic version of back-to-nature ideologies. Jewish students, kept out of German dueling societies as unworthy, formed their own student fraternities (*Verbindungen*) and trained for self-defense. From early on, too, Zionists and "assimiliationists" had divided into fiercely ideological camps, their conflicts sharpened by their distance from realities and by the *précieux* and emotional style of their human relations. Earlier conflicts between old and young, "bourgeois" and "authentic" lifestyles, capitalism and several versions of social or national-social Utopias had by now been transformed into coexistence between parents and children and their acknowledged need for separation.

Before the Third Reich arrived, representatives of the Jewish community had coopted youth movement (*Jugendbewegung*) elements to extracurricular Jewish education at about the same time that saw the YMHA and settlement house movements in the United

States. An American organization, The United Order of B'nai B'rith, through its German affiliates, had in fact used American models to stimulate "valuable leisure-time activities" and "*Bildung*" (intellectual and emotional refinement) among Jewish city youth. In the 1920s, the Würzburg rabbi and other communal officials had tried to reach apprentices and employees they saw in danger of sliding into social and cultural alienation. A Zionist youth group had sprung up shortly after World War I, drawing in part from students and East European immigrant youth, but had disintegrated after a few years. Similarly, an adult-sponsored youth association (*Jugendverein*) had come and gone at the end of the Weimar Republic. It had declared itself "neutral" in political or ideological terms in order to include as many diverse young men and women as possible, and had formulated its ultimate goal for social and political action as *gesamt-jüdisch*, that is, all-embracingly Jewish but vague enough to accommodate the chaotic realities of international immigration.

The youth association in Würzburg reflected several layers of the organizational type "youth group." Rabbis and congregational leaders had faced centrifugal trends among Jewish youth away from Judaism. Their first system of religious instructions was never allowed to grow to maturity: teaching stopped most of the time—orthodox excepted—when the boy reached thirteen years of age and parents felt that they had discharged their duty to a Jewish learning that was becoming irrelevant for their social ambitions. Youth movements offered a way out of this de-Judaization The embourgeoised upper-middle class saw in the new youth groups a remedy for the loss of their most active youth to the political left whose intellectual attraction they could not match. The disintegration of the German political center paralleled this loss of substance and dynamism in religious liberalism. Community leaders wanted to organize youth who were being marginalized economically by the structural changes in business organization; commercial employees saw themselves increasingly barred from advancing to ownership and independence in the retail field where Jews were most heavily concentrated, and dropped into the proletariat. All Jewish groups, especially the new Zionists, joined the general (German) trend to begin party-political education with public school children—a trend probably begun by European socialists even before World War I. Jewish political (that is, ideological) groupings such as Zionists, or German Jewish nationalists in their several shades, or Eastern European Jewish left-wing and labor movements, were part of this trend.

If some or all of these historic currents had left any traces in our Würzburg youth movement, my playmates and I were blissfully oblivious of our world-historic or cultural connections. We hiked together, played together, and dutifully attended the services conducted by youth for youth on Sabbath afternoons that Rabbi Hanover had instituted. A newly appointed youth rabbi (*Jugendrabbiner*) and a recent Jewish law school graduate, deprived of a job by Nazi discrimination, took a hand in organizing us after 1933. Hermann Neumark, a somewhat older philosophy student, served as spiritual guide and intellectual mentor to our cheerful ignorance of contemporary Jewish thought. The Gemeinde made a few rooms available for meetings in its (new?) administrative center, a house beside the synagogue yard. We redefined and "organized" what we had done previously—sports, weekend or biweekly hikes into the forest and hills surrounding the town—and met after synagogue and on Sabbath afternoons and evenings in the *Gemeindehaus* without benefit of adult supervision. The groups grew—all non-Jewish outlets were barred—a few youngsters became "organizers" and "leaders," students and other ideologically motivated parties approached us to join their political or religious persuasion, but the middle-of-the-road attitudes of our elders prevailed. We joined a neutral organization, the *Verband*. It corresponded to the idea of the nondenominational *Einheitsgemeinde* (mainstream, including all ritual denominations) that had a tradition in nineteenth-century Jewish Würzburg. By 1935, we probably had about eighty youngsters in the group since parents were glad to know their children were safe, protected against being accosted by the new fanatics beginning to appear on the streets.

The Verband of which we were a Verein had its main strength in South German towns and villages, and may have reached a total of about 6,400 members at its peak around this time. The older Verband had had a widely noted influence on German Jewish politics shortly after World War I, when it was led by young lawyers and returning veterans, but now, in 1934–35, it was distinctly on the decline in numbers if not in the brilliance of its young-Turk intellectual leaders—they included some respected professional names.

Some of these had joined radical leftist parties when they failed to turn the still-establishment Verband around. Before 1933, Zionism or *chalutziuth*—collective settlement in Palestine—had not been issues for debate.

For us, coming in from private and personal thoughts and activities, the Berlin center of the Verband and national and regional convocations of its leaders taught new perspectives on German politics—intellectual socialism and radical collectivism—and the then key issue of German Jewish versus national Jewish identity. Berlin published a periodical and sent out mimeographed materials whose contents, if they were seen by a censor in Goebbels's Ministry of Propaganda, would pass only because the Jewish press was not supposed to reach the general public. In the often Aesopian language applied, Jewish periodicals of all kinds were, in fact, the only semifree press in the Third Reich until suppressed in November 1938. This semifreedom applied especially to the Zionist press. The Nazi government, at the time, proclaimed the segregation and emigration of Jews as its goal. Some German radicals saw in Zionism an irredentist movement that would serve two Nazi goals, helping rid Germany of Jews and creating a cauldron of irreconcilable national conflict in a British mandate. (Some Jewish and some Nazi ideologues would pretend to believe in the cooperation of kindred nationalisms.)

This opened a window to the real world for the teenagers celebrating their togetherness under new sponsors. It made good sense at a moment of transition in Jewish political consciousness. The shocking violence of the first six months of 1933 was stopped when the secret rearmament had demanded a smooth public image for camouflage and import/export. Until the Nuremberg laws of 1935, even seasoned Jewish political functionaries would have some reason to hope for some taming of the beast. But only a few illusion-prone people expected a future for the young in Germany. Palestine, until 1936, absorbed more German Jewish immigrants than any other country. Reorienting the young toward Zionism would not prevent their fleeing elsewhere if the need arose. The silence among churches, universities, the army, the nationwide economic power coordinating organizations, and all others who were once friends and neighbors was just too penetrating to plan a Jewish future in a Germany going mad.

Thus, for about a year or two—I am unable to be more precise, but before I left town in the fall of 1936—we "learned" Zionism from the material issued or recommended by Berlin, debated German and Jewish nationalism, agonized over Orient and Occident, love of country and history, and went to convocations where an admired group of theoreticians and serious ideologues took time out to pry us out of our comfortable homes. We studied the history and sociology of Zionism and Palestine from readers and source books, sang Palestine songs, and learned some Hebrew in the different modern (Sephardic) pronunciation. We also tried to understand Labor Zionist and radical-revolutionary East European authors in translations and excerpts, but of course lacked the knowledge or the guidance that would place them—and Marx's *Communist Manifesto*, the only Marx we read at the time—into their several contexts. Ours was a most theoretical, "soft," nationalism; Martin Buber, the humanist aesthete, Richard Beer-Hoffman, the poet of tribal roots, Stefan Zweig ("Jeremias") touched chords our idealistic minds could absorb. At the end we had made "the decision for Zionism" after much travail, opting for Jewish-Arab understanding and the common struggle for freedom from national oppression and economic exploitation—so debunkingly realistic and so hopelessly remote from reality. We were too young to make decisions on emigration on our own. Jewish emigration from Nazi Germany was a family migration. After the first three years into the Third Reich, emigration to the Holy Land had declined, and overseas countries became the preferred and realistic targets of migrant families.

The most significant gain from our Zionism, in retrospect, was not that the Verband contributed a respectable if not overwhelming number of émigrés to the reconstruction of Israel and thus saved them from being murdered in the Holocaust, but that it eased the separation from our cultural roots, the art and the landscape, the language and the literature, and the social comforts of the rooted life, and that it protected us—helped to protect us—against losing our self-assurance, our "identity," before the enemy and his clangorous hatred. Still, we did keep finding lasting cues in continued explorations of the literature and art of a past Germany. Our intellectual mentors, ten to fifteen years our elders, still had their feet on these grounds, too. It helped us avoid the agonizing pains the parent generation had to go through without coming out on top. We changed their emotional coordinates.

Ours became a humanizing national counter-Utopia, the dream the best of German Zionists, Robert Weltsch, dreamed of, peaceful coexistence of Arabs and Jews, and most forcefully injected into Jewish consciousness in 1933.[3] Even if it seemed to us then that we were among the privileged few to escape contamination by the aggressor, the community as a whole gave an unblemished account of itself, and I am not sure any longer that I can isolate the youth movement from the broader cultural context in all its tragic configuration.

During my Würzburg years, we had never made Nazism or racism the subject of debate; the historic or intellectual places of racism and Nazism never appeared on the agenda of our seminars or convocations. "The Germans" as yet did not exist until you had left the country and reflected on the enormity of what had been happening to you. There were good and bad persons, friendly and grumpy ones, pomposity, strutting, and posturing besides decency and quiet friendship. The biology of race simply made no sense and had not penetrated language or daily life. I do not know if anybody ever used it to rationalize his rejection or hatred of Jews; antisemitism had deeper, more complex roots than race, in history, economics, religion, folklore, body images, social relations, or societal tensions and propaganda images.

I trust that nearly every one of my friends of that time would remember incidents in which he or she was mistaken for an "Aryan," in situations that made the "other" look faintly or grossly ridiculous. I once managed to make the director of a vocational junior college ridiculous in front of his students. I had to attend one year of a vocational school, the so-called "eleventh year" following the Gymnasium. The entire school was assembled in the largest auditorium when he demonstrated "Aryan" racial features on me during the obligatory hour of "race science" the Nazis had added to the curriculum. The whole class snickered. His embarrassment became complete when he challenged me in the following "race" hour to greet him with the Hitler salute the class had to yell at him

---

[3] Robert Weltsch, "Tragt ihn mit Stolz, den Gelben Fleck," editorial, *Jüdische Rundschau*, April 4, 1933, p. 1.

in unison, and I trumpeted back at him that I was "Jewish, Herr Direktor." (Being punished with a double four-hour arrest did not diminish my glee and may not have diminished his embarrassment, as he continued teaching "race science" the rest of the term.) Anecdotal, to be sure, but our clocks ticked differently. They had power and the means of physical and propagandistic coercion, but they did not control our character or our self-assurance. Zionism had grown out of Jewish assumptions with us, not imitation or identification with German nationalism. We were not yet aware of the historic divisions between cultural and political Zionism, and between ideological and practical trends. What we were reading in our texts suggested that they complemented each other. Even if some of the neo-romantic poetry, or some of the philosophical literature written by Jewish writers which we stumbled on, or to which we were guided, *did* rhapsodize about the bonds of blood over the generations, we placed it into the religious and biblical tradition, not racism: we did not require antitoxins against defamation.

Given the loneliness and anomie that beset adolescents in many of the urban and cosmopolitan environments I have been able to observe in my peregrinations, ours was a privileged coincidence of conditions, making for community for a short moment in time. While the institutions of the Gemeinde quite splendidly pulled the community together to face an increasingly hostile city, we were protected by this community and free to live out the impulses and test the consequences of our changing orientations and self-understandings. Our growth certainly involved us in pain. But it was on our own terms that we faced adulthood, not on the dictates of the increasingly noisy and hostile propaganda and politics of the regime. They were too crude to replace the cultural subtleties of centuries that emancipation had made part of education and Bildung among German Jews. In the 1950s, I interviewed enough former members of our youth movement in the United States to feel certain that, if my glasses were rose-tinted, so were everybody else's.[4]

---

[4] Herbert A. Strauss, "The Jugendverband: A Social and Intellectual History," *Leo Baeck Institute Year Book*, 6 (1961), 210–25.

3

Youth Movement and Zionist Student Collective: Berlin, 1936–1938

IN THE FALL OF 1936, I left Würzburg for Berlin. I had been offered the administration of our national youth office, when the previous executive, Martin Seliger, left for the Hebrew University in Jerusalem. The decision to leave Würzburg came easy enough except for the separation from Anne. I had felt happy and comfortable at home, but was bored and routinized in my commercial occupation, and saw little ahead of me that held any challenge. Leaving the Gymnasium had barred all avenues for study abroad. My family had never tried hard to emigrate, and the emigration office in the Gemeinde had no advice for me. Moving to Berlin looked like a continuation of the communal life I had found in our youth group, and a challenge as well. I would be responsible for designing study and discussion programs for about sixteen hundred young people, and preparing meetings, seminars, and encampments on a national scale with increased responsibility for administration. What I had enjoyed when it was leisure I surely would enjoy when it became an occupation. I was just past eighteen years of age.

The conditions we agreed upon were entirely noncommercial. I would join a Socialist-Zionist student "collective" (we did not use the word at the time), to be housed and fed, and receive an allowance for whatever I needed in shoes, clothing, carfare, and so on. My job carried no salary; expenses would be reimbursed by the youth group treasury. I would have an office in the building housing the central organization representing all Jews in Germany, the Reichsvertretung der Juden in Deutschland.[1] Like the other stu-

---

[1] The Reichsvertretung der Juden in Deutschland was founded in 1933 by German Jewish community leaders to create a central coordinating, defense, and administrative agency. Different from Eastern European *Judenräte* (Jewish councils),

dents, I would be enrolled in a culturally progressive institute for Jewish graduate study, the Lehranstalt für die Wissenschaft des Judentums, a "liberal" institute for Jewish graduate study, the only German Jewish institution dedicated to Jewish scholarship without formal affiliation to any of the denominational units (orthodox, conservative, Reform). This would prepare us for teaching in a kibbutz in Palestine where we would hope to emigrate with a youth group assembled by the international education and emigration agency Aliyath HaNoar–Youth Aliyah—emigration of youth— founded by Henriette Szold, the American communal and Zionist leader in 1934.

I arrived at the Berlin railroad station (Anhalter Bahnhof) as night was setting in, expectant if exhausted from the lengthy railroad trip, and made my way to the address I had received from Berlin, Elsässerstrasse 53, IV, Beth Hatalmidim, student home. The reception was not too friendly; the director (on loan from a kibbutz in Palestine) had not been informed of the date and hour of my arrival, and was unprepared. They turned an empty armoire on its face, put a mattress on it, and heaved it into a corner, in the informal style Israelis and hikers are accustomed to. Two women about my age provided the little sympathy I needed not to feel quite lost. The first impression of traffic pushing its way through crowded,

---

it was not set up by a Nazi government or police agency or by SS or Gestapo orders. Its history shows that until 1938, its leaders retained an independent voice vis-à-vis Gestapo or government orders. Its power base was its connection with Jewish social service and funding agencies in England and the United States and the Nazi government's policies in the 1930s. During this delicate period of secret (and illegal) rearmament and extreme scarcity of foreign currency to buy needed metals and other raw materials on the international market, Nazi propaganda sought to create the image of an orderly and civilized society bent on peaceful revision of the peace treaties of 1918–22. That terror and murder were not yet government policy permitted a relative cultural and religious autonomy to the Jewish community in Germany. It rested, of course, on an extensive discriminatory narrowing of individual and organizational freedom of action, and on penetrating antisemitic pressure to force Jews to emigrate. But at least until late 1937/early 1938, the Jewish community in Germany was able to defend itself and to create an effective system of mutual aid, social service, aid to emigration, and independent cultural and religious activities even as Jews progressively lost economic freedom and the political and constitutional place that had been guaranteed to them by more than a century of Jewish emancipation in Germany. The "community under stress" remained active and unbowed until the long dark night engulfed culture and community. The Reichsvertretung has an honorable place in their final agonies.

slightly foggy streets. with headlights diffused in haze, was over-whelming and intimidating.

The job I entered upon the next morning was within easy reach of my new home. My office was located near Bahnhof Zoo station in Charlottenburg at Kantstrasse 158, directly adjacent to the busy railroad and elevated tracks that linked Central and West Berlin at this point. The only person I knew in Berlin before I arrived was my mentor, Paul Eppstein, a sociologist and social work expert at the Reichsvertretung.[2] As in Elsässerstrasse, I had to improvise the office I was supposed to use: typewriter and chair, small shelf and table, wastepaper basket in a corner of an unused room, and access to a telephone in Eppstein's office, presided over by Mrs. Myrantz, a beautiful, elegant, and somewhat madeup woman, unlike any of her colleagues I had known in Würzburg. The most important item for the job was a copier in another room used by the whole floor. It was the typed-stencil-and-inked-drum variety run by hand, proba-bly advanced technology for its time. Since the Hochschule would not open before late October or early November, I concentrated first on the organizational tasks at hand.

The youth groups of the Jugendverband—I sketched the Würz-burg branch earlier—were concentrated in the south and southwest of the country, covering the belt of Southern Jewish settlement across Bavaria, Württemberg, Baden, and the Rhenish Palatinate. Most of the larger cities also had affiliated groups, but our group was concentrated primarily in the numerous country towns that at that time still served as commercial centers for the rich agricultural areas around them (grain, feed, wine, hops, lumber, livestock). Youth groups had sprung up increasingly when Jewish youth were cut off suddenly from the sociability they had enjoyed before Hitler. Jewish youth was more isolated in the countryside during those years than city youth, given the face-to-face intimacy of Christian village society. A Jewish youth association filled the gap and pro-vided constructive leisure time and links with Jewish youth in the region and across state borders. It did not need the concerned mind of a Jewish mother to recognize that the trend for better-off families

---

[2] Herbert A. Strauss, "Jewish Autonomy Within the Limits of National-Socialist Policy: The Communities and the *Reichsvertretung*," in *The Jews in National-Social-ist Germany*, ed. Arnold Paucker, Sylvia Gilchrist, and Barbara Suchy (Tübingen: J. C. B. Mohr [Paul Siebeck], 1986), pp. 125–52.

to move away from the countryside to towns and cities might make lasting companionship harder for their daughters.

Teachers and cantors, the arbiters of ritual and learning in these small communities, properly worried about the isolation of their charges from the culture of their environment and from Jewish intellectual and political life, creating a semblance of an *ethnic* German Jewish culture at the very end of the German Jewish period of history. Palestine had become a major attraction for Jewish émigrés from Germany between 1933 and 1936, and although traditional Jewish folk culture was still strong in the countryside, Zionism and modern Hebrew were relatively new subjects and had grown beyond the stage where ritual incantation and contributions to the *Blaue Büchse*, the ubiquitous blue tin can used for fund raising by the Jewish National Fund wherever Jews lived, would suffice.

The Jewish substance present in villages and small towns did not need strengthening. What was needed were programs dealing with current events, modern Palestine, contemporary Jewish songs, political literature, and advice on emigration opportunities. Frequently, teachers would lead the groups. This limited their youth movement character, but gave them substance. During my first round-trip to the major centers I recognized that information on trends not available in the Jewish press—inside information on organizations and channels, emigration chances, reports from abroad—would serve as the basis of lasting cooperation between us. The number of young people was diminishing rapidly, as was the number of adult congregants left behind. I appreciated their traditional hospitality; they recognized my Southern dialect, my youth, my ignorance, and my earnest good will to be of service to them in more than trivia. During the two years the Nazis still allowed Jewish youth organizations to function (until November 1938), I must have taken three or four turns around the Jewish South, often a lonely and exhausting trip rewarded only by the friendships it made possible.

For towns, the program would need an added component of Jewish tradition and custom, since "assimilation" was to be replaced by a Jewish identity that would accommodate the several strains of Jewish politics on neutral ground—that is, use, almost invent for German Jewry, an idea symbolizing the unity of the Jewish people wherever they lived and their responsibility for each other. Overseas countries were replacing Palestine as the preferred target of emigration for Jews from Germany in 1936, but it took until 1939 for the United States and England to lift restrictions on immigration enough to make a difference. In the few big cities, our youth organization played a different social role from that in the towns. There they were often marginal or social catch-alls, their members tolerating intellectual efforts as interruptions of the sociability that was important to them. For most of them, Palestine offered less attraction than overseas settlement.

For the history of this Jugendverband[3] "my" years were an intellectually insignificant afterglow of the fireworks of the 1920s and early 1930s, but they marked the transition to a new realism and were shielded from cynicism by a new awareness of what Judaism could mean when entirely unexpected brutalities reemerged in the twentieth century.

For the eager provincial in Elsässerstrasse who soon changed to a regular bed and won some friends among his fellow "collectivists," Berlin became the great adventure that would form his life for the next seven years. The town was huge, dirty, and incoherent, even aside from the Nazi government's presence. My new home lay in an earlier center of Jewish migrant settlement near the Stettiner Bahnhof, the Bahnhof Friedrichstrasse, and the thoroughfares from the east and northeast of Prussia and beyond from where Berlin's Jewish population had recruited itself right up to the 1920s. By the 1930s "my" area had long become a workers' and proletarian quarter, different from the proverbial crime centers around Alexanderplatz except for the flourishing run of prostitutes that populated the access roads to the Stettiner Bahnhof. Jewish families had come also from the eastern parts of Prussia, to judge from their German dialects and pronunciation, and kept shop, prayed, worked, and brought up their children. The Lehranstalt at Artilleriestrasse 14 I began to attend as a nonmatriculated student in November 1936, and its orthodox equivalent at Artilleriestrasse 31, had as much been left behind by population drifts in the city as the ornate main synagogue of the Gemeinde and its administrative center around the corner in Oranienburgerstrasse. Gentrified Berlin Jewry lived farther west and had built new centers there.

---

[3] See above, pp. 55–60.

By 1936, Berlin Jewry kept making up in numbers what it was losing to emigration, and the city remained, or became once again, the center of Jewish life and Jewish culture, supported by a critical mass of Jews found nowhere else in Germany in such numbers. They were extremely diverse in every way. Some were old family and old wealth, refined to decadence and often converted to Protestantism for admission to gentry families. Some, at the other extreme, had just come off the trains and lived, like immigrants everywhere, in compact districts, creating their own differentiated culture and a renaissance of Yiddish literature, art illustration, or music. The most generally visible Jewish presence was in retail trade, from the department and specialty stores they had pioneered as a new type of distribution center to dwarf mom-and-pop shops that lined many streets even in the 1930s. Berlin had been home to the bohemian literature and the significant painters, actors, directors, and musicians that had made up "Weimar culture," and even if their work was now banned and they themselves exiled or persecuted, one could still meet many people who had been witnesses to their glow. Berlin Jews had contributed to the world status of the University of Berlin, to Jewish scholarship, to the legal and medical professions, often out of a social and political conscience that no Nazi's ever matched.

Berlin and the state of Prussia had returned Socialist/leftist majorities to government most of the time of Weimar. To penetrate the cultural webs that held them together would take more than a generation—the Nazis had been in power for only three years when I arrived in 1936. It was my first metropolis after the polis I grew up in. The military spectacles and the glittering shows the Nazi government and the Nazi Party staged for larger movie audiences in the provinces contrasted starkly with the workers' quarters in all their grime. My "collective" lay within walking distance of major run-down slums. It was separated from them by respectable working- and lower-middle-class blocks running north and east. These districts and their people impressed me indelibly as they had impressed the radical sons of the Jewish bourgeoisie of the 1920s, whose experience I was unwittingly reliving. The social symbolism I ascribed to the embourgeoised Jewish West like Charlottenburg, or, as the case may be, to their more or less tasteful villas in quarters like Grunewald or Dahlem, appeared much less devastating for Jewish class relations than the aesthetic and economic tensions in the city in general: Jewish poverty seemed less desperate, less threatening, more chintzy, lower middle class. Jews had no landowning class; wealth was as recent as that of most of the bourgeoisie; and in the nineteenth century, Berlin "society" had seen them as *arrivistes*, upstarts, with parvenu manners and values one tolerated because their marriageable daughters had dowries.

In the poor quarters, down-and-out Polish Jewish immigrants had huddled together during and after the First World War. They appeared reassuring to me, people clad in orthodox black, women in kerchiefs, decaying basement stores advertising religious objects in frayed Hebrew wall inscriptions flanking the staircases leading down below. It captured the sympathy we had cultivated in our youth movement, our enlarged circle of Jewish commitment. Our neighbors seemed more alive than the Wilhelmian "baroque" eclectics in the West.

Yet, it turned out that my social access to Jewish Berlin was mostly with the respectable Jewish middle class that differed from Würzburg's Jewish population only in its more moderate interest in religion and its sharper critical appraisal of the world around them, that is, in its Berlin cosmopolitan habit of debunking establishments. I met them first as the functionaries my work brought me in contact with, and during my studies and through some of my teachers at the Lehranstalt für die Wissenschaft des Judentums. From 1939 on, I rented rooms in Charlottenburg and found myself quite at home there. To my surprise, most of my neighbors' parents or grandparents, or they themselves, had come to Berlin as I had, in search of cosmopolitan freedom and opportunity, quite a few of them from South and West Germany.

But "my" Berlin was not only the new Jewish environment that did not stop fascinating me, in part because it was so different from mine, or the new circles of friends that youth makes so easily. Precisely because I had entered a "collective," I felt often lonely and isolated by all the strangeness around me, spoiled as I had been by the Gemeinschaft I had left behind that had become unacknowledged second nature, and by the lovely environment we had appropriated with the possessiveness of rooted growth. Berlin became an adventure on another level. I took long walks in Tiergarten and Grunewald and along the Havel and Wannsee and Glienicker Sea area where one could still swim without concern or fear of being molested, and I discovered the rich collections of classical art and paintings and, once again, appropriated them during numerous weekend visits to the Pergamon Altar and the Ishtar Gate. Rembrandt's helmeted man, or the Nefertiti, seemed like part of my own environment. I would sometimes line up at 6 A.M. to buy the cheapest tickets to performances of the State Opera Unter den Linden, or the Schauspielhaus to be engrossed by Gründgens's Hamlet—the regulars among these early risers would begin to recognize one another and discuss with great conviction and expertise the merits of what they had seen and heard from the top rank of the house. I also saw quite a few plays in the less ostentatious but often superior performances put on by the Volksbühne (people's theater) that had played such a significant role in Weimar Berlin. The performance I remember best was by a white-haired actor named Wüllner in Goethe's *Faust*, possibly including Part II, although my memory has fused this Berlin *Faust* with a performance I would attend in the Zurich Schauspielhaus in the mid-1940s. My music life, though, with rare exceptions, centered around the 78s, still in "mono," often scratchy, on the hand-wound phonograph, and the classical repertoire, Beethoven, Mozart, Bach, Corelli, Scarlatti, to which I listened with lights dimmed, lost in thoughts and feelings. And I continued to be a voracious reader of German literature across the board, without benefit of linguistic or literary scholarship, as the cheap editions slowly began to fill third-hand shelves. Berlin allowed you to live in a self-made cocoon.

The Lehranstalt[4] in which the student collective enrolled when the term began was one of three university-level institutes for higher Jewish learning in Germany. Its statutes committed it to the pursuit of "pure" scholarship in Judaic studies (*Wissenschaft des Judentums, Judaistik*). Its nineteenth-century founders, a sophisticated class and culture, had valued civil-service–style objectivity more highly than "mere partisanship." They had declared their independence from the denominational groups that divided modern Judaism everywhere, but failed to beat the dialectic Hegel was well

---

[4] Herbert A. Strauss, "Die letzten Jahre der Hochschule (Lehranstalt) für die Wissenschaft des Judentums, Berlin, 1936–1942," in *Wissenschaft des Judentums— Chokhmat Yisrael: Anfänge der Judaistik in Europa*, ed. Julius Carlebach (Darmstadt: Wissenschaftlicher Buchverlag, 1992), pp. 36–52 (including references).

aware of: "pure" Wissenschaft by itself was viewed as taking sides. In practice, the Lehranstalt trained liberal and reform rabbis and teachers in Wissenschaft while periodically renewing its commitment to the humanistic ethos of European classicism and its precise historical methods: by this long-since-diluted philosophical tradition, Jewish Wissenschaft had chartered its own independent course.

In the following I shall replace the name, which had become a household word among Jewish scholars, with the designation Hochschule, the original name chosen to express the academic aspirations of its founders. Lehranstalt implied teaching, an occupational training center. Prussian authorities had refused to legitimize the designation Hochschule shortly after its foundation in 1872, and Nazi authorities had followed their precedent. It was Hochschule only during the Weimar Republic.

The Hochschule was the only institution of Jewish higher learning in Germany that a mostly nonpracticing agnostic group of young Zionist Socialists could profitably attend. The orthodox and conservative curricula of the two other institutes, in Berlin and Breslau, respectively, would have had little meaning for a collective "learning its Marx" in order to fit into the sharply divided ideological camps they would join in Palestine. Their Zionism, Zionism in Germany, youth movement Zionism, had originated in a highly symbolic and moralistic perception of reality; it had been "idealistic" and had searched for the roots below their uprooting also in Jewish ritual which they proceeded to reinvent. In Palestine, youth groups and kibbutzim had begun to experiment with new secular forms, replacing the accustomed ritual on Sabbaths and holidays, using texts that could be interpreted in national terms and would renew the spirit of communality of the ancient tradition. None of this would have made sense to traditionalists, and at first it appeared artificial to me until I realized that this was one way to adjust ancient forms to contemporary sensitivities. It was an object lesson in the creative interplay between tradition and innovation in religion.

When, with the nonchalance of youth, I first entered the Hochschule building in Artilleriestrasse 14, within walking distance of our student home, I had no knowledge of its history and mission, and no inkling of the influence it would exert on my future life. The building that housed it, four stories high, presented a tastefully

Wilhelmian façade that blended well into a continuous row of houses lining the street. It barely revealed its institutional character. The Hochschule was the purest expression of a period and a class in German and Berlin Jewish history, and the most sophisticated expression of the place of Jewish Wissenschaft in the great European currents of thought and culture since the early nineteenth century. The Hochschule was founded in 1872 on the model of a German university: throughout the nineteenth century, German Wissenschafts-ministries—Education and Wissenschaft fell under the jurisdiction of the states, not the central government—had pointedly refused to honor initiatives by Jewish scholars to establish a chair or an institute for Wissenschaft des Judentums. As a Prussian ministry opined in mid-century, legitimizing a Jewish Wissenschaft by such a step contradicted the policy of complete absorption, the liberal government goal of the time.[5]

Still, Wissenschaft had grown without university support as young Jewish scholars, educated in the humanities at German universities, embraced the method and spirit of neoclassicism, *Neuhumanismus*, and its quasi-religious ethos. Judaism would renew itself through a critical reconstruction of its primary sources. It was the heady and pristine belief of this classicism that critical historical studies and precise philological methods would confirm the "eternal truth" of the Jewish religion and its claim to universal ethical principles of timeless validity. Even when historical studies, history itself, would begin to destroy this timelessness by discovering the plural nature of world civilization, when history turned relativistic and became historicism (*Historismus*), the Hochschule held fast to its ethos.

Shortly before Hitler seized power in 1933, the institute celebrated sixty years of scholarly brilliance and worldwide recognition as a model for cities whose Jewries, from Budapest to Cincinnati and Jerusalem, supported similar high-mindedness. The Berlin institute was able to attract renowned faculty whose publications— one measure of excellence—and graduates reflected unstable balances among general, European, American, German scholarship, and Jewish learning. "Assimilation," coexistence, symbiosis were seen as resting on mutual respect between Christianity and

---

[5] See above, note 4.

Judaism, on the large reservoir of Jewish education and learning that students and faculty had carried into Hochschule modernity from their orthodox origins in rural communities and in Eastern Europe. However, the Hochschule's intellectual brilliance frequently was achieved at the price of financial stringency and near-destitution, especially in post–World War I Germany. Gemeinde administrations or elected representatives withheld support— Berlin and a few regional assemblies were exceptions—on the pretext that the Hochschule by-laws provided for the admission of non-Jewish students. It survived the postwar run-away inflation of the early 1920s only with American Jewish financial assistance. In turn, some of its prominent faculty members (Ismar Elbogen, Julius Guttmann) were appointed as visiting professors, or advisers on personnel and curricula, in New York Jewish theological institutions.

After the "Great Inflation," the Hochschule found fiscal and institutional calm for a few years before the Great Depression once again dislocated it in unexpected ways. Its enrollment suddenly increased to a point where faculty and board felt constrained to warn against "academic proletarization" and unemployment for rabbis and teachers. Unemployed high school graduates in Germany and in other countries saw an opportunity for a constructive use of enforced idleness, while some top-level faculty accepted positions elsewhere even before Hitler's seizure of power.

Paradoxically, the Third Reich presented the Hochschule with challenges and opportunities. It managed to avoid being dissolved and stayed open ten of the twelve years of Nazi rule. In the mid-thirties, its faculty and students would increase in number and diversity beyond anything in its history; it would add new disciplines to its curriculum by creating a humanities and social science general education division and appoint university teachers and researchers to the faculty who had been dismissed by the Nazi laws of April 7, 1933, and September 15, 1935. Graduates of this period would serve in Germany and around the world as rabbis, teachers, scholars, and organization and communal officials. The Hochschule preserved the integrity of its heritage, minuscule in size in an ocean of brutality but persevering in its scholarly commitment to Jewish studies and its openness to the world. I do not know if many faculty and students were aware of this unique but brittle brilliance, or of what would be in store for them.

In 1935–36, our "collective" increased Hochschule enrollment by about fifty students in two years. I believe all my fellow "collectivists" ended their freelance studies and emigrated to Palestine as our organizations had planned for us. They may well have been aware of the attraction university-level study would exert on young German Jews, and made successful efforts to keep us identified with the cause. We maintained contacts with the central Zionist administration located in Berlin Charlottenburg's Meinekestrasse 10, and visited agricultural training centers for kibbutzim in Palestine that had been located in the environs of Berlin. We also frequently listened to lectures and discussed current political events with Zionist labor leaders from Israel and Germany. Among them were a brilliant young lawyer from Nuremberg, Georg (Giora) Josephtal, and his wife, Senta Punfud. Georg would join a kibbutz in Israel and embark upon a singularly productive career at the top of Zionist and Israeli politics and diplomacy, including Ben Gurion's cabinet. He died of kidney disease at age fifty, potentially the most prominent Jew from Germany in Israeli politics, a preserve of immigrants from Eastern Europe. Senta served as a Labor Party member of the Knesset. Georg's political analysis of Jewish communal affairs and Zionist politics were my first introduction to contemporary world politics, fascinatingly different from my Würzburg perspectives and our concept of Judaism as a humanistic religion. Equally memorable was my first encounter with Eastern European styles of rhetoric represented by Boris Eisenstadt, a former Danzig Zionist leader sent from Palestine to Jews in Germany. After 1948, he was elected to the Israeli parliament, the Knesset, on the Labor Party ticket. Though he was no less penetratingly analytical than Josephtal, his fiery and passionate delivery contrasted sharply with Josephtal's. Georg's surgical brilliance, the new experiences they imparted to us, stand out in my memory to this day.

The "collective" was dissolved after about a year, presumably because it had completed its task, and I moved on to new assignments, small jobs, and study. Precisely because it resembled a secular monastic system without private property, collective life was relaxed and meaningful for what I wanted to be and do at that time. We lived among German working people and coped with the simple conditions our old building imposed on us: we bought our supply of coal—pressed brown coal briquettes—in a nearby coal cellar and carried them on our backs four or five flights of steps to the apartment, fifty or one hundred pounds at a time. I frequently ate in fast-food restaurants especially late at night or early in the morning, and stood at high, round tables talking with neighbors on their way home from a late shift or late pleasures. I still bought my small supplies in mom-and-pop stores and knew the proprietors. It may have been the romanticism of the totally different and new that made contacts easy, but I felt the freedom of owning nothing and being planted with two feet in my Gemeinschaft and my plans. Nazism, at any rate, in this working-people's environment, would pop up only occasionally, when a brown uniform or a Nazi Party pin in a lapel would flit through. It was still early into the catastrophe, 1936 and 1937.

4

General Studies: Berlin, November 1936 to September 1, 1939

THE HOCHSCHULE I ENTERED with my fellow collectivists in November 1936 would have been a unique, and a uniquely attractive, academic institution, even if these had not been "extraordinary times, a time of oppression that called for extraordinary measures," as one of our history professors, Ismar Elbogen, phrased it in 1938. In the mid-1930s enrollment was at its peak; students, faculty, and curriculum at their most diversified, to a point where some classes were relocated in nearby Jewish public and middle schools (amusingly enough, students of the orthodox *Rabbinerseminar* expressed religious scruples over attending classes in the Hochschule building). The dismissal of Jewish teachers from public schools had led some older men to take up studies at the Hochschule. They prepared for teaching in Jewish schools, or just made use of their time while waiting to emigrate. Of regular students I recall some who would emigrate or flee before the war broke out in September 1939. Some of them would contribute in a major way to liberal or Reform congregations abroad, to Jewish scholarship and organizations, or to universities in England or the Western hemisphere. There were also some older Christian theologians, including a woman pastor or theological student, probably of Dutch or Scandinavian nationality. The last class presumably entered in 1938 or 1939. I remember about six to eight of these younger men who had obtained the Abitur certificate in one of the Berlin Jewish schools and had, of course, been barred from entering a German university. Most "regular," that is, fully matriculated, students had already been at the Hochschule for some years when I entered, and held pulpits in Berlin or outside it as temporary or tenured auxiliary rabbis or preachers, or teachers. In the summer term of 1937, enrollment reached an all-time high with fifty-eight full-time matriculated and eighty-three nonmatriculated (part-time) students. A year later, it had fallen to forty matriculated and twenty-two nonmatriculated students, presumably through emigration. In 1939, seventeen matriculated and fourteen nonmatriculated students were left.

The faculty was composed of five permanent chairs in the major Judaistics disciplines. The maximum number of seventeen full-time or part-time instructors (*Dozenten*) was reached in 1937–38. The small number of women among students increased until 1939. A much-noted graduate, Frau Rabbiner Jonas, may have been the first ordained woman rabbi at the Hochschule or, for that matter, at any Jewish theological institution. Her robust sense of humor was said to have helped her over what was viewed by most as an awkward position. She officiated mostly in social service situations.

Sources kindly put at my disposal by Dr. Renate Grumach, Berlin, the widow of Dr. Ernst Grumach, a faculty member, and Dr. Irene Shiroun, Jerusalem, his daughter, allow insights into some of the intellectual and administrative issues that occupied faculty and students at the time. The lists of courses (*Vorlesungsverzeichnisse*) issued each term or year, and printed in the annual *Berichte* (in irregular intervals from the mid-1930s on), confirm my recollection that the Hochschule held fast to its traditional curriculum and that the demanding standards of its past, if anything, were tightened.[1]

Admission was based on university requirements, that is, students needed to submit the certificate of matriculation (the *Abiturzeugnis*), the comprehensive graduation examination of a nine-year high school, preferably a Humanistisches Gymnasium like mine. If students needed additional preparations, attendance at a preparatory division (*Präparandie*) was required. The course of studies was divided into a core requirement lasting probably four years or more, and advanced study involving specialization in a major and a minor or minors. Each division required a comprehensive multi-hour examination often stretching over many weeks or even months. For graduation, the bylaws prescribed proof of successful completion of studies at a university in a related field, that is, a printed dissertation and a doctorate. In addition, two written master's-length theses

---

[1] Hochschule Annual Reports (*Berichte*): 45 (1928), 46 (1929), 47 (1930), 48 (1931), 49 (1932), 50 (1936), 51 (1938).

tested proficiency in Talmudic studies and another discipline. My printed certificate for the examination in core subjects dated June 18, 1940, suggests the comprehensive spread of requirements: philology (linguistics, *Sprachwissenschaft*), biblical criticism (*Bibelwissenschaft*), Talmudic criticism (*Talmudwissenschaft*), *Midrasch* (Midrash), *Liturgik* (liturgy—prayers and service, calendar, customs), philosophy of religion (history of religion), Jewish history and literature. I presume it took at least six to eight years to complete all requirements for a rabbinical degree and a certificate for teaching religion in a government-run Gymnasium, the high school/junior college hybrid. University study and written theses had been superimposed on a lengthy series of oral examinations in major subjects that might stretch over some years, A plan to add examinations in non-Judaistic subjects taught in a separate division mentioned in the 1938 *Bericht* was never formalized. The November pogroms of 1938 destroyed expectations of this kind, too.

As long as it was allowed to survive, the Hochschule reflected the ideal image of the German rabbi, and probably the highest standards that Wissenschaft des Judentums had reached in some of, if not all, the disciplines it offered. The doctorate had been prescribed by government decree for tenured rabbis in nineteenth-century German states intent on turning Jews into educated German citizens. German state-church relations also required that rabbis function as arms of the state in several official contexts such as the civil registry of marriage and inheritance law. The Hochschule's curriculum may well have been an outstanding symbol of the link between dynamic Jewish learning and universal scholarship. That the Hochschule expanded its Judaistics offerings and sought to find a substitute for the previously required doctorate was, of course, not unique to this German Jewish liberal institution. It has been observed that in many instances Nazi persecution threw Jewish institutions on their own hidden resources wherever persecution did not completely destroy them, as in late-1930s Germany.[2] I benefited greatly from this paradox.

Yet, that this inclusive curriculum could not survive unchanged into the twentieth century would have become obvious even if per-

---

[2] Salo W. Baron, *Bibliography of Jewish Social Studies, 1938–1939* (New York: Jewish Social Studies Publications, 1940), p. 3.

secution would not have changed the composition of the student body. Generational change alone would have opened new vistas, as would internal developments like Zionism or the extreme demographic decline in world Jewry. Curricular reform emerged as one issue in the 1930s.

Surviving faculty sources reflect the currents eddying about the debate on this reform. One set of issues was the demand made by Talmud studies on students' time and the limited usefulness of these studies for later rabbinical practice. Ismar Elbogen (see below) and an organized representation of students supported a proposal for comprehensive change. It would equip graduates with new skills they would need in emigration countries: proficiency in Spanish and English, and training in independent study especially in countries that lacked libraries and other tools for scholarship. Greek and Latin would be dropped from the curriculum, and "examinations merely testing rote learning like 'history, history of religion, history of education, Religionsphilosophie'" and so forth would be abolished. Comprehensive final examinations stretching over months and years would be split into two, one each for rabbis and teachers. University-style lectures would be replaced by colloquia and seminars, and emphasis shifted from disinterested scholarship to practical training in homiletics, the teaching of religion, and social work.

In the spring of 1938, when Elbogen advanced these wide-ranging and revolutionary ideas, time was already beginning to run out for the Hochschule. Elbogen would leave in the fall for New York, and the November pogroms of 1938 would create an entirely new situation for Jews in Germany. Only a few of his suggestions were subsequently carried out, and "practical courses" in English, Hebrew, Spanish, Jewish social work, and gymnastics (*sic*) added to or intensified without revolutionizing the curriculum. Students unable to take language and "practical" courses in addition to the traditional curriculum and to spend thirty-six (*sic*) hours per week in class would be asked to leave. "It would amount to a selection of the fittest."

Although today I share Elbogen's views of traditional curricula and learning by rote, it was my good fortune that his colleagues on the faculty and the Board of Overseers (*Kuratorium*) held to more traditional views until their work, too, was severely restricted or destroyed by the pogroms of 1938. In 1933 and 1935, government decrees and the Nuremberg laws severed literally thousands of Jewish university teachers and researchers from their academic institutions in the greatest brain drain of German intellectual history. It allowed the Hochschule to expand its Judaistics faculty by appointing new instructors from among this group and adding courses in Arabic, Assyrian, Ethiopian, Syrian, and Egyptian hieroglyphics (hieratic writing), and a three-term sequence of lectures on Islamic history and culture. The additions constituted the largest increase in Judaistic and Semitistic subjects in the history of the Hochschule.

Entirely new in Jewish institutional history was the development of new courses into a small humanities division, Division of General (that is, non-Judaistic) scholarship, the *Allgemeinwissenschaftliche Abteilung*.[3] Several currents contributed to its foundation. Elbogen, himself an undisputed research scholar and writer in several Judaistics disciplines, probably had few allies in his fight for curricular modernization. Influential faculty and board members may have agreed with his disappointment about the declining quality of preparation and talent among the larger number of students entering the Hochschule in the 1930s. But they sought to raise the course requirements rather than adjust them downward. (Complaints about being swamped with students seeking substitute careers during the economic depression before 1933 already appeared in the *Berichte* in the late 1920s.) Now the dismissal from German universities of numerous Jewish research scholars, both those experienced and those beginning promising careers, created a supply of university-level talents. After 1934, the phenomenologist Arnold Metzger, a former assistant of Edmund Husserl's and a philosopher in his own right, taught at the Hochschule on a grant made available by his wife's largesse—her father owned a popular retail shoe chain in Berlin. The 1938 *Bericht* credits the Metzgers with the initiative for the new division. Appointing dismissed professors and lecturers relieved real human suffering—some were on the Gemeinden's welfare rolls. At the same time, they would adequately provide the university studies Jews could no longer undertake, and strengthen the traditionalists in their demands for higher standards. The fu-

---

[3] Richard Fuchs, "The Hochschule für die Wissenschaft des Judentums in the Period of Nazi Rule: Personal Recollections," *Leo Baeck Institute Year Book*, 12 (1967), 3–31.

ture, one presumes, did not appear entirely dark for German Jewry in the mid-1930s. Some of the exchanges preserved in the faculty correspondence of the period are absurd if read *ex eventu* and not as documents of steadfastness in the face of a deteriorating situation. If—*if*—there had been a future, appointing a humanities faculty might have laid the groundwork for a major academic innovation—if there had been a post-Nazi German Jewry. The administrator entrusted by Hochschule and Reichsvertretung with bringing the new division into existence has described the circumstances of the time.

The label Division of General Scholarship—Allgemeinwissenschaftliche Abteilung—was used only in internal communications and was carefully avoided in the printed or mimeographed lists of courses issued each term. They had to be approved by Gestapo and police officials in Berlin, and even as early as 1936, Nazi bureaucrats had resorted to severe reprisals, including internment in a concentration camp, if guidelines or censorship rules were infringed upon. The new courses were given innocuous and often half-true labels and disguised in traditional Jewish studies categories.

For the next five semesters, the new faculty offered courses in Greek and Roman history and the history of the Ancient Near East; Greek, Latin, and Hellenistic literature; Greek and Latin linguistics; general European history and historiography; history of religion; international relations; theories of government; philosophy; psychology; education; political histories of the Mediterranean in relation to European history; and history of Eastern Europe. Some of these titles stood for subject matters, textual analysis, or specializations deemed too close to forbidden subjects to be revealed. By far the largest number of courses were in the humanities and in history. The social sciences were underrepresented, even if some of the teachers, like the economist Franz Oppenheimer, were well-known leaders in their fields.

That the Hochschule rested mainly on two pillars—its new history, literature, and philosophy *and* its greatly respected Wissenschaft des Judentums tradition—appeared to answer precisely to my needs and self-understanding. My orthodox youth I would trust for knowledge of the religious tradition; it turned out that my Hebrew preparation was very helpful in the Wissenschaft courses I took. Like others brought up in orthodoxy, I did not know too much about the intellectual roots and the Enlightenment-driven beliefs of Reform Judaism. I probably carried a notion with me that it was no more than a less demanding orthodoxy born of convenience and wealth. It would take time for me to shed these notions. At that moment, I needed to know more about human nature and its link to religion, about contexts of history that would trace the present to a past that held the key to its purpose. Zionism and socialism served to explain the political or economic future I had chosen in Palestine. The few bits of diaries surviving from that time do refer to the "biological world-view" that had penetrated thought and "exude[d] nothing but barbarism" but really was "not worth an argument." My thoughts circled around questions like meaning and death—religious questions transposed into Wissenschaft, history, culture, comparative religion, aesthetics, ultimately experiences and emotional certainties.

Still, my living I had to do on my own, and my Zionist-socialist focus on the future outside "European civilization," did not suppress my gratitude for the excitement I found in my lectures and seminars and in being attracted to teachers whose personalities and thoughts I felt speaking directly to my meanderings.

It would be borne in upon me only after the school was closed by Gestapo fiat and I had left Berlin and Germany what an extraordinary experience I had had not only in my personal life and development, but also as a witness to the agony of a sophisticated academic civilization and the culture of which it had been a supreme expression. When I began to take courses at the Hochschule in 1936, teaching and research had reached a peak, Wissenschaft was still borne by the dynamism of the intense scholarship of the preceding decades. Persecution had affected its operation primarily in the administrative relationship to the police agencies which the Third Reich imposed on Jewish institutions, and to nazified elements of the older educational bureaucracies charged to superintend them, as well as comparable German institutions. Nazi chicanery and the ever-present threat of lawlessness did change administrative procedures that used to be routine and now were turned into repressive controls and censorship. At any time, an ill-educated bunch of police bureaucrats could, and did, imprison respected or renowned scholars or professionals, or deliver them to the life-threatening tortures and mistreatments characteristic of concentration camps from 1933 on. As yet, this exposed situation did not affect teaching and research in their self-regulating substance, even if publications were suppressed and writers or editors reprimanded if some primitive fanatic recognized deviations from his political line.

Until 1938, I studied in an intellectually autonomous community of scholars in Jewish Wissenschaft and became a beneficiary of a great German tradition in the humanities, at a university under external threat but preserving its autonomous internal traditions. Teachers *did* have to cope with the insecurity that Gestapo arbitrariness might turn into threats to their lives in an instant. Lectures might be infiltrated by agents or paid informers, and publications denounced. But they disposed of many techniques of equivocation, Aesopian language, and obvious historical parallels that would make the insiders' day long after they had left the classroom.

In the course of 1938, the situation was changing clearly enough for wary eyes to see. Professors looked on as indestructible pillars of the Hochschule emigrated; the number of students declined rapidly; decrees and chicaneries increased: the economic stranglehold tightened; the *Anschluss* (annexation) of Austria shocked, although little information on the atrocities committed by the Austrians against Jews—in Vienna, for example—transpired under tight censorship. The pogroms of November appeared almost as the logical conclusion to this crescendo. German Jewry was entering the pre-Holocaust phase of its history. Yet, while all this took place, the Hochschule carried on research and teaching and scheduled examinations; students and faculty debated the reform of the curriculum, papers were written, some were even published, while the Jewish community around us was being destroyed. Its last agony was a monument to courage and hope against hope and dogged persistence by our teachers and administrators. Most of them did not survive the camps to which they would be deported. Nor did most students, whose number had dwindled to fewer than twenty. The descent into this abyss must be told separately. The two phases must be kept separate. The institutional forms were preserved while the substance shrunk; the intellectual brilliance of faculty and students and some of the greatly expanded curriculum of the years 1935–39 persevered; the intense concentration of an institution under extreme stress tightened as its lifelines snapped in the final agony of the Jewish community.

The rollbook for the "ausserordentlichen Hörer [nonmatriculated student] Herbert Strauss aus Würzburg" for the summer term of 1937 reflects a breathless enthusiasm and intellectual curiosity: it lists twelve courses for twenty-six hours a week, including three seminars. Attendance was certified by the customary signatures of the professors entered at the beginning and the end of the term in the rollbook. Five courses dealt with Jewish subjects and were given by the Judaistics staff: philosophy of religion (Max Wiener); Genesis, Proverbs (Moses Sister); Jews in Modern Europe, 1500–1750 (Ismar Elbogen); the Talmud as a source of history (Ismar Elbogen). I also took a course in philosophy (the body–soul problem [Friedländer]); a course in educational theory (Friedländer), history of economic theory (Franz Oppenheimer); a seminar on economics (Franz Oppenheimer); a seminar on Latin historians of the Middle Ages (Hans Liebeschütz), theories of society: ancient world and Middle Ages (Hans Liebeschütz); and the Mediterranean in modern history (Arnold Berney). I do not remember if I kept up this pace for the following three semesters as a nonmatriculated student.

Only one of three rollbooks for this period survived persecution and emigration. That I did attend for three terms as a nonmatriculated student is noted in an entry in my certificate for the intermediate examination dated June 18, 1940, and instructors' certifications (*Seminarscheine*) I earned from Professors Friedländer and Berney in psychology and history, respectively. In American colleges or graduate schools, a workload of twenty-six hours a week would seem excessive, if not ludicrous, considering the papers and examinations the student would have to prepare. In German or Swiss universities with whom I would become familiar later on, only "Exercises" (*Übungen*) and proseminars and seminars needed papers or examinations. Since my work load included only four such preparations, and I had thrown myself into the work without reservation, it was quite manageable. Much of what went on in these courses has become blurred in my recollection, but most of the teachers I remember well enough to recall my impressions and reactions.

In late 1937, the first flush of freedom must have begun to recede. I was admitted to the (Hebrew) entrance examination for the Jerusalem Teachers' Seminary Beth Hakerem. The Hochschule was authorized to administer such examinations. Those passing could apply for a student "certificate" (visa) to the Jewish Agency for Palestine whose supply of entry permits for workers or craftsmen had been severely strained after the 1936 Arab riots. Guided by Dr. Gustav Ormann, the Hebrew instructor, I immersed myself in a crash course in modern Hebrew language and literature.

I obtained a grammar written in Hebrew and remember the enjoyment—perversely—I drew from the flexibility and logical playfulness, as it seemed to me then, of a language whose consonants will extend meanings if supplied with the appropriate vowels and prefixes and suffixes. I began to read Jewish newspapers but found them difficult, as style and vocabulary had moved some distance from the classical. Dr. Ormann made me read modern literature and poetry and some classic nineteenth-century Yiddish novelists and humorists in Hebrew translations. The pièce de résistance was contemporary Jewish history in the Hebrew language. I remember plowing through Ben-Zion Dinur's (Dünaburg) nationally conceived history. That Dr. Ormann directed me to read many of the collected essays of Ahad Ha'am (Asher Ginsburg) (in five volumes of most subtle and elegantly simple Hebrew), and that I found much political and cultural sustenance in them, I understand today as a sign that I was beginning to move away from the flirtation with Marxism and the simple life of the pioneer. I did notice his social Darwinism and his view of Zionism as a cultural renewal movement, an assertion of pride in a nation that would not be exclusively concentrated in a Jewish state or exhaust its social philosophy in international diplomacy to secure a charter from the powers of the day. It gave Zionism the same ethical and cultural note that we had learned from Martin Buber and our youth movement and that the best among Zionist leaders then and later represented.

On April 20, 1938, I appeared before the three examiners commissioned by the faculty and passed the all-Hebrew examination before the historian Ismar Elbogen, the philosopher Max Wiener, and the Hebraist and Bible scholar Moses Sister with the mark "good." I do not recall what I was examined about, but retain a sense that it offered a pleasant, almost playful, occasion to display a newly found dexterity. I also applied soon after for a student certificate and for admission to the seminary, but cannot recall any longer why this attempt proved fruitless. I had to wait until I would hear from Jerusalem or the Jewish Agency in Berlin (Palästina-Amt). The Beth Hatalmidim had been dissolved, and I found a temporary job in a residence home for boys learning a craft in preparation for their emigration under the auspices of ORT (acronym for Organization for Rehabilitation and Training, originally the Russian Obtchestvo Rasprostaneniya Truda sredi Yevreev), the respected Eastern European agency long active in programs of vocational education and retraining. I left the job and went through a period of real hunger, not wanting to admit to home or others that I was literally starving. It ended when a fellow student and good friend, Hans Lamm, informed the Reichsvertretung and the head of the Jugendverband, Paul Eppstein, of my pigheadedness, and things were regularized. The emerging conflict I was facing at the time was well summarized in a telegram our organization received at our last national meeting around this time. It read: "Koakh lehagshama atzmit ze koakh lehagshamat geulatenu"—The strength through which you realize yourself is also the strength needed to bring about our national salvation.

The emissary of the Labor Party in Palestine who sent this lapidary admonition to rally us to the cause was no doubt well advised to appeal to the philosophical basis of the youth movement: Buber's personalism was linked in our minds with communitarianism and service to the new nation, free of the capitalistic distortions that we saw as warping the directness of dialogue and encounter. It was thus linked to our self-understanding. I do not believe that it achieved what its author had intended: emigration from Nazi Germany to Palestine weakened after 1936, and became mainly a family migration to overseas countries and Germany's European neighbors. The examination I had taken would become a step among many away from the communitarian Utopia I was preparing myself for, even if I did not understand its significance then. Beginning in 1936, I had become friends with many young Berlin Jews—my studies and my youth work had opened up many friendships and communalities, and I gained a sharply edged sense for the personalities of my teachers, who would become significant persons in my emotional life. I traveled several times a year to Würzburg to be with my parents, my sister, and my friends, to take a rest from the nervousness of the town, and to eat the family food. I was, of course, informed about the international events of that fateful year, 1938, from German newspapers, almost our only source besides the considerable and often intense talk in our rumor society in Berlin. In reality, I was miserably ignorant of the danger of war brewing especially in that year. Emigration took first and urgent place in our Jewish community. Many more people than ever before packed their "household goods" into containers (then called lifts) and left for the United States and other overseas countries. Rabbinical students at the Hochschule were helped to continue studying in the United States at Hebrew Union College; others secured positions. Jews in Vienna had been crudely mistreated by the citizens of that treacherously *gemütlich* city and were fleeing in droves across the border. My very close friend Paul Eppstein participated in an international conference called by Franklin D. Roosevelt to direct Jewish emigration into internationally agreed channels, and to dissuade the Nazi government from their contemptuous and chaotic expulsion of Jews from Germany and from despoiling German Jews before allowing them to leave. He returned from Evian-les-Bains in great despondency, although U.S. immigration authorities had agreed to admit Jews to the limit of the "German" and "Austrian" quotas that had been written into the law since the 1920s. Even my father now urged me to apply to the U.S. consulate in Stuttgart (whose district included Würzburg). It had no results. We received registration numbers in 1938 that would be called years later, even if a German employee at the consulate had not been proven corrupt and sold lower registration numbers to well-heeled applicants.

Now my father also agreed to separate from our sister Edith. After I left, she grew even closer to him than before, closer than to mother, who had rather strict ideas about growing into womanhood. As for many parents at the time, it was heart-rending to decide to have a child leave home and hometown, leave the country, and face a foreign culture in a foreign country under harsh conditions. Since girls were in demand for youth *aliyah* groups at the time, precisely because traditional views of women's vulnerability and dependencies lingered on among German Jews, it was easy to have her included in a group connected with the *kibbuz me'uchad*, the majority Socialist Labor Party settlement system. In the summer of 1938, we had a joyful, carefree month together in Berlin before she left with a group via Italy for Palestine. She was a beautiful blond young woman, rather tall for her age and physically fit, an all-round sportswoman. These four weeks were one shock of recognition: we had numerous traits in common—the energetic and optimistic approach to life, the communitarianism, the trust in people, an ironic sense of humor, the moral sense of the culture that shaped us as yet undimmed by the ugliness of life away from the cocoon, the matter-of-fact Jewishness, and the taste for the aesthetic and literary experiences available to us. Two years had made a difference in our lives: family was the narcissism of loving oneself in the other. We knew that we would not have to separate forever, but I would skirt disaster by staying on in Berlin; she would skirt death when she settled in the swamp area of Lake Huleh, in northern Galilee, and contracted a glandular infection that finally turned into cancer of the lymph gland. The Jewish Agency for Palestine had sprayed her area of the settlement near the swamps of Lake Huleh with DDT, then recently discovered in the fight against the anopheles mosquito that caused widespread malaria among Arabs and Jews in the area. It was a singular medical triumph of the Jerusalem Hadassah Medical Center that she regained her health after a radical neck dissection and lived a full life with her Russian husband (from the Caucasus mountains), her three children, and numerous grandchildren. She was just past her fifteenth birthday when we met last in Berlin before the war. She died at age seventy in Chulatha of lung cancer, having smoked cigarettes all her working life.

After the war, when I was earning enough money to travel, we met regularly in Israel, Europe, New York, or Chulatha. In the 1950s, mother lived for some years with Edith's family in a small kibbutz two-room apartment but could not adjust to so different a culture, although she greatly loved the sociability extended to her by the parent generation. She could not accept the radical communitarian kibbutz way, as practiced at the time, of taking children away from their parents at an early age and bringing them up in a children's house until they graduated from high school. After some years mother returned to us in New York. My own regular visits with Edith reaffirmed our deep emotional links to each other. She died in 1991. I spent a good deal of time with her in her last year.

Visitors to her grave in the Chulatha cemetery face the steep incline of the Golan Heights across the Jordan River plain, and the distant, often snow-capped peaks of the Hermon Mountains.

We had fully expected in the summer of 1938 that it would be my last summer in Germany, too. At the end of the spring term I returned home. Life in Würzburg was placid on the surface, but quite a few families were packing up and leaving for America, as immigration restrictions were eased enough to shorten the long wait bureaucrats and politics had imposed on them. I spent some of the time paddling down the Main River for a week or two with Dina Ehrenreich (Mrs. Dina Meyer), a Berlin youth-group friend and a spirited companion.[4] The peace of the water and the rural landscape on its banks offered welcome contrasts to the tense and threatening headlines and radio reports that inundated us in Berlin. Neither I nor most of my friends were alert enough to read the signs right. I had just turned twenty years of age, and was very much concerned with my private affairs: the humanistic world I had entered through my studies and readings, the business of growing up, celebrating the arts, the seasons. I thought I had coped enough with "reality" by preparing my emigration to the teachers' seminary in Jerusalem.

Nothing in my entire education had ever systematically dealt with politics or foreign affairs *in contemporary settings*. In the Gymnasium, history instruction had stopped with the French Revolution and Napoleon. What I was reading on my own did not teach me an understanding of the present. Some of my appalling ignorance and unconcern was no doubt idiosyncratic, my own stubborn separations and reconnections. Yet, all our talk about what the Nazi newspapers peddled through well-manipulated headlines every day fell far short of what I would learn later from listening to educated and incisive political commentators over the radio, especially in wartime Switzerland. I lacked the concepts to place events into perspective. Five years of growing up in Nazi Germany had drowned me in political propaganda and turned me into a political ignoramus at the same time. You immunized yourself by adopting a jaundiced cynicism, but you knew of no way of filling the resulting void, you did not know of the void. "They" defined the framework of your opposition and your expectations. I should have been afraid of a new war as early as that beautiful summer of 1938.

The courses I was taking at the Hochschule in both divisions were entirely nonpolitical. The Secret Police and the education au-

---

[4] She and I learned of each other's survival only in mid-1998; she had come upon the German version of these memoirs in Manchester, her hometown in England since 1939.

thorities would not have allowed the school to stay open otherwise. Some teachers announced their courses under ambivalent titles and went on to teach what the educational bureaucracy of Third Reich Berlin would have considered trespasses into forbidden territory had they known. Most of such deviations from the script were too subtle, too humanistic, too hidden in historic analogies or "Aesopian" language to do more than satisfy the teacher's tender sense of rebellion or timid insubordination. Even peppering your lectures or seminars with "subversive asides," once you knew that nobody in your class was a police informer, was no substitute for the systematic, conceptual alternative that would grant independence from the daily din of propaganda. One or two instructors in the Division of General Scholarship did teach subjects that might have applied to the contemporary scene and assisted us in formulating a liberal framework. One of these free men was Franz Oppenheimer, by then of venerable age and of a dynamic stage presence matched by none of his colleagues. Oppenheimer taught his well-known system of Ricardo-derived agrarian economics and literally preached his version of agrarian collectivism. He had played a role in settlement policies and debates in Palestine since before the First World War. Unfortunately, his doctrines were inapplicable to an understanding of the Nazi industrial and imperial command economy, even if he fascinated his listeners with provocative asides on the Third Reich.

The other man was the historian Arnold Berney, with whom I took several courses on foreign policy. If I recall correctly, he used von Ranke's concentrated essay "The Great Powers" ("Die grossen Mächte") written in the 1840s to develop his own views of foreign affairs as a calculus of power politics, modified by grains of moral restraint: they would turn into balance-of-power politics in the end. With this seminar, Berney restated the foreign-policy rationale German national elites had used to justify a moderate (Bismarckian) German hegemony in the concert of Europe, and were using again after 1933 to interpret Hitler's unlimited appetite for *Lebensraum* in traditional power/political terms. It was clear that Berney's liberal interpretation of the power play, seen from a German perspective, could not serve as a true alternative to the propaganda framework we needed to penetrate.

None of the other courses came that close to contemporary issues, but in most classes teachers would deal with the issues by one technique or another, from ironic comments on the events of the day to the use of historic parallels, explicit asides, Aesopian language, or philosophical abstractions. To us, even these small gestures meant relief, ineffective as they were without any call to actions which would have been senseless in any event. It is impossible to reconstruct the atmosphere of intimidation and anxiety for which these often capricious antics might have offered relief. The Secret Police destroyed German Jews for lesser offenses in the 1930s.

In the fall, vacation over, I took the train to Berlin in perfect inner peace: at home I had been doubly spoiled now that Edith had left, and mother and father lived untroubled lives. Jews kept leaving Würzburg for larger towns to prepare their emigration faster, or for overseas destinations, just as they had in Berlin. While newspaper headlines screamed of crises and war, the town moved along in its accustomed speed and with its *gemütlich* charm. I would see Edith in Palestine when the visa from Jerusalem would arrive soon, and would continue my education at the Hochschule. It was a smug moment, with the unusual examination in Hebrew behind me. That the Munich Conference at the end of September averted war had a peculiar effect on my perception of Nazi policies: just as they had heaped nonsensical abuse on us and tried to teach their nonsensical race doctrines, their noisy grandiloquence did not have to be taken seriously, its main purpose being to deceive and manipulate. It was "just propaganda." The middle distance of the future was under my rational control; *their* future could be expected with personal confidence for the long run.

FATHER

On October 20, 1938, in his sixty-third year, father was taken into police detention by the Criminal Police of Würzburg. Two weeks later his police detention (*Polizeihaft*) was reclassified as protective detention (*Schutzhaft*) and his "case" transferred to the Secret State Police (Gestapo) Würzburg, a field office (*Aussenstelle*) of the Gestapostelle Nuremberg/Fürth. *Schutzhaft* was the cynical euphemism for arbitrary and indeterminate police detention on trumped-up charges. The arrest began a train of Nazi police persecution that ended with his deportation to Warsaw on April 14, 1942. The record of his agony has survived among the archives of the Würzburg Gestapo. Bavarian State Archives now administering these files made a complete copy of the documents available to me. What follows is based on these files.

The formal order for father's arrest originated with the Berlin center of the Gestapo, the Geheime Staatspolizeiamt Berlin, Prinz Albrecht Strasse 8. It carried the typed signature of its chief, (Reinhard) Heydrich, and was dated November 4, 1938. The arrest had been requested by the local Würzburg office of the Gestapo: his behavior in the police precinct office (*Dienstelle*) was "insolent and provocative" following his appearance, and "was in line with his known previous behavior. . . . Jewish insolence . . . has not yet learned how to behave in a state that merely tolerates him as its guest . . ." (Gestapo Würzburg to Gestapa Berlin, October 21, 1938). The Berlin detention order (*Schutzhaftbefehl*) adds the comment to the standard printed formula justifying arrest for an indefinite time "that he [Benno Strauss] had publicly expressed his hostility to the state through arrogant and insolent behavior, and has thus grossly [*größlich*] violated his right to be tolerated as its guest."

A report sent by the Nazi Party district office manager, August Söldner, and his wife, Lina (*sic*; later, Karoline), to the Würzburg Gestapo details the nature of his subversive behavior:

Karoline had told August upon his return home for lunch that father had dropped a tobacco leaf on her freshly washed stairwell—she was the concierge—and had exchanged a few testy words with her when she berated him for it. August felt that father had done this on purpose to sully the Aryan dignity of his wife. As a Nazi Party official, he demanded that the police report to him what steps they had taken against this person (October 15, 1938).

Father denied the allegation and pointed out that he had merely brushed off the (unsmoked) tip of his cigar before lighting it. In a letter written from the Würzburg prison, he apologized for his inattention and offered to make amends. He reported later that one of his Gestapo interrogators had done exactly the same thing to his cigar and then told him, "This, Herr Strauss, is why you are detained." (The man's father had gone to school with mine.) Father pointed out that his accuser had been "36 to 45 feet" away from him when the incident occurred and would have been unable to see the small tobacco leaf (Protocol, October 20, 1938). A petty Nazi Party employee had to appease his wife by denouncing father and placing the weight of his party position behind the denunciation. Both police and Gestapo would be vulnerable if they did not show the proper zeal demanded by the local party bureau and Heydrich's order.

Depositions made by father stressed his nonpolitical past (he voted Liberal-Centrist until 1918, then Social Democratic, but had no formal affiliation), his army and procurement services, his unblemished life, and the hard times he had been in. This may have helped him avoid transfer to a concentration camp for the moment. That he was already in prison, that is, under Gestapo control, also may have helped him avoid being rounded up by the Storm Troopers on November 9–10, 1938, and sent to a concentration camp. The woman informer deposited on October 20, 1938, what her husband had reported previously, and disputed father's rebuttal.

In several documents, father assured his interrogators that he would emigrate at the earliest possible opportunity, and that his son—I—was working to secure an immigration certificate to Palestine where his daughter, Edith, had already settled on a kibbutz.

On November 29, 1938, mother went to the Gestapo and surrendered a hunting knife and father's military dress sword to comply with a Nazi decree dated November 11, 1938, that Jews had to deliver all weapons in their possession. Father had asked her to do so in a letter from prison. The two other weapons my father had reported to the prison police—a six-shooter and a knuckleduster—my mother had thrown into the Main River the day father was taken into custody (Protocol, November 29, 1938).

On January 7, 1939, after seventy-nine days of arrest, he was released from the Würzburg Ottostrasse prison, "to effect a change of his residence to a foreign country" (Protocol, January 9, 1939). On November 15, 1938, he had named Palestine as the emigration target for which his son (I) had submitted an application to the Palästina-Amt in Berlin. His passport application, completed in early January 1939, named Bolivia (Hollendo) as his goal. (With the help of a friend's father, I had procured a visa from a Berlin Travel Agency specializing in such semilegal travel permits.) Father was ordered to leave the country within eighteen days following his release from prison, and "strongly admonished to abstain from obstreperous behavior in the future." He failed to comply.

In September 1939 he volunteered for work. I do not know if anybody advised him to do so for his own protection. He was assigned work on a construction site for the Municipal Building Department (*Tiefbauamt*).

On November 11, 1939, he was rearrested on order of the Berlin Gestapo Amt (Gestapa) dated November 15, 1939 (*sic*). His personnel card carries the entry "12.14.1939 emigrated to Palestine." He was released on December 12, 1939, from this second imprisonment. Had a Würzburg Gestapo official tried to close his case, or get the petty Nazi denouncer Söldner off the police's back? The then president of the Israelitische Kulturgemeinde, Würzburg, Dr. Richard Müller, a lawyer and friend of mother's who survived persecution with the help of his non-Jewish wife and son, may have intervened on his behalf. On July 3, 1940, father was admitted to an agricultural training center near Berlin (Radinkendorf) that was under Jewish administration and had sheltered the remnants of the Jewish Gemeinde of Schneidemühl. They had been expelled from their town overnight after Germany invaded Poland in September 1939.

On March 5, 1942, the Gestapo Central Office (Gestapa) in Berlin reactivated the protective custody order of November 1938 and had my father rearrested. "Emigration is not possible in the foreseeable future in view of the general prohibition against emigration. . . . Strauss is to be 'packed off' . . . [*Überstellung*, a monstrous Nazi phrase] to the Sachsenhausen concentration camp." A letter to the Berlin Gestapa referred to as coming from Würzburg dated September 27, 1941, is not included in the file. Could it have originated with the denouncer? It refers to an SS Brigadeführer (Lt. Colonel?) and major general of the police, Dr. (Benno) Martin of Nuremberg, as the source for the order to rearrest my father.

On March 31, 1942, the Gestapo Potsdam arrested father once again in Radinkendorf. He was "evacuated from Potsdam in agreement with *Kriminalrat* Forster, the 'Referent' [case worker] on April 14, 1942."

The destination of my father's transport does not emerge clearly from this file or other postwar documentation. Würzburg Gestapo chief Völkl (who committed suicide in 1945) noted "evacuated to the East (4.13.1943)." Father's Würzburg Gestapo personnel card states as its final entry "emigrated to Palestine on 12.14.39," that is, two days following his release from the second arrest. The file mentions his transfer to Radinkendorf, which took place on July 3, 1940, only as late as March 7, 1942 (Memo to Gestapo Nuremberg/Fürth), in response to requests from the Berlin Gestapa for his internment in the Sachsenhausen concentration camp. As a result, the Berlin Gestapa file listed father as having been evacuated with Camp Radinkendorf by special transport (*Sondertransport*) to Trawnikii/Lublin "on 4.14.43." A card based on this information, and filled in after the war in Berlin by an employee of the American Jewish Joint Distribution Committee, was entered later in the central documentation file of the International Red Cross-International Tracing Center, Arolsen near Hanover (Letter of April 31, 1955). An (undated) typewritten list of Würzburg Jewish Holocaust victims also deposited with the Arolsen Tracing Center includes "Benno Strauss, July 20, 1876, died in U.S.A."

None of these entries is correct. Mother and I said good-bye to father before his deportation during an unbearably controlled and unbearably painful five minutes the Gestapo allowed us to talk with him at the Levetzowstrasse Synagogue collection point in Berlin before his transport left. Previously, we had had several reunions of great poignancy in my Berlin furnished room while he worked in Radinkendorf, mother coming by train from Würzburg, and I had traveled to Würzburg at regular intervals from Berlin until September 19, 1941, when the Jewish badge was introduced and travel became more hazardous for Jews than just a violation of their curfew.

The fact was that on April 14, 1942, father was deported by the Potsdam Gestapo to the Warsaw ghetto. Both mother and I received terse notes from there, written on postcards and, at one point, a small photograph of him. For a while, we were able to write back and send some small parcels containing unrationed food. His last message to mother said that he was "being moved" (*in Marsch gesetzt*). It was dated late May or early June 1942, and was the last we heard of him. In June 1942, the SS began to deport Jews from Warsaw ghetto to Treblinka extermination camp.

After 1945, several German courts dealt with the behavior of August and Karoline Söldner. They were interned at Hammelburg, north of Würzburg, in a detention camp for members of the Nazi

Party hierarchy, and were classified by a local citizens' court (one of the denazification tribunals set up by the U.S. Military Government—*Spruchkammern*) at the camp as minor offenders, "kind human beings," helpful in keeping adversaries of the regime out of the clutches of the Gestapo. My father's day of death had been fixed by a Würzburg court, the *Amtsgericht*—functioning as court of registration – as December 31, 1942, and on May 1, 1949, the criminal division of the *Landgericht* Würzburg, court of first instance, sentenced August Söldner to a two-year prison term for "aggravated deprivation of freedom with fatal consequences and false accusation" (*schwere Freiheitsberaubung mit Todesfolge und falsche Anschuldigung*). Karoline Söldner was sentenced to a term of nine months in prison as an accessory (*Beihilfe*) (*Main-Post Würzburg*, January 7 [?], 1949).

A letter I received in New York in January 1949 from Walter W. Urlaub, a civilian employee (investigator and adviser) of the U.S. Special Branch Advisory Team for Lower Franconia, then controlled by the American Military Occupation authorities, attests to the German court's considerable efforts to establish the facts and punish the perpetrators. These showed that the Söldners exhibited "no trace of remorse or uttered any word of regret." The prosecutor quoted "the old and true German proverb" that "the informer is and remains the greatest scoundrel in the land" ("Der größte Lump im ganzen Land, das ist und bleibt der Denunziant") and demanded penalties of six and two years of aggravated imprisonment at compulsory labor for the guilty couple. Special Branch also requested a retrial of the perpetrators before the Denazification Court (*Spruchkammer*) under Occupation statute: the earlier mild finding had not considered the Söldners' denunciation of my father since it was "unknown to the court at the time." The prosecution failed to convince judge and jury, who under German law deliberate together, the jury being composed of a few selected jurors, that a revision was indicated. They accepted the argument that the couple had been interned since the end of the war and had lost all their property, and that Söldner was "induced by the loquacity of his wife to commit the denunciation, not by egotistical motives," and so on (*Main-Post*, June 28, 1949).

My mother and the then president of the Würzburg Jewish congregation were praised for their "absolutely detached and highly proper [*hochanständig*] testimonies at the trial free of any trace of hatred." My mother acted according to the code she taught us. Privacy was part of her pride, and she knew that German courts value decorum. But was her unwillingness to speak in public of her contempt for evil men and deeds not in some ways as damaging as Mitscherlich's "Unfähigkeit zu trauern"—the postwar Germans' "inability to mourn"?[5]

Sentences imposed on SS General Martin and his subordinate policemen, whose command included Würzburg, by a Nuremberg Court were overturned on appeal, "since the defendants had been unable to recognize that they had violated the law [*Unrechtmäßigkeit*] when they carried out the deportations" of Jews from Franconia—a total of 4,500 men, women, and children, few of whom survived the war (*Main-Post*, June 4, 1951).

THE POGROMS OF NOVEMBER 1938

With father's imprisonment, Nazi brutality had violently upset the life of our family: against our advice, father had passed up the opportunity to leave Germany for Latin America, although barely three weeks after he was seized, the violent events of *Kristallnacht*, "Crystal Night," should have destroyed all illusions about a Jewish future in Germany.[6] In early November, I returned to Würzburg to support mother in whatever could be done to end his imprisonment.

I was still in Berlin when the Gestapo rounded up about 17,000 Jews of Polish nationality at the end of October and deported them, men, women, and children, old and young, under inhuman and brutal conditions to the Polish border. Their suffering was increased when the Polish government refused to admit its own citizens to their own country. They had to camp out in the no-man's-land between the borders as the Eastern European winter descended.

---

[5] In 1967 two German psychoanalysts related the indifference they perceived among Germans toward the Nazi past to dynamic mechanisms they summarized as "the inability to mourn." Cf. Alexandre and Margarete Mitscherlich, *Die Unfahigkeit zu trauern: Grundlagen kollektiven Verhaltens* (Munich: Piper, 1967).

[6] Ronald Flade, *Die Würzburger Juden: Ihre Geschichte vom Mittelalter bis zur Gegenwart* (Würzburg: Stürtz Verlag, 1987), p. 315.

Their fate was still in the balance when I tried to persuade the Gestapo and the local judicial authorities in Ottostrasse prison to dismiss father to prepare his emigration. One encounter frightened my mother: a young law bureaucrat had torn into me saying that we would after all only spread atrocity stories (*Greuelmärchen*) about the new Germany abroad when we emigrated, and I stated that what we would have to tell would only be the truth. I was too mad to fear the worst when he left the room in a rage, to return after a few minutes without reprisals. I presume the scene neither helped nor delayed father's release, who, as I read in his Gestapo files many decades after 1938, drew their ire because of his insolence, the same quick rage against the insolence of others. Like father, like son.

The Crystal Night atrocities took a bloody turn in placid Würzburg as the thugs intruded into Jewish apartments and houses and demolished glass and furniture before arresting the men. One of our good acquaintances, the sixty-three-year-old Julius Lebermann, was beaten by a mob of Party members and died a few days later of his wounds: he had retired from his wholesale wine business for reasons of health in 1931. The uncle of a schoolmate of mine, Alfred Katzmann, a much-decorated veteran of World War I, age forty-three, threw himself out of a window when they came to arrest him, and Claire Rosenthal, the wife of a lawyer, despaired of his ever returning from the concentration camp and swallowed poison. She was forty-nine years old when she died.

I fell between the cracks of the terror system because I had not registered with the police when I came back home, and my Berlin landlady had not volunteered my address. On November 10, I went to Domerschulgasse and observed through the open gate that firemen were still dousing a large heap of ashes that used to be the furniture and the books they had taken out and burned. The synagogue itself was presumably too close to other buildings and could not be burned down without risking a major conflagration (I later learned that orders to that effect had been issued by Berlin). I stood among a small crowd of passive and mute onlookers when the incident involving Josef Gössmann reported earlier occurred. By that time, the rector of the university, SA-man Ernst Seifert, a member of the medical faculty, had left the synagogue compound: he would claim before a postwar court that the crowd had pushed him into the synagogue, and that he had never as much as seized an iron rod to take part in the demolition. It was the usual cowardly denial of the respectable.

My father never explained in depth, and I did not ask, why he stayed on in Würzburg. Above all, he did not want to leave without mother, who had maintained so much of our lives in balance, including, of course, some of our livelihood. By now, he depended in part on her resolution and energy, and he was probably realistic about the difficulties of starting a new life in an exotic Latin American country whose language he did not speak. He would not function outside the culture that sustained him, not out of patriotism—the word would have appeared pathetic to him—but because he could not imagine himself anywhere else. These were the only roots he had struck, his family, his friends, his community; parents, sister, son were buried in the cemetery. I don't know when his habitual good cheer yielded to the insight that he was facing a deadly system run by trivial murderers.

I returned to Würzburg twice to be with mother before he was released from prison in January 1939. The Nazis had achieved the result they had wished for with these pogroms: in Berlin as in Würzburg, everybody felt under extreme pressure to emigrate, even if one had to leave impoverished or go to a country one first had to locate on a globe, or had to circumvent immigration laws or bribe officials to get away from Germany and into some settlement country. It was as if people knew that these brutalities would be visited thousandfold on all who failed, unto death.

When I had returned to Berlin after my first visit I was on my way to visit Paul Eppstein in his Ludwigkirch Strasse apartment but met him in the entrance hall to the building. He was on his way to meet his colleagues from the Reichsvertretung—they avoided working in their offices for fear of being nabbed, and met in one of the private apartments: "Next time, we two will meet in a concentration camp." A few weeks later, when no staff member of the Reichsvertretung was under arrest any longer—the Gestapo needed the organization—I would have to see Eppstein urgently once again. He might know what to do about a citation to appear at a Gestapo office in Burgstrasse. Nobody ever could predict what would happen to a Jewish client there, and I remembered the encounter in the Würzburg prison a few weeks earlier. He suggested flight through an underground connection to Holland, but cautioned that I should follow my "instinct." I went with barely suppressed fear. Two bureaucrats in a stale office wanted to verify father's statements about his son in Berlin.

Paul Eppstein was the most remarkably "pure" intellectual I had met during my German and Swiss years; he and his wife, Hedwig, both Baden Jews, were my elders by seventeen and fifteen years, respectively, and had guided the Jugendverband into Zionist and socialist channels. In Berlin, our loose acquaintance had grown into an unequal friendship that, at least to me, bridged the gulf separating the provincial from the cosmopolitan. On Saturday afternoons, their apartment in Ludwigkirch-Strasse, for a while, became an intellectual and artistic home to me while I lived in "my" collective in the North and administered "my" youth group. Eppstein had taken a social work position with the Reichsvertretung after Nazi law deprived him of the instructorship at Mannheim Commercial Hochschule he had held since age twenty-five, a rare occurrence. That he had written on Marxist-Leninist epistemology I admired less than the humanity he lived and combined with a sharply critical view of politics and social conditions. Many senior officials of the Reichsvertretung were leaving their work behind and emigrating. Hedwig had been in New York to inform herself about a position at the New School for Social Research, where a coven of mostly Social Democratic intellectuals taught social science courses on an advanced level. Her observations were sufficiently negative to discourage Paul. He put his life on the line for the Jewish community, above all for its youth, advanced on the career ladder, and, at the end, became de facto the equal of Leo Baeck, the president of the Reichsvertretung's board of directors. The style of these two men, their values and their talents and personalities could not but clash, the "*grand rabin*'s" (grand rabbi's) sense of his religious mission and his idealistic philosophy of culture versus the relentless realist disdaining all masks in meeting "the other" in or outside his office hours. Baeck's sermonesque style dismissed anxious petitioners glowing with hope that the help he had vaguely promised would arrive—although both sides should have known that serious protection against persecution or deportation was beyond any Jewish official's power. Eppstein displeased Baeck by his close friendship with his secretary, Mrs. Myrantz, and his preference for social assistance to youth rather than the aged if only one of these two groups could be assisted or helped to survive under inhuman Gestapo dictates. In Theresienstadt, their differences probably became unbridgeable. Eyewitnesses and oral history records in Jerusalem archives suggest that both men battled Gestapo impositions in Berlin in the 1930s with unfailing courage and integrity to the point of risking their lives.

I had lost touch with Paul and Hedwig by late 1942. In January 1943 both he and Leo Baeck were deported to Theresienstadt-Terezin, which served as an internment camp for older Jews from Central Europe *and* as a holding pen for the Auschwitz extermination camp. Baeck never once wrote or spoke about his life there. Eppstein's place in history was fixed by a single book written from a hostile perspective. The author was Hans Günther Adler, a Czech-Jewish fellow prisoner who wrote an at first widely accepted history of Theresienstadt after the war.[7]

We may never know more about Paul's role in Theresienstadt than what emerges from this jaundiced and angry presentation. Given the differences in age and sophistication that separated us, I would not presume to speculate on its psychological verisimilitude. Paul's predecessor as "camp senior" was a well-established Czech Zionist leader, Jacob Edelstein, who had been in this position since the camp was founded in September 1941, according to reports on his initiative. In November 1943, he was arrested by the SS administration of the camp, and on June 20, 1944, shot to death, after being forced to witness the murder of his wife and daughter. The Nazis had accused him of replacing names on lists of inmates the SS had selected for deportation to Auschwitz and the gas chambers. Paul's survival may have depended on the camp guard's backing just as much as Edelstein's. One major accusation was that Paul took part in a notorious deception the Nazis tried to engineer with a propaganda film presenting the camp as a happy, contented old-age home, whose impact the journalist Adler probably overestimated—as if inmates, whatever their position, had been able to resist. Had living in constant danger of being mistreated or murdered changed the humanitarian friend we knew and loved? Or had living in an atmosphere of power struggles forced survival strategies on him that came to dominate his behavior?

---

[7] Hans-Günther Adler, *Theresienstadt, 1941–1945: Das Antitz einer Zwangsgemeinschaft* (Tübingen: J. C. B. Mohr [Paul Siebeck], 1955).

In the end, Paul Eppstein knew too much of what the Gestapo and the SS had perpetrated against the Jews to be left alive. He was murdered on September 28, 1944, in Theresienstadt by the three Austrian SS officers in charge of the camp. It was the day after Yom Kippur. Hedwig Eppstein and Mrs. Myrantz were deported soon after to Auschwitz and murdered there, presumably upon arrival. Paul died without leaving a record. Leo Baeck died in 1956 without having written or spoken about his life in Nazi Germany and Theresienstadt, 1933–1945.

The violent acts we have become used to summarizing in abstractions like "deportation of Jews of Polish nationality" and "Crystal Night" did not destroy the Hochschule as they destroyed the four other institutes of Jewish graduate studies, two teachers' seminars and two rabbinical schools. The building was left untouched. Neither furniture nor library was destroyed. Paul Eppstein and Leo Baeck, two of the mentors or friends to whom I owed much guidance until they and I were forced to leave Berlin in 1943, albeit under very different circumstances, remained models in my intellectual and, in Paul's case, emotional life, even if I did not have to be in contact with them for weeks or months on end. It may well have been my youth: studies at the Hochschule that answered to my intellectual interests and needs usually also led me to read the instructors' publications in their biographical contexts. The extraordinary stress which the events and atmosphere of persecution inflicted on a group whose players left the stage and emigrated one by one, as in Haydn's *Abschieds-Symphonie* (Farewell Symphony), probably lowered barriers between faculty and students in unique ways. With a handful of my teachers, relations also became personal and private for some time. My experiences at the Hochschule thus linked the personal and the intellectual in ways that never recurred in my academic career. And they were punctuated by often heart-wrenching farewells.

The first of the professors the Hochschule lost even before Crystal Night was Dr. Moses Sister, who was swept up in the deportation of Polish nationals on October 27–29, 1938. He had taught Old Testament in modern Bible-critical style, but fully immersed in traditional Eastern Jewish learning, presumably his background. He was probably more of a teacher than a research scholar, and my Würzburg Hebrew training and Bible reading carried over into an easy relationship to teacher and subject. What mattered most for my admiration for him was his iconoclastic sense of humor and his liberating ironic barbs against the rabbinical correctness and respectability of German Jewish establishments. We often would walk home part of the way, and as I understood the sensitive core of his *Lebenskunst* (delicate balancing acts), in exile as it were, he disabused me of what he called my "romantic infatuation" with Polish Jewry. He suggested the standards by which I should try to experience the German Jewish/Polish Jewish relationship and the tragedy of Polish Jewish conditions and its human destructiveness. In Berlin I saw him as a free spirit, vulnerable, an outsider, an authentic socialist intellectual, a refined philologist with a deep feeling for the Hebrew language, a temperamental debunker of ideologies and interests that would determine your purpose and use you. He was forced away before I was able to tell him of the pleasures he had given me. Luckily, he left Poland for Israel in time. I had some impersonal correspondence with him in Tel Aviv, dated April 26, 1939, but was unsuccessful in tracing his whereabouts in the 1950s when I tried again.

Quite the opposite mind and personality I met in another of my teachers who fled Germany in November 1938 to avoid being interned in a concentration camp. He had taught modern history in the General Scholarship Division from early on, and represented a combination of German liberal nationalism, political Zionism, German conservative *Realpolitik*, and esoteric German poetry in the upper-case style of the circle around Stefan George, Friedrich Gundolf, and Karl Wolfskehl, or Richard Beer-Hofmann and Martin Buber. Dr. Arnold Berney was dismissed from his teaching position at the University of Freiburg in 1933 and had written and lectured since for Jewish education groups on Jewish and Zionist subjects.

At the Hochschule, Berney usually appeared in the Nehru-style dark jacket that had been a hallmark of the *George-Kreis* (George circle). His style of lecturing was somewhat formal and at times intense and pathetic, in the way of traditional German mandarins. He was the scion of a Baden Jewish family of wine merchants of impeccable German patriotism and equally impeccable Jewish religious liberalism, and an attractive personality of considerable charm and sensitivity. I remember at least two courses I took with him in 1937–38. One was announced as "Ranke and Rosenzweig," and was in reality an introduction to international relations concepts developed from Leopold von Ranke's text "The Great Powers," a mid-nineteenth-century classic. The other was a course on the significance of the Mediterranean Sea in the diplomatic relations of the Great Powers. As I learned many decades later in the Jerusalem archives where his widow permitted me to study his papers, his major scholarly work had been a humanistic reinterpretation of a seventeenth-century Elector and of King Frederick II (the Great) of Prussia (1740–86): His thinking might have made a major contribution to post-1945 German liberalism, a counterweight to Hans Rothfels's more power-oriented conservatism. He was unsuccessful in obtaining an appointment at Hebrew University, in spite of excellent recommendations. Their chair on modern history (held by Richard Köbner, another German refugee) did not march to a drummer of German Realpolitik. Berney worked for a British army unit in Palestine during the early war years and wrote a private "war diary" that also clearly articulates his distance from the political correctness of the Western Allies in World War II: the frame of reference was the German conservative (revisionist) view of the power politics of World War I written from a German perspective.

The paradox of his thinking in the context of pre-Holocaust Jewish life in Germany consisted not only in his superb if unlikely fusion of the different elements of his liberal Jewish heritage and his centrist-conservative German politics and history with political and cultural Zionism. That his conservative anti-Nazism was given room at the Hochschule testifies to the open space in which opposition to the regime in Germany was as yet undifferentiated at this early stage. That the Hochschule offered Berney a berth, however few students could be expected to be interested, also reflects liberal open-mindedness at its best. He died at age forty-three in Haifa (or Jerusalem), "likely, had he been put on, to have prov'd most royally."

In the summer of 1938, a teacher who might have been a major influence on my studies emigrated to the United States to take a research professor's position at the Jewish Theological Seminary in New York. I had used his one-volume, clearly written *History of the Jews in Germany* when it appeared in 1935 to prepare myself for our group meetings, and was eager to meet the author. I did not know then that Ismar Elbogen had been with the Hochschule since 1902 and won universal respect for his scholarship in centers of Jewish learning around the world, and that he was easily the most broadly knowledgeable and most productive scholar during this last phase of Wissenschaft des Judentums. His course on modern Jewish history was a brilliant demonstration of historical methodology: he would concentrate on a sentence from a history text, mostly his own, and spend the hour in anchoring it in the relevant sources, the different interpretations and their implications for related fields of scholarship, its place in the context of Jewish as well as German or European history. He came as close to being an omnimath as any other scholar I encountered, in a matter-of-fact way that made it seem effortless. What attracted me to his personality was this totally unpretentious sobriety, the almost serene modesty of a man at peace with himself and with ironic distance from the world around him. Another course I took in my first term, "The Talmud as a Source of History (Sanhedrin)," applied the same method to the text, precise philological-historical chronologies and an immense store of associations in the traditional Talmud-learning mode. When I ventured on several occasions beyond his concrete approach and risked a generalization, he would ask gently where in the world I would know this from, his small eyes below the dominating forehead twinkling in ironic amusement. I knew that he had grown up in the province of Posen (Poznań) and assumed that he had a traditional Jewish youth for a basis of his learning. His father had indeed been a Hebrew schoolteacher, a *melamed*, in a province that produced many outstanding men and women in Jewish life, and I felt quite at home with the qualities he projected. He was "a naturally religious" man like many of my Würzburg elders, maybe in a more relaxed, less defensive fashion, closer to the dynamic communal roots and the folk humor of Eastern Jewry, less impaired by the need to bridge forced separations.

The card catalogue of the library listed numerous of his scholarly publications, including his works on Jewish liturgy which had become standard. The subject did not interest me, except for the perspective it provided for the services I had shared with my Würzburg community since I was able to walk. Linking philology with history confirmed all I had learned up till then.

Elbogen did not write from a Jewish national, Zionist perspective, although in lectures he talked quite respectfully of the resettlement of Palestine, which by then had been accepted by mainstream German Jewry. His concept of Judaism remained religious, even if he dealt with social and institutional analysis in his histories. I believe he never wavered in the optimism of reason and the popular Enlightenment of his origins. It determined his religion, and as late as the mid-1930s led him to formulate his lifelong trust in the scholarly culture culminating in the cross-fertilization of the German Enlightenment and purified Jewish traditions: Jewish studies would not be complete without recourse to general history and the humanities. Wissenschaft des Judentums never lost sight of its cultural and philosophical underpinning: the master of detailed and precise philological analysis kept warning against mindless reductions to positivism. I could not quite believe he meant it when he said that anti-Jewish (antisemitic) attacks would cease once the purity and truth of Judaism would be recognized—thus making it a Jewish problem rather than the Christian or gentile problem it really was.[8]

When he presented a lecture on the occasion of Leo Baeck's twenty-fifth anniversary at the Hochschule in 1938 and celebrated the Talmudist Hillel (first century C.E.) as one of the founders of the Jewish tradition precisely because of his modesty and gentility, he was describing his own personality and its attraction. He died in New York in 1943, before he would be able to grasp the full measure of destruction visited upon his world.[9]

In November 1938, the Hochschule was not touched by the centrally planned and directed pogrom that had closed its sister institutions in Berlin and in the country: one dare not ask whether its destruction then might later have saved lives among the students and faculty. I was certain that I would be leaving Germany as I had planned when my studies in Berlin ended, and returned to Artilleriestrasse 14 to explore what the school would recommend for the interim after I had come back to Berlin from Würzburg later in November. In the *Lehrerzimmer* (staff room) to the right of the entrance on the ground floor I stumbled upon an impromptu meeting of faculty and staff members voicing great anxiety about the

---

[8] Ismar Elbogen, "Deutschland," in *Germania Judaica* I, ed. Ismar Elbogen et al. (Breslau: M. & H. Marcus, 1934; repr. Tübingen: J. C. B. Mohr, 1963), pp. xvii–xlvii.

[9] Ismar Elbogen, "Die Überlieferung von Hillel," in *Festschrift für Leo Baeck* (Berlin: Schocken Verlag, 1938), pp. 67–68.

obvious vulnerability of the Hochschule to any willful acts of vandalism.

Present were Professor Eugen Täubler, Dr. Hans Fabian, and Mrs. Jenny Wilde. They proposed to entrust valuable library and archival holdings to faculty, staff, or students who would take them through German customs as part of their usually extensive private libraries when they emigrated. The least risk would be taken if a foreign national would be involved in this act of self-preservation. I suggested that the professor of Talmud studies, Dr. Alexander Guttmann, an Hungarian national, would be the best choice for including Hochschule rare books in his collection without being detected by Berlin customs agents. Guttmann's father had himself been a well-known teacher of the subject at the Budapest Theological Seminary. The son probably had a valuable private collection of rare books on his own.

The conspirators survived war and Holocaust. Jenny Wilde, the elderly chief librarian of the Hochschule returned from Theresienstadt. Her young assistant, Lenore (?) Sperling, did not return from deportation. Hans Fabian, the administrative secretary of the Hochschule and liaison to the Reichsvertretung, was ordered back from Theresienstadt following his deportation by the Gestapo, and forced to work in the (once respectable) office of the *Oberfinanzpräsident* (president of the main district [state] treasury). He had to assist in sorting out the legal and real estate tangles created by the theft of Jewish property "ceded" under duress to the German Reich by the victims upon deportation to the death and labor camps of Eastern Europe.[10]

In 1945, Hans Fabian made his administrative skill and his Berlin temperament available to the new Berlin congregation that rose again out of destruction, and helped see it through the difficult and dangerous years of separation from the Communist-controlled East. He probably never felt at home in New York to which he had

---

[10] The Landesarchiv Berlin stores all (?) questionnaires Berlin Jews were forced to fill out while being detained in holding camps like Synagogue Levetzowstrasse prior to being taken to deportation trains. The Archiv kindly made copies available to me in 1994 of the two twenty-six–page printed questionnaires that had been filled out and signed by Louis and Johanna Schloss, Lotte's parents, in Levetzowstrasse on October 24, 1942. Appended were the formal confiscation proceedings of their property, involving several regional jurisdictions, in the bureaucratic language of the tax collector. It was the last written document they left behind.

emigrated after some years. We co-edited a *Festschrift* to the Berlin Gemeinde in 1970, but he remained sensitive to personal insinuations about his forced labor for the Berlin Revenue office. His Berlin-style humor and snarl served to mask his rage at writers like H. G. Adler and their facile pretense to superiority.[11]

Eugen Täubler taught at the Hochschule until the spring of 1940 and left for a position at Hebrew Union College in Cincinnati during the summer. I attended most of his courses in biblical criticism (*Bibelwissenschaft*) and in Jewish or Near Eastern history courses from 1938 to 1940 and was overawed by his critical use of the Bible as a source of Near Eastern history. He struck me as the image of a German university professor because he adopted a rather formal and distant style both inside the classroom and out. I was thus greatly surprised when a visit I paid him at the Hochschule to say good-bye and announce my formal withdrawal from the school turned into a most personal counseling session.

Although unlike other young men I had not been interned in a concentration camp in November 1938, I was now straining to leave Germany more urgently than ever. The Palästina-Amt informed me soon after November 10 that I could not expect a student visa under the circumstances. I should instead apply for a permit to enter England in a visa category that the Home Office considered non-competitive with British labor, like domestic servant, butler, or agricultural trainee. In the second half of November I had fallen head over heels in love with Dorothy (Dörte) Greifenhagen, a Berlin girl about my age whose family was preparing to migrate to England. She was friends with some *chalutzim* (pioneers) I had lived with in the student collective. Our first, longer meeting during a Nazi-imposed day-long curfew turned fast into intense and tempestuous love: I would follow her to England where her family would be received by a maternal grandmother, an Englishwoman by birth and nationality. We would marry, and try to get to a kibbutz in Palestine after passing through a *hakhshara* collective, the training period needed for obtaining a workers' permit for permanent settlement. The few months we had together until she left

---

[11] Hans-Erich Fabian, "Zur Enstehung der Reichvereinigung der Juden in Deutschland," in *Gegenwart im Rückblick: Festgabe für die Jüdische Gemeinde zu Berlin 25 Jahre nach dem Neubeginn*, ed. Herbert A. Strauss and Kurt R. Grossman (Heidelberg: Lothar Stiehm Verlag, 1970), pp. 165–79.

Berlin in the summer of 1939 almost immunized me against the emotional impact of the panic flight of Berlin Jews to overseas destinations and England. His Majesty's Government had reversed its immigration policy after the November pogroms and was admitting large numbers from among political and Jewish refugees. I would have been one of about 64,000 German, Austrian, and Czech victims saved by Neville Chamberlain's government between November 1938 and September 1939.

I thought that our plan was well laid and that heaven would protect the lovers, no matter what Brecht and Weil had tunesmithed in *The Threepenny Opera* about first and second plans. My Hochschule time would end, father would use his visa, Edith had successfully extricated herself from the collapse of Jewish life around us. Some time in February or early March 1939, I went to tell Täubler and take leave of him. He seemed less forbidding since the November conspiracy in the Lehrerzimmer: Were our plans realistic? Were refugees who had found an asylum not second priority over against those still in personal peril in Germany and Austria? Was the Colonial Office not making every effort to deflect migration pressures from Palestine, since they expected to partition the country into an Arab and a Jewish sector, and placate the Arabs?

But then: I would certainly get into England to work as a butler or other household aid, but was I sure that working in an agricultural collective in Palestine was what would allow me the best use of my abilities? The faculty had noted my Hebrew examination and the work I had done in my classes, although I was only a nonmatriculated student. It need not end there: Leo Baeck and other officials of the Hochschule were talking with Cambridge and London rabbis and academics about taking the Hochschule *in toto* to England, library and some faculty included. If there were a place for me there as an assistant, would I really want to go through with my plan? "Many could do what I would do" but I had "das Zeug zu einem Wissenschaftler"—what it takes to do scholarly work. National salvation and self-realization? Old Professor Hemmerich in Würzburg talking about the New Testament and "Mit dem Pfunde wuchern"(make full use of your talent)? Just when I had learned for a few terms how free one feels if one "realizes oneself" instead of a schedule?[12]

---

[12] Christhard Hoffman and Daniel Schwartz, "Early but Opposed, Supported but Late: Two Berlin Seminaries Which Attempted to Move Abroad," *Leo Baeck Institute Year Book*, 36 (1991), 287–304.

I would keep his confidential information to myself, I promised, and would work on getting to England as quickly as possible (to be with my love, I thought). I was, of course, honored but I knew myself and my intellectual gaps well enough not to take their offer quite seriously, however flattering it had been. Just in case the permit would take time to arrive, Professor Täubler concluded, the faculty wanted me to know that they would wave the requirement of the Gymnasium-leaving certificate if I wished to change my status to matriculated student.

On April 15 1939, I took the rational course and enrolled in the degree program of the Hochschule, which waived its fees and granted me a monthly stipend whose amount I have forgotten. Professors Täubler and Ernst Grumach would guide my studies. It was understood that I was preparing myself for scholarly not rabbinical activities. They may have felt some wry astonishment that after November 1938 any student endowed with a minimal sense of realism—which, of course, I was not, even if my actions had been perfectly rational—would stake his time on an entirely impractical career, scholarship, instead of retraining for something "real" like a craft or agriculture. I did not expect to stay on in Germany or with the Hochschule, and could not take Täubler's perspectives quite seriously. But it would not hurt to follow his suggestion while I waited for the visa.

My rollbook records a course on Genesis, chapter 49, and on the period of the Kings (Täubler), a seminar on Maimonides's *More Nevukhim* (Guide of the Perplexed) (Baeck), and two Talmud courses with Professor Guttmann. Under the circumstances, I remember few details of these courses, certainly of Professor Guttmann's whose texts were small lagoons in a big sea of apparently inexhaustible involution. I do remember being impressed with the almost word-by-word, certainly phrase-by-phrase and sentence-by-sentence analysis of Genesis 49, even if all details have evaporated—I did not expect to specialize in biblical criticism (*Bibelkritik*).

With this small course load, my time was very much my own, and we used it well. I had no work left in the Reichsvertretung's building at Kantstrasse 158 but kept seeing Paul Eppstein regularly. My small organization had no assets of its own, all the office equipment had been on loan from Eppstein's division. I heard little from South Germany: it was *sauve qui peut* getting out of the camps, lining up for hours and days for visas, documents. transportations. I still remember the lines before the Hilfsverein der Juden in Deutschland (Relief Association of Jews in Germany) and the travel agency in Meinekestrasse (Lloyd Triestino/Pazifik und Orient?) that could help with visas for a consideration to Latin American consular officials. My father was a beneficiary of such beneficent corruption. Equally beneficent but incorruptible were the Berlin customs agents who had to supervise the packing of "lifts" with household goods for overseas shipment. I helped at least half-a-dozen times with the melancholy work of "liquidating" a household and its heavy freight of a happily lived lifetime, and became aware of their agents' ironic Berlin disdain for their task and their open sympathy for the victims—once the Gestapo agent had cleared out.

The Hochschule also seemed empty and dispirited now that I knew that it might emigrate, too. Dörte left by boat from Hamburg (to Southampton?) probably before the term had ended. It seemed such a short distance to England from the pier, and time aligned on our side.

The summer term of 1939 ended in mid-July as indicated by the dates entered in my new "*Testatbuch*" (*Anmeldebuch*, matriculated student's attendance register) by my professors. Some weeks later, I was notified that I had been granted a permit for England and should present myself at the British Consulate General in Tiergartenstrasse, Berlin, to have it entered in my passport. Generally, a Jewish emigrant had to spend weeks or months assembling the documents he would need to submit with the application for his passport and obtaining the permission of numerous German authorities to leave the country. To have the application accepted, one had to prove that a visa had been granted. The Nazis made sure that the émigré would be robbed of much of what he had owned and worked for. Generally, only household goods could be taken abroad. Even there, Gestapo inspectors made sure that their confiscatory regulations would be observed.

None of this applied to a student who did not pay taxes and had no household or property to transfer abroad. I assembled the documents requested in the application form and submitted it between August 10 and 15, 1939, to an office headed by Adolf Eichmann and located at a house confiscated sometime in the 1930s from the B'nai B'rith, the Brüdervereinshaus (the House of B'nai B'rith

Brothers). I remembered having attended some exciting lectures on "contemporary historical writing" by Paul Eppstein, Fritz Bamberger, and others in its large second-floor meeting hall before 1938. I marched up the Wilhelminian staircase and was told by one of the Jewish helpers recruited from the staff of the Gemeinde to return in three weeks. I pointed out that I had only personal documents since I was a student without household goods or property to transfer, but it did not shake his routine convictions that applications take three weeks to process. When I became restless—the newspapers turned quite alarmist and prepared their readers for "revenge" against Poland—and returned to the Eichmann office a week or ten days later, the official did not move from his chair and desk: it could not be ready yet, blah, blah, blah. By Friday, September 1, the German army had invaded Poland, and I was finally handed the passport bearing a date of about a week earlier. The official was apologetic. By an unlikely accident, this same official, with his young wife, turned up in Bern, Switzerland, as a refugee in 1944.

It was too late in the day to obtain the stamp in this passport from the British Consulate General in Tiergartenstrasse. When I tried to visit there Sunday morning, September 3, the Consulate was surrounded by German police. A small group of persons—some on the same errand as I—waited across the street under trees lining the street. At noontime, the doors of the Consulate opened and several men—I don't remember seeing a woman among them—left the building. The British ultimatum to Hitler to withdraw from Poland had expired at 11:00 A.M. British daylight savings time. I was seeing the outbreak of a new Great War. As I drifted off with the others, that vague sense of alarm and heightened anticipation and readiness for a new situation began to rise up in my body. That afternoon I visited the offices of the Hilfsverein der Juden in Deutschland located in the neighborhood of my old student home. They assembled a group that had been similarly caught by the outbreak of the war and sent us overnight to their Cologne branch office, which detached us to the Dutch border, guided by an official. We were made to wait the afternoon in the open of a beautiful fall day only to learn in the end that the Netherlands were unable to grant us the customary transit visa. Great Britain refused to honor all visas granted to enemy aliens. I returned to Berlin the next day.

When I had arrived at Cologne's main railroad station in the dawn of the previous day I had heard the first German air raid sirens wailing off. It would be the first of many such alarms I would hear regularly in wartime Berlin for the next three-and-a-half years. I heard it with a mixture of joy and fear as I would hear the sirens to come, hope and danger fused, weekly and daily, the results of the raids slowly showing. This first one may well have been a false alarm.[13]

Subsequently, I followed the advice of friends to seek entry to Sweden with the help of a Berlin lawyer who claimed to have connections with Stockholm, without success. Meinekestrasse knew no constructive way out and advised waiting. A few months later, at the suggestion of Ernst Grumach, with whom I was beginning to take courses, I moved into his apartment building, a Gartenhaus (rear building, part of a quadrangle around a courtyard) in the Charlottenburg district, Schlüterstrasse 53, and took a furnished room with Mrs. Neumann, a widow.

---

[13] Herbert A. Strauss, "Jewish Emigration from Germany: Nazi Policies and Jewish Responses," *Leo Baeck Institute Year Book*, 25 (1980), 313–61; 26 (1981), 343–409.

5

Wissenschaft des Judentums: Berlin, September 1939–January 1942

WHEN I RETURNED from the Dutch border on September 6 or 7, 1939, it did not occur to me that the exit door had snapped shut for good. I returned to a greatly diminished circle of friends and fellow students, to teachers I respected, and to an institution whose well-knit, four-story building and restrained fin-de-siècle façade had become part of my daily life. Since I had arrived proverbially penniless in the fall of 1936, the city and its cultural life, even its sometimes loud-mouthed, tinny, nasal, aggressive talk, had grown on me, as had its beautiful surroundings. And I returned to a Jewish community that had taken me in by its very cultural diversity and its institutional strength. There were probably still about 70,000 Jews in Berlin when the war began. I felt secure and protected by a world of civilized living. Berlin Jewish culture, the culture of Jews in Berlin, was isolated by six years of persecution and emigration, and had turned inward. With November 1938, the sudden growth of Jewish literature on religion, history, and tradition stopped as abruptly as it had begun in 1933. But religious life went on unimpeded in district and institutional synagogues still standing after the pogrom night of November 1938 and in numerous small prayer groups around the city. The Gemeinde centers, mostly in Berlin-Mitte (central Berlin) and -North, intensified their social services, as people ate up their savings and members became older. Less visible to the public, the central administration of Jewish organizations and Gemeinden in Germany, now reorganized from the Reichsvertretung and called Reichsvereinigung (Reich Associations), coordinated and provided financing to its constituent organizations, and remained the conduit for assistance money transferred by Jewish organizations abroad. Jews in Berlin still constituted a critical mass.

Outside, Berlin's theater and music culture appeared to go on unchanged in its classical, educated-middle-class mold, even if Jews
had been banned from theaters and concert halls, a ban I disregarded when the occasion arose, or I joined friends of friends for a
performance. As far as I could observe, it appeared a fact to me that
just as in Würzburg's Catholic folklife, what would be called Nazi
"culture" had no presence in the traditional classical concert repertoire or the equally traditional theater programs of those years. (I
learned much later that popular film and entertainment and programs of classical music were promoted by Goebbels's Propaganda
Ministry to boost morale and offer escapes from reality.)

In November 1939, I registered for my second semester in the
degree program of the Hochschule and found the student body
shrunk considerably, to about twenty to twenty-five students. The
Division of General Scholarship—Allgemeinwissenschaftliche Abteilung—had disappeared, since most instructors had left Germany
after November 1938. Franz Oppenheimer offered a *privatissimum*
(private tutorial) on David Ricardo to a few students in his apartment. I was privileged to be among them. He left in 1939 or 1940
for the United States via Japan. Ernst Grumach soon became my
major teacher when Eugen Täubler left in 1940 for a teaching position at Hebrew Union College in Cincinnati, Ohio. My first major
Talmud teacher, Alexander Guttmann, emigrated to Cincinnati in
1940. By then, of the original Judaistics faculty, only Leo Baeck was
left. He succeeded in appointing new lecturers from among two
groups, retired scholars and rabbis in Berlin Gemeinden, or young
men and a woman of scholarly or educational promise.[1] The curriculum was expanded to include "Practical Courses" like public
speaking, Spanish, English, modern Hebrew texts, Jewish social
work, gymnastics. They were taught by part-time instructors. Especially memorable for me was a lecture series on Jewish Communal
Services in Germany (Jüdische Gemeinschaftsarbeit in Deutschland). It consisted of seven lectures offered by leading functionaries
of the Reichsvereinigung and the Gemeinde and was scheduled for
a late afternoon hour on seven consecutive Tuesdays, open to the

---

[1] Rabbi Gross (Hebrew, Semitic languages, Talmud); Mrs. Rotbart (Hebrew);
Meier Spanier (*Didaktik*); Leopold Lucas (Medieval Jewish History); Julius Lew-
kowitz (Jewish religious philosophy); Rabbi Gescheit (Talmud and *Shulkhan
Arukh*); Leo Wisten (public speaking).

public.[2] Of the teachers who signed my class book between the summer term of 1939 and the summer term of 1942, of the substitutes appointed to replace émigrés, and of the seven communal officials appointed as guest lecturers in 1940, only Leo Baeck, Ernst Grumach, Alexander Guttmann, Eugen Täubler, Moritz Henschel, and Leo Wisten survived the war in Berlin, emigrated, or returned from concentration camps. Mrs. Jenny Wilde returned to Berlin from Theresienstadt after 1945. The others perished miserably in concentration camps, disappeared following their deportation from Berlin to Eastern Europe, or were executed without trial. Even if this had not been the most exposed human situation I would ever face, these men and women would remain in my memory, etched against the decay, the threats, and the sudden jolts that surrounded their lectures, seminars, and tutorials as they created stability.

The sober methods we learned from them in the quiet and unfazed dialogues of their small classes decoded past *and* present realities for us. Our intellectual space had no walls that needed piercing, except for the challenge of understanding complex thinkers and their forbiddingly alien languages, the otherness of ancient religious thought and practice, the cultural codes of past symbolic communication. I felt serene and secure inside classes and out, almost euphorically, almost naïvely pushing aside our preoccupations, the constriction of our space, the fear, the threat, the reduction to being almost prisoners. Even the lectures on communal service I soaked up with rapt attention in 1940. They reached below the rational to moral levels of my Würzburg Jewish education, even if they did not convey the blood and tears of these men and women: many of them, of their own free will, had opted to stay on in Berlin Jewish service;[3] all of them knew how precarious their lives would become, surely, after the November 9 pogroms of 1938 and the outbreak of the war. Talking of their work, they had stressed problem-solving, self-help, practicality, what could be accomplished in our adverse condition. Was the abyss over which they were suspended any different from ours, their listeners? I was reading Kierkegaard and Heidegger then: was our condition not just—"just"—a sharp-edged exam-

---

[2] The lecturers were Otto Hirsch, Arthur Lilienthal, Paul Eppstein, Julius Seligsohn, Conrad Cohn, Paula Fürst, and Moritz Henschel.

[3] Ernst Gottfried Lowenthal, ed., *Bewährung im Untergang: Ein Gedenkbuch* (Stuttgart: Deutsche Verlagsanstalt, 1965).

ple of what they perceived as the poor condition of man and his world? I did not know the words "extreme situation" as applied to persecution and concentration camps at the time.

My self-education in the social sciences would have to wait until I worked for three years on a research project at the Social Science Graduate Faculty of the New School for Social Research on New York's 12th Street in the late 1940s.[4]

A two-term intensive reading of Heidegger's main oeuvre in Ernst Grumach's philosophy seminar allowed me to see the sober technical side of the work and its place in the philosophical tradition; of Heidegger's embrace of the Führer in 1933–34 I learned only from the intermittent if insensitive debate about his philosophy and its clone, "l'existentialisme," in New York opinion journals from the 1950s on. Like Pascal and Romano Guardini, whom I took up to broaden my understanding of Kierkegaard's *Fear and Trembling* and *Sickness unto Death*, I studied Heidegger's *Being and Time*) (*Sein und Zeit*) against the solid background of my Jewish tradition and my emotion-based concern with the meaning of religion in my world, not for their nihilism, Protestantism, or Catholicism. With time my readings changed my view of what constituted the religious experience: it comes through our own religious literature at rare moments of communal and personal crisis. In some ways, it seemed to affirm my orthodox origins more strongly than the ethical and harmonistic understanding at the core of Jewish Reform and liberalism. It spoke more to our exposed condition.

In retrospect, I may have manned my own *Narrenschiff* (ship of fools) to bounce off the despair of these writers from my sense of buoyancy during these years. In early September 1939, I returned to a strenuous schedule of courses and seminars guided for the first time by teachers with whom I was able to develop a personal rapport. I was also drawn into the service of the Jewish community in seemingly natural continuity with my youth movement work. Shortly after my return, I was among the students and Gemeinde members who were asked to volunteer their labor for a statistical assignment that had been imposed upon the Reichsvereinigung.

---

[4] Jacob Goldstein, Irving F. Lukoff, and Herbert A. Strauss, *Individuelles und kollektives Verhalten in Nazi-Konzentrationslagern: Soziologische und psychologische Studien zu Berichten ungarisch-jüdischer Überlebender* (Frankfurt: Campus Verlag, 1991). This is a translation of a 1948–51 research report.

The Gestapo, for whatever reasons, on short notice, had requested summaries from census sheets on Jews in Germany; our task was to transfer masses of dry local and regional data to summary sheets, a routine assignment that needed no brains. Later on, I would be asked to help distribute ration cards—if memory serves me right—from Gemeinde bureaus. In September 1941, I was asked to give out small pieces of yellow cloth cut from larger sheets, each of which bore the word *Jude* in absurdly distorted lettering, the Nazi idea of shaming the Jews by turning Latin capitals into pseudo-hebraized script. From mid-September 1941 on, we had to wear this six-pointed "Jewish star" sewn to our clothing (some people developed systems to make them removable). From the fall of 1940 on, I served as an auxiliary rabbi. Nobody thought we were "collaborating" by serving the community, as some blithely superior moralists opined from the distance of many miles and years later. The conflict between "is" and "ought," which I felt on several occasions, clearly etched on my memory, was not between helping the Nazis and resisting them, but from being forced to symbolize "normality" and quiet self-possession for our predominantly elderly fellow Jews whose "fear and trembling" was closer to reality than our stiff upper lip.

The most important event in my personal life was meeting Lotte when we both were to help with the statistical work. I had been drafted for it by Leo Baeck; and she, by friends in the Gemeinde. We both had fallen in with a rather cheerful and easygoing group of young people. We had volunteered for night work and noticed each other for quite opposite reasons: I had withdrawn into my shell to withstand the boring and meaningless assignment; she, with a lovely voice and a provocative irony, challenged the rest of us to stop feeling sorry for ourselves. She was spirited like no other girl I had met previously, with a touch of innocence contrasting charmingly with her prim way of simple elegance. She had sparkling dark-brown eyes, a beautiful dark face, and a *petite* personality that stood out in the crowd—she later claimed the same for my impression on her—and seemed to manage in our dreary environment and our disgusting countinghouse to express an emotional self that would captivate me then—and ever since. We met and had many serious walks and talks with each other, sparked by her many-sided interests and cheerfully admitted ignorance about most of the things that mattered to me. She was, in fact, a voracious reader with a sense for human life that at the time I felt as a new and feminine dimension of dealing with reality. I was unable to resist her.

The Schloss family, Louis and Johanna, had been living in the North German town of Wolfenbüttel what seemed the contented life of small-town Jews, not unlike my own experience, but the family was not religious or Zionist, although Lotte's brother, Shaul, had emigrated to Palestine and settled on a kibbutz of the Labor Party, Mapai. Her parental house was adjacent to the local synagogue, a large late-nineteenth-century building, as she described it, but the 125 Jews left in 1932 did not fill the house or worship very often. Lotte lived across the street from the Grandducal Library where Gotthold Ephraim Lessing, more than a local culture hero for Jews in Germany, had served some unhappy years as librarian. Lessing did not seem to have left much of the legacy of toleration and Enlightenment he represented in German theater (*Nathan der Weise*) and intellectual history: Braunschweig had elected a Nazi state government from 1930 on, and the Schlosses had left their hometown because antisemitic rowdyism and the economic boycott of Jews had driven them away. In Berlin they lived in Berlin-Kladow, a then semirural suburban settlement near a village, Kladow, at an idyllic spot bordering the Havel River. A brother of Johanna Schloss's, a successful Berlin textile entrepreneur, had emigrated early and left his country house to the use of his family.

As our friendship developed into an intense emotional relationship—as yet quite informal and open—our first fascination with each other moved from play to seriousness. We lived an hour apart as the bus went, and had to watch the 8:00 P.M. curfew the Nazis forced upon us, at least to some self-protective extent; but we were together to stare down the series of military successes that seemed to tighten the fences around us but let at least the British Broadcasting Company's daily news and commentaries get through— different from the one described in Orwell's *1984*, with its complete isolation from the world of reality. We sought each other's company on May 10, 1940, when German armies attacked in the West, and on June 22, 1941, when they invaded the Soviet Union, and told each other all the news we obtained that might offer some light or hope, rumor, gossip, observations, foreign sources. We shared our food when we could—Lotte turned out to be a master cook—

and the Schloss family as well as my mother helped us with vegetables, butter, meat, and other delicacies in short supply or tightly rationed. Even before the final crises came upon us that would threaten the lives of our parents and ourselves, the storm around us had brought us together in our need for emotional and intellectual support.

Thus, it would probably be right to say for both of us that we hoped to survive, I more confidently, and maybe naïvely, than Lotte. I do not believe that any of my fellow students, my teachers, my acquaintances would imagine the anonymous death suffered in utter forlornness that was in store for so many of us. It made rational sense to expect to survive and escape the worst, even if my ability to visualize my future diminished more and more in the course of the years in wartime Berlin. "Optimism" does not denote my condition, nor "pessimism" Lotte's, even if there were enough people who said that they expected the worst, or, conversely, saw encouraging trends in military and political events, surely not without justification; the war was being lost by Germany, Austria, and Italy from 1941 on. For the Jewish community, the timing of this loss was the obvious central question: exchanging BBC news heard or listened to clandestinely and at the risk of being denounced by the ubiquitous informers or found by SS listening-squads cruising in radio cars; spreading the latest rumors; finding an occasional foreign newspaper on a Charlottenburg railroad newsstand, even if it was only the *Pester Lloyd*, a German-language paper from Hungary; interpreting the daily army bulletins (*Heeresberichte des Oberkommandos der Wehrmacht*) and the war maps they conjured up—all this concerned us. Would we outlast "them," the Nazis? Would "they," the British, the Russians, the Americans be fast enough?

During the earlier war years, the main rumor exchange for me was some fellow students and two teachers with whom I developed closer relations, Eugen Täubler and Ernst Grumach. One of Täubler's main sources was Leo Baeck, his close friend and fellow Poznań Jew. Baeck, it was learned after the war, had been in touch with conservative and military resistance groups like Carl Gördeler's and was asked to provide advice on their plans for a post-Hitler Germany. Grumach, probably through his Greek and Cretan studies, had contact with former colleagues or fellow students who would pass him information.

My memory tells me that deep down I was relatively confident and upbeat until I left for Switzerland in mid-1943, but subject to deep bouts of despair and hopelessness. My sports activities in the past and swimming and hiking in Berlin had left me in excellent health and with an athlete's confidence in my physical resilience. Various influences on my education had trained me to suffer emotional storms with outward calm, and given me the self-control that would become vital when I had to hide in Berlin in 1942–43. On a spiritual and deeper layer, I believe that my fundamental feeling for my environment had been shaped by the belief in a providentially ordered world that must have come to me before I could articulate it, the serenity that lay below orthodox belief and ritual, and the rhythms of prayers and holidays during the sacred year. It would stay with me as my basic feeling tone long after my youthful beliefs had disintegrated.

I do not remember when it dawned on me that the very existence of the Hochschule, its survival in Berlin until June 1942, was nothing short of miraculous, for me personally and as a fact of German Jewish history. I do not know the precise reasons why it was tolerated for so long. Several searches in German (and former East German) archives have not yielded files created by any of the government agencies, or the Hochschule, that may have suggested answers. When the other institutes of rabbinical training and higher Jewish learning in Berlin, Breslau, Cologne, and Würzburg were closed down after the 1938 pogrom, the Hochschule was kept open, and none of its Judaistics faculty imprisoned in a concentration camp. One biographer, Leonard Baker,[5] has suggested that the Berlin Gestapo treated Leo Baeck with caution, remembering that, in 1935, when he was arrested for a short time, high-level American and Anglican Church protests impressed the Nazi government sufficiently to free him forthwith. More immediately, enrolling prospective *chaluzim* (pioneers) in preparation for emigration to Palestine fitted the then Nazi policy goal of pushing all Jews out as quickly as possible. The Nazis may have wanted to keep one teachers' training school open as long as religious services and instruc-

---

[5] Leonard Baker, *Days of Sorrow and Pain: Leo Baeck and the Berlin Jews* (New York and London: Macmillan/Collier, 1978); see also Strauss, "Die letzen Jahre," p. 69, note 4; and *Leo Baeck Institute Year Book*, passim, s.v. Leo Baeck.

tion were tolerated. They ended it in 1942 when all pretenses were dropped. One would also like to know if Leo Baeck, the only leader capable of such a feat, had used his prestige or his connections to extract a promise from some group in the polycentric Nazi power jungle to keep the Hochschule open. The school's closing in mid-1942 affected Leo Baeck more than any other measure to which I could observe his reaction over the years. The abrupt end of the remaining Jewish school system was the clearest signal that the end of Jewish life had come.

The Hochschule during its last years bore the stamp of Leo Baeck's personality and character. He maintained the curriculum in Judaistics and appointed substitute lecturers. Baeck kept teaching to the very end—beyond the date at which he signed my class book in July 1941. (I had received a leave of absence from the Hochschule in 1941, to attend the Jüdische Oberschule, a *Gymnasium*-type secondary school.) Leo Baeck was then sixty-six years old. In public appearances in the lecture hall, the classroom, or the pulpit, he represented the upper-class tradition of German public speaking, difficult to understand (though possibly for some tooth problem), abstract, philosophical, even in the simplified rhetorical figures that recurred in his sermons. He was a tall, slim man. A white beard would underline his dignified distance, his never-failing grace and politesse in professional contacts giving confidence to the many men and women who sought not only his advice but also his intercession on behalf of a relative or friend. Those who failed to discount his professional pastoral need to give comfort to the distressed would often misconstrue what Baeck held out only as vague promises, "to do what he could" in circumstances vastly beyond his control.

At the time, not only did I respect, I venerated Leo Baeck for his command of the universe of European humanism.[6] I saw character traits in him that epitomized the German Jewish symbiosis, and in which I recognized some of my own ideals. That the Hochschule had become a symbol of stability and pride in ourselves was to an eminent degree a projection of Leo Baeck's attitudes. He lived a

---

[6] Hans Liebeschütz, "Judaism and History of Religion in Leo Baeck's Work," *Leo Baeck Institute Year Book*, 2 (1957), 8–20; and his "Between Past and Future: Leo Baeck's Historical Position," ibid., 11 (1967), 3–27.

highly disciplined life, beginning early in the day with writing, or reading Greek philosophy or the great tragic writers, and kept to a tight daily schedule that would accommodate a large variety of activities. In conversations with students, he would at times point to his services as a German army chaplain in World War I as a model of what was needed in our own extraordinary circumstances. Although, by today's standards, he would be an "old" sixty-six years, his apparent frailty concealed great physical energy. I believe that he saw himself in the image of the *grand seigneur*, the gentleman, imparting sobriety, coolness—*Haltung*, in the untranslatable German phrase—that would master chaos even if it could not conquer it any longer. I would see him climb up the staircase to the Hochschule library to visit the librarian, Mrs. Jenny Wilde, or concern himself with students' worries, and when I was down and out in a slum area of Puerto Rican Manhattan during my early penurious immigrant years in New York, he would come for dinner to us, climb up the rickety stairs, and endure the small catastrophes our two-year-old Janie would fling at him from her high chair. The few letters I exchanged with him after the war also reflected this style, the self-protective veneer of a person perpetually engulfed by people in need. His letters, as far as they are preserved in archives, are almost empty of content. The values he projected were imposingly pastoral—*Seelsorge*. The inscription he had placed on his memorial tombstone in Berlin's Weissensee cemetery—*migeza rabbonim*, from the tribe (race) of rabbis, in the tradition (from the stem) of rabbis—touches on the "essence" of his personality, essence having been a preferred tool of his generation in its interpretations of complex and diverse bodies of thought like "Judaism" or "Christianity." He adhered to conservative/orthodox ritual practice in the tradition of the German Jewish *Einheitsgemeinde* mainstream that had fused the different denominational trends in the Hegelian spirit of the *Kaiserreich* (empire). His traditionalism was probably closer to conservatism, in American terms, than his association with the more radical Reform (progressive Judaism) movement suggested. Also traditional in terms of Jewish emancipation was the central emphasis he gave to scholarship in educating rabbis who would transcend the *Seelsorge* mold and add through research and publications what the ever-changing present demanded to keep the unchanging core of Judaism (its "essence") creative. He celebrated the Pharisees as revolutionary traditionalists in the image of Jewish Reform, following an interpretation advanced much earlier by Leopold Zunz, and reinforcing the analysis Robert Travers Herford had published in 1912.[7] In his view, the very nature of Jewish theological thought demanded roots in the culture of each period *and* in the contents and methods of the intellectual tradition of Judaism, stretching to the horizons of the sea of learning.

Another of Baeck's preferred descriptive strategies, seeing polarities in apparently indivisible phenomena—*ein Zwiefaches*, a duality, two-in-one, a dialectic tension—served to tie intellectual trends together that were at the core of nineteenth- and twentieth-century modernity in culture and religion. When I met Baeck, his ideas had long since reached their final form. He was recognized as a, if not the, leading rabbi in Germany and the intellectual leader of the World Union for Progressive Judaism. The reconciliation of opposites in culture and religion reflected his role as the great political harmonizer, even if this meant not taking sides when doing so would have been "right," for example, his more than ambivalent attitude toward Zionist rabbis before World War I. His assertion of control through reconciling conflicts, and his attitudes toward contending trends in communal life reflected the political ethos of German educated and social elites before World War I: the Kaiser and the courts, tenured civil servants (*Beamte*), the military and the law, the mandarins at the universities, and landowning gentries derived their claim to power and recognition from claiming to be "above the interests" fighting each other for profit or lacking a moral grasp of "the whole." "Dignity" and "nobility of service and personality" (*Würde und Adel*), the highest encomiums recurring frequently in ceremonial German Jewish discourse, reflected the depth to which Germans-Jewish symbiosis in thought and in society had shaped our social character through the values of a bureaucratic and gentrified Hegelianism.

But Leo Baeck's public persona was not his only "essence." It was said at the time that in negotiations with the Berlin Gestapo which he was forced to conduct as president of the Reichsvertretung and its successor, the Reichsvereinigung, Baeck used his dig-

---

[7] Robert Travers Herford, *Pharisaism: Its Aims and Its Methods* (New York: G. P. Putnam's Sons, 1912); see also his *The Pharisees* (New York: Macmillan, 1924).

nity with enough shrewdness and tactical skill to be dubbed "the old fox" by police and colleagues alike. I had no occasion to observe his activities in political situations, but I remember the shrewd and not always charitable comments on men and affairs he used to make when I rode with him after class on the elevated railroad (*Stadtbahn*) from Friedrichstrasse station to Bahnhof Zoo, the station for his office and my rented room. But I do not recall when I discovered that his concern with individuals was secondary to his concern for Judaism and institutions like the Hochschule, on which he had staked his life. He demonstratively refused the advice to emigrate tendered him during his frequent trips to London; the captain would stay on the bridge. Luckily, unlike many of the best among Jewish officials who acted out of the same sense of duty and perished, he survived in Theresienstadt. Most rabbis of established reputations had fled abroad after the November pogroms of 1938, or were forced by the Gestapo to abandon their congregations, presumably to hasten the emigration of the congregants. Some rabbis had acted out of their sense of responsibity and had gone with their over-aged congregations or with institutions like orphanages and old-age homes into camps like Theresienstadt, or into the gas chambers. Quite a few who thus perished were advanced in years themselves, and had been retired. Rabbis Regina Jonas, Peter Joseph, Hans Harff, Hans Löwenthal, and Manfred Gross, recent graduates of the Hochschule, were cut down before they reached their potential. The more than thirty rabbis serving the German Jewish community who paid the ultimate price for their devotion in the Holocaust have never been properly honored by the surviving German Jewish émigré community. Are community leaders and rabbis conflicted about taking to the boats while one-third of their charges perished? Do the pogroms of Crystal Night really represent the deepest trauma in our destruction? There is no place to hide behind Baeck's and Eppstein's clear-eyed courage in the face of the ultimate threat.

Baeck's decision to stay with the remnant in Germany may have contributed initially to the delay in the attempt to transfer the Hochschule to Cambridge in 1938–39. He had hesitated to accept the condition that he would direct research and teaching. The rescue attempt was delayed, then abandoned with the German invasion of Poland. By then the plan to transfer the Hochschule had already failed. Its main English sponsor, a renowned Bible scholar, Herbert Loewe of Cambridge, had died, and the chief British rabbinate opposed the project strenuously.[8] In the fall of 1940, Baeck appealed to my obligation to serve and my sense of duty to the community, and I became an auxiliary rabbi in the Berlin Gemeinde. My task was to preside over services and act as a preacher on the Jewish holidays. He knew that I would not take up a rabbinical career and assured me that I was included in plans for the transfer of the Hochschule to Cambridge. For now, I was needed to maintain religious services.

This step was only a small part of his broad policy of maintaining the community in existence, *coûte que coûte*. I do not know if Baeck had the information or the premonition I lacked in 1938–39 to anticipate the total physical destruction of our community. By then the urge to emigrate had taken on near-panic proportions. Some countries, notably England and to some extent the United States, had eased their rigid exclusion practices, either because public pressures against immigrants were lessening, or because rearmament suggested coming labor shortages. Even so, the "paper walls" erected after World War I and the Great Depression were not dismantled; they were merely pierced in some countries for selected groups of applicants. As early as the fall of 1938, Jewish social workers had reasoned in the last issue of the German Jewish journal *Jewish Social Work and Social Policy*[9] that the impoverished community left behind, after all those able to leave had left the country, would become an over-aged remnant and would have to be cared for by Jewish assistance once their savings were gone. (A few weeks after this last issue was published, Nazi laws ended all Jewish economic activity in Germany and Austria, and made this speculation an instant reality.) Until it was *verboten* by a Himmler decree in October 1941, Jews in smaller numbers still emigrated, primarily to the United States, even via such unlikely routes as the Trans-Siberian railroad and across the Pacific Ocean, until the German attack

---

[8] See above, p. 108, note 12.

[9] *Jüdische Wohlfahrtspflege und Sozialpolitik*, 4 (1933–34)–8 (1938). The last issue (October 1938) reports on a Jewish social workers' convention meeting shortly before the pogroms of 1938, revealing the presumption of civility we all labored under. For the general trend of social policy, cf. my "Jewish Autonomy," and note 2, p. 64, above.

on Russia in June 1941 barred this escape route, too. A few succeeded in reaching the United States via the neutrals in Western Europe, Vichy France, Shanghai, or Japan. In the summer of 1941, Berlin still had a critical mass of Jews and an active Jewish religious and communal life. Our condition appeared to justify the stability Baeck had imparted to the Hochschule.

The last and fatal turn was reached with the attack on Russia, and the mass deportation of Jews from Berlin beginning in October 1941. Our armchair strategists properly interpreted the check of the German armies before Moscow and Leningrad as major setbacks, even if we could not know its near-catastrophic seriousness, or the illusions of a general staff that had failed to provide German troops with winter uniforms. The *Oberkommando* (high command) had expected another blitzkrieg. Too late they collected winter clothing in Berlin, and presumably the rest of the country, from the civilian population. That winter, Grumach deduced properly that the invasion of England had been abandoned for good. Parallels with Napoleon's Russian strategy were rife and eagerly studied. Our waiting time would be shortened.

When the first transport of Jews was assembled in Berlin in October 1941, Nazi deception could not hide that a new stage in brutality had been reached. As in other countries, and in the extermination camps, everything was done to mislead the victims about the fate that awaited them. The mockery and bestiality of these deceptions involved layer after layer of German accessories "just doing their jobs" or their "duty." Some departments of the Jewish Gemeinde bureaucracy had been dragooned by the Gestapo into assisting them in preparing members for deportation. This, in turn, became part of the system of deception that tranquilized us. Would the familiar Gemeinde administration in Oranienburger Strasse, with its imposing synagogue building, deceive its members about "resettlement," the term used on the forms the Gemeinde had sent to persons whose names had been supplied by the Gestapo on those notorious lists?

Deportees had to cede their property to the Reich to defray the alleged expenses of being maintained in the East. They were issued a list of the clothing and utensils allowed each person: it supported the illusion that our organization and energy would prevail, as they had prevailed since the war began. Each person or family received written notice from the Gemeinde that they would be *abgeholt* and brought to the Levetzowstrasse synagogue before being entrained for the East. *Abholen* had ambiguous connotations: a friend coming by to fetch you for a walk, the police arresting you. The victims were to wait for the *Abholers* in their apartments, suitcases or backpacks at the ready. As a rule, *Abholers* formed a team made up of police officials and helpers designated by the Jüdische Gemeinde. Eighteen months later, the last 35,000 Berlin Jews, except for a trickle of persons the Gestapo considered "war essential" or privileged, and the thousands who were hiding out, had been deported to their deaths in Eastern European ghettos and camps. An additional 14,900 had been transported to Theresienstadt, the "old-age" ghetto. Fewer than 5,000 of almost 50,000 deportees returned.

Nobody could imagine the brutality and cruelty with which Berlin police riot squads (*Überfall-Kommandos*), the security detail (*Leibstandarte Adolf Hitler*), and the Berlin Gestapo would treat their victims, especially during the final round-up on February 27–28, 1943. It has been abundantly documented before the Allied Tribunals in Nuremberg, the war-crimes trials held in post-1945 Germany, and the Eichmann trial in Jerusalem.

It was during these nine months, from October 1941 to June 1942, that the Hochschule co-existed with the Holocaust of Berlin Jews, the ultimate denial of its stability.

From the distance of half a century that has burned the murder of a people into the world's consciousness, the emotions still revolt against what my memory has retained: most of us fell for the Nazi deception, accepted the assistance given by the Jüdische Gemeinde in the expulsion process as a sign that our people would find harsh conditions in this unprecedented catastrophe, but that we could survive it. How else would the Gemeinde lend its assistance to "resettlement"? It was said at the time, and told for a fact after 1945 in scholarly works, that Leo Baeck had reluctantly supported the Gemeinde in doing the Gestapo's bidding. It would give the inevitable a human face. I never tried to verify this because it was irrelevant. Whatever the result, it would not relieve my pain over the outcome. By 1941, Baeck was in no position to order the Gemeinde to desist. His power had been diminished by Eppstein's rise within the operational hierarchy of the Reichsvertretung and he never had control over the quite independent Gemeinde administration. It must have been an attempt to ease the victims' pain in the over-whelming maelstrom of force that engulfed them, helpless victims all.

The war would end in defeat for Germany. We had drawn our confidence from numerous facts, relevant or not, and from propa-ganda assertions over the BBC that pointed to this end, and that had called into being a veritable underworld of rumors. It dominated all talk intimate enough not to be overheard. The documents and the studies published since 1945 support the judgment that I was not alone, or an exception; that in what we thought of as our twentieth-century world, and in what the civilized Jewish world thought in 1941–42, genocide and Holocaust did not exist as words for an un-imaginable reality.

It is possible, of course, that growing up in an atmosphere of persecution and aggressive anti-Jewish propaganda since age fif-teen, when the Third Reich began, had accustomed me to living on several levels at once. It had taught me to fight each step of the deteriorating condition imposed on the community with the split consciousness and the alertness one needed to deal with each step affecting our lives. As yet, concern, anxiousness, fear, the black self-tortures that come with the physical lows that dot anybody's vital landscape at night formed the counterpoise to my German Jewish self-confidence, the "reality-principle" as it were, for which the Hochschule paradoxically was the emotional symbol. Its normality assured us of a world under the control of reason and order. It became one influence for rational action and thus for the control of anxiety that would have affected the cool front, the stiff upper lip, if it had been given free rein. Like Nietzsche's wise fool, we should have tolled the bells to let anxiety warn reason that death was abroad. Suppressing our feelings or, rather, not letting them alarm us for the realities that were engulfing us, pushing them to the mar-gins of our consciousness and everyday behavior, appears to me to describe at least my own condition at the time, and, I trust, the condition of many of my colleagues. If we had faced up to the catas-trophe, would some of us, would I, have prepared for the few op-tions we had—including illegal hiding and illegal flight across a border? I knew some people who talked incessantly of escape. Few succeeded in the end; most of those who did at first hide under-ground were recognized or denounced and sent to their deaths in the East. My friends and I did talk about going underground, but it was feeble emoting and abstract protest. I would not have gone into hiding if circumstances would not have forced my hand. Reason reinforced by past experience came down on the side of the known and apparently smaller risks of facing one crisis at a time as it arose, based on past experience. Emotions and reason remained stable, "under control," and minimized the threat that we might have deduced from the minimum of information and the rumors we had.

That there were moments of intense panic I would not have remembered were it not for a personal letter and a small memoir that survived the war by accident. The letter is mostly typewritten; the memoir is in my handwriting. Both carry precise dates. The letter was begun on October 10, 1941, and written on nine subsequent evenings and nights, the last being October 18. The note is dated December 26, 1941.

In 1941, I was gripped by a tense concern with the fate that would await the first group of Jews in Berlin put on notice that they would be deported to an unknown destination in Eastern Europe. Among the acquaintances given notice was a close friend of ours and her husband, Mr. and Mrs. Herzenberg. Mrs. Herzenberg had been my English teacher for about a year, and I had come to admire her as a person and love her inspired teaching. As we understood soon after, the transport was sent to Lodz. The Gestapo had selected the most vulnerable among Jews in Berlin, the stateless persons for whom no government would intercede, and for whom no German administrative agency had any responsibility.[10] Mr. Herzenberg, an engineer, had fled Russia soon after the 1917 revolution. Like the "White Russian" émigré colony that led a dynamic intellectual and political life in Berlin in the 1920s, the Herzenbergs had been stripped of their Russian and German citizenship, respectively, and had become "stateless."

The week between October 10 and October 18 threw me into a deeply felt panic. The twenty-four–page, single-spaced typewritten letter was driven by forebodings about the Herzenbergs' fate, the fate of our community, my own fate, and my wish to let the recipi-

---

[10] In 1942 the German Foreign Office advised the Gestapo in the Netherlands to begin deportations with stateless Jews since it "would attract less attention" ("weniger auffalen"). Cf. Robert M. W. Kempner, *Edith Stein und Anne Frank* (Freiburg: Herder, 1968), p. 53.

ent, Dörte, know about my emotional condition and my thoughts in the face of their deaths and my own. It reflects much of my personal preoccupation with the reading and studying I was doing at the time, with the comforts of religion in the face of your own impending destruction, with Nazi politics and philosophical-religious literature from Kierkegaard, Dostoevsky, and Schopenhauer, to Heidegger. And it reaffirms a basic belief in the core of the religious world view I had found in my post-orthodox thinking. But it also refers to "our knowledge" of "what happened to our brothers in the East," relates our condition to the fate of the Armenians in World War I: "During these last two years, we have sometimes had the feeling of being acutely threatened, that we would die soon— nothing in particular giving us reason to feel that way, but always something—but against death life always asserts its particular [*eigentümliches*] right and imposes it on us: it makes external conventions [*äussere Schranken*] relative, and strengthens the sense of loyalty to oneself" (p.11).

I mention my fear that this was only the beginning of such expulsions, and that I would die while so much still needed to be felt and thought. I tried to place this fear of death into the perspective of what I was able to distill from my own readings at the time. In the end, the letter affirms the Nietzschean *amor fati* for the Jewish mission and its history, whose "only purpose and subject [*Substratum*] [was] man":

> "Every Jew is a king in the realm of faith; he has arrived at an independent judgment about himself and the world; he has started early to recognize the terror of naked death; he knows that nobody can escape the last solitude of dying, neither splendor nor happiness, and no ideology provided by the state [p. 19].

> The executioners play no role in the greatness of our suffering . . . ; they don't need to be considered. . . . War, any war, improves nothing. . . . even if the Jewish view of war and the state is unreal and utopian, it is warmer, and on another level, where historians like Mommsen or Burckhardt see the grandiose battles of opposing forces and principles, the Jewish faith [*gläubiger Jude*] perceives only confused human suffering and eternal hankering after falsehood and vanities. . . . The only possible response to the imminence of our death . . . is the leap into faith, maybe a piece of hate-edged love [*Hassliebe*], and gratitude for a nation that involves man in this situation, the

Jewish nation, whose group character was never as apparent as in the cauldron of this catastrophe. We are Jews—we are ashamed that blind love of life has found only petty responses, but proud of our people, whose genius [*Fähigkeiten*] and inner pride have not been demoralized by an eight-year war of nerves [p. 20]."

I know now, I learned after the war, that I could and should have known about our being mass murdered. Hitler had announced his intentions in a speech heard by millions of Germans over the radio as early as January 30, 1939. He repeated those snarling threats of "death to the Jews" on several subsequent occasions, while internal Nazi information on this genocide in progress appeared in clear text in the Nazi Party press. Millions had heard his threats over the radio. The foreign press had reported them. I had heard them, but I could not take them seriously. I did not read the Nazi Party press and was not privy to their office decorations: they used Hitler's death threat against the Jews as one of those prettily framed posters that conveyed the "motto of the week" to all Party offices. None of those brave souls would remember reading about mass murder after the war.

I do remember clamming up at the malicious sneers, the almost subhuman viciousness with which Hitler spat out his elemental and primitive roars—but I did not take them seriously. The shock did not translate into external reality; my alarm system did not stay high. I had learned to disregard the often repeated, incessant, and raucously mean oratory because it seemed to have no relationship to my reality or the environment I had lived in since 1933. I learned to discount it. Hitler's had been one more propaganda "message" that seemed as remote from reality as Jewish "world power," the "Anglo-Jewish war," or the "Jewish-Bolshevist menace." But the panic of 1941 penetrated my consciousness from within myself. Now the brave front helped me to deny, in fact became itself, "reality." The extremes of coping with present and future crises one by one, and the chaos that had to be controlled for the sake of survival, constituted the true poles of my thoughts and feelings during these years.

In retrospect, of course, the chaos *was* the reality, and stability the illusion, at least from one perspective. Was Leo Baeck "wrong" when his biblically stiff neck and his gentlemanly disdain for the

Nazis guided the Hochschule, its faculty and its students, its curriculum and its library, through nine of the twelve years of Nazi rule in Germany? "It is the misfortune of Jews," I heard him say, "that our enemies are always *so kleine Leute*" (such insignificant people). Was he "wrong" when he bet against time with his and our lives? When he lived his theological belief that the essence of Judaism remains unchangeable, whatever the historic circumstances? Nobody except Mahatma Gandhi had ever suggested that voluntarily dissolving the institutions and ending the organizational life of the community was an option worth considering—even if the Nazi authorities had not retaliated with hostage-shooting and murder against this kind of resistance.

Then, when deportations began on a large scale in October 1941, did the Jüdische Gemeinde administration have the option not to make employees available to assist in the process? Did Baeck know of the mass murders of Berlin Jews—his moral and religious wards—in the ghettos and camps to which they were brought? Did he make the morally right decision when he withheld the truth? Why did he keep students and faculty at the Hochschule in the dark about whatever he knew? Why did he keep me in the dark when I visited him in his home near Schöneberg Park (Am Park 15) in January 1943, after I had been in hiding from the Gestapo for over two months? Would his making public what awaited us in Eastern Europe have saved lives, even if it would have cost him his own? Could he have found a way to make public what he must have known, for example, through foreign journalists from neutral countries assigned to Berlin? Baeck was in contact with the military and political conspirators then preparing the attempt of July 20, 1944, on Hitler's life. Could the few students and teachers who held out at the Hochschule to the end have saved themselves if they had known the truth? Would being told have given them an unfair advantage? Who would have suffered if they had escaped?

I liked and respected Leo Baeck too much and for too long for such questions to occur while the extreme situation lasted in Germany, and while I was studying in Switzerland. I also remembered the murderous retaliations the Nazis had visited upon Jewish communities or their leaders if they had offered collective resistance. My perspectives changed only as more time elapsed and the distance increased to the length of the ocean. After the war, I met

Leo Baeck at the first international meeting I attended, the 1946 conference of the World Union for Progressive Judaism in London. I served as one of the *ad personam* delegates from Switzerland. We celebrated his survival. After my emigration to the United States, I saw him again in New York in 1947 or 1948. It became clear then that I could not gain perspective on my Berlin experiences without placing Leo Baeck into the context of history and morality. He never spoke about his last years in Germany in public, and he avoided requests for oral history interviews submitted to him in Jerusalem by Kurt-Jacob Ball-Kaduri, a respectable German Jewish scholar-journalist, a former Berlin lawyer.[11] My own judgment vacillated considerably during the earlier postwar years, until I saw his behavior in terms of the irreconcilable dilemmas of decision-making in situations beyond his control, balancing the consequences of one action against the other, against its estimated effects on human life and on institutions, and the anticipated behavior of the forces involved. His ultimate dilemmas may well have been between stiff-necked preservation of the institution, the superior rights of the community, and individuals in need, essence versus existence, traditional versus human reality inextricably intertwined here and now.

This new perspective, striving to do justice to a dilemma that I could not fully comprehend because basic information was not forthcoming at the time, did not open up easily. In 1947 or 1948, the correspondence and the personal relationship with Leo Baeck came to an end, as I was living through the professional and cultural changes of my new condition as an immigrant starting at the proverbial bottom. In 1947, I accepted a fellowship from the U.S. National Health Service, Mental Health Division, in Bethesda, Maryland, to take part in a project studying the concentration camp experiences of Hungarian Jewish camp survivors and the so-called Buchenwald children through autobiographical documents and a carefully structured program of interviews and tests. The burden of what emerged during three years of work on this topic at the New School for Social Research in New York City changed many of my basic attitudes.[12] Occupying a pulpit in the tradition symbolized by

---

[11] Kurt-Jakob Ball-Kaduri, "Leo Baeck and Contemporary History: A Riddle in Baeck's Life," *Yad Vashem Studies*, 6 (Jerusalem 1967): 128–29.

[12] See above, note 4.

Baeck now became a moral impossibility as well. The Hochschule was not refounded in Cambridge as a scholarly academy, and I did not follow up referrals to a rabbinical position Baeck had proposed, based on his certification of my graduation of the Hochschule, the incomplete lengthy final examinations, two research papers, and the Abitur.

This did not touch the immense gratitude I felt for Baeck the teacher and scholar. In 1940–41, he offered two lecture courses on history and philosophy of religion and a seminar on medieval philosophical texts that spoke directly to my intellectual situation. Baeck examined me on these subjects when I began taking the graduating examinations of the Hochschule. Thanks to Ernst Grumach, who probably removed the protocol from the files of the faculty when the Hochschule was closed, all but one entry in Baeck's handwriting, on the "Schlussprüfung [final examination] des Herrn Herbert Strauss begonnen: 10 February 1941" has survived. It was presumably among the papers I was able to smuggle into Switzerland in 1942 or 1943 through a diplomatic mail pouch. Baeck had tested in: Introduction to the Talmud, History of Religion (*Religionsgeschichte*), Pedagogy, and Philosophy of Religion (mainly of medieval Jewish Spain including an interpretation of Maimonides's *Guide of the Perplexed*). Each entry noted the main areas I was asked about and conveys an impression of the breadth of each hour-long examination. History of religion spoke most directly to my intellectual needs. I still remember the excitement I felt as I saw that Würzburg had reflected a universal human experience: that older layers or forms and attitudes could be recognized that had survived into the present, however transformed by new contexts, and that religions yielded a common core to comparative analysis. I had followed the literature Baeck had mentioned in his lectures. If I had had to choose a major then, I would have elected comparative religion and history of religion as my academic vocation!

The protocol entry reveals Baeck's style. Beginning with general reflections on "principles" or the state of research, he would first explore "primitive" or prehistoric and simple forms, then evoke associations on key terms of analysis and, in the end, on philosophical or complex issues and problems to identify the "core" (essence, *Wesen*) of a phenomenon in the great religions as they reach into the present.

The Baeck I was privileged to study with at age twenty-two also offered the clearest historical interpretation of the Jewish origins of Christianity. I took his course interpreting the New Testament's Epistle to the Galatians and studied his brilliant articles on the "nature" of Judaism as a "classical" religion as compared to Christianity as a "romantic" religion. He placed Paul into the conflicts of his time through the isolation of such key concepts as law and grace and their place in Jewish thought. The essay on classical and romantic religion offered sweeping definitions of their terms and their place in European intellectual history (Renaissance, eighteenth century, humanism, aesthetics). Baeck integrated this history into the "essence" of Christianity and Judaism. These, too, were established by well-founded and broadly documented reductions of a large body of quotations from texts and different periods of cultural and religious history, but were seen as revealing the central tenets of each religion—their essence.

This precisely was Baeck's main strength, the interpretation of vast data of cultural history on a highly abstract level in an ordered temporal sequence. He had studied with Wilhelm Dilthey, a master of interpretative cultural history, and had spent time, in the 1920s, in an esoteric gathering of like-minded cultural philosophers, Keyserling's School of Wisdom. His lectures created their own universe, more real than the contradictory and confused intellectual discontinuities from which concepts and lines of development had been abstracted. Political and social realities occurred only as asides. Our present troubles were hardly ever mentioned. They did not enter Baeck's intellectual world, where Greek, Christian, gnostic, stoic, or Manichaean philosophers or texts were engaged in timeless disputations with Judaism.

In the 1980s, I was handed a suitcase containing the papers, certificates, and other documents Ernst Grumach had taken from my room in Schlüterstrasse 53 after it was sealed by the Gestapo as confiscated Jewish property in 1942. Ernst and Mrs. Grumach had kindly stored it in their attic in Berlin and had moved it with them from one apartment to another. I had not known of its existence. It was one of many such traces of a long-dead past tearing at my heartstrings when I returned to Berlin for a teaching assignment in the 1980s. Included were about a dozen sets of notes I had taken in lectures between 1939 and 1941, in ink or pencil, mostly in longhand (except for a few stenographic lines to catch up with the speaker), and Hebrew or Greek citations. In some of these lecture notes, Leo Baeck appears as the supreme philological-historical analyst, displaying a stunning array of references and quotations, and applying stylistic and literary criticism to biblical and post-biblical texts with an intellectual certainty distilled from decades of theological system-building. One or two lectures reveal his *summa theologica* simplified and concentrated for the classroom. Excerpts from a series of lectures on "The Ideas of Judaism" offered during the summer term of 1940 may explain the intellectual and personal charisma engulfing his listeners while German armies occupied Belgium, Holland, and France (my rollbook, included in this suitcase, had Baeck's signature [*Testat*] for May 24, 1940, and July 27, 1941, the first and last lecture of his I attended).

Here are my notes on that lecture course on "The Ideas of Judaism" offered by Leo Baeck at the Hochschule für die Wissenschaft des Judentums, Berlin, Artilleriestrasse 14, in the summer of 1940. Part three of the five-part lecture was not included in the surviving notes, for reasons I can no longer reconstruct. My enrollment in this lecture course is noted in my rollbook.

[B.C.E.] 586 separated epochs in Judaism: the religion of the Israelites and Judaism. Previously, the division between Judaea and (North) Israel does not appear meaningful in the history of religion. Psalms and prophets would not have failed to mention it if the tradition of the ten lost tribes had had a basis in reality. After B.C.E. 438 (return from Persian exile) the number "12" dominates public consciousness and is being applied retroactively to several groups of data. Although Talmudic and prophetic religion differ in essence—the word *Gebot* [command] does not appear in prophetic literature—their evolution like that of the Catholic Church, shows no break. The prophets were included in the Bible canon and thus kept alive. New only were the forms of religiosity, like *Kern und Schale* [core and shell]: Talmud, Midrash, philosophy of religion express identical thoughts and are forms of expression only. The language changes; the contents remain the same.

The concept of development, in European thought: eighteenth-century optimism a belief in the good and in man's power to realize it. Romanticism and *Restauration* put an end to the optimistic implications of development ("and we shall not be able to return to this faith").

Darwin, Malthus, Ranke, Nietzsche, Treitschke: "Fit is who wins the war." Only few ideas endure in the development of mankind. "Development occurs if a great individual embodies a great idea." Renaissance is a new embodiment of an idea—all development is renaissance, rebirth of the idea, new confrontation with old contents through a different personality (Moses in Hillel's *Lehrhaus*). "The miracle of renaissance appears in Judaism as the continuity of actually existing historical *Faktizität*" [webs of facts].

2.

Universalism has remained an idea that never stops benefiting mankind. Numbers do not count but the inclusiveness [*Weite*] of the ideas. Similarly, the word World Religion [*Weltreligion*] does not imply numbers but a quality: Calvinism in the U.S. Constitution, Holland, Switzerland, England, rise of capitalism. Jews show similar dynamics, beginning with their influence on the (Christian) Church, to socialism. All democratic development originates with Calvin, everything authoritarian with Luther (1914–1940).

Renaissance mediates the dynamics of an idea. In Judaism, too, there was no break but a continuity, a talent to effect renaissance.

Aristotle: ἡ φύσις τέλος ἐστίν. In contrast central to Judaism: The One and Eternal enters into the plural and the temporal. There is an Eternal, a Being [*Seiendes*], Thoughts [*Gedanken*] are the linguistic form of this eternity and being; the Bible is such an idea, Plotinus expressed Plato better than Plato himself; Herman Cohen [expressed] Kant better than Immanuel Kant. The idea of unity was given, *eheye asher eheye* [I am becoming what I become, or I am to be what I shall be] (Exodus   ). Being can be defined only through itself, the struggle for expression, *rishon ve'akharon* [the First and the Last].

The concept of unity had been found in other (cultures), too, but seeing it as uniquely and exclusively "Being by itself" [*Sein an sich*] is Israelite: that the One and Unique enters into the world of the Plural . . . Plato's εἶδος remains transcendental . . .

And the ethical *Gebot* [command] runs a parallel to the ontological: it enters the *Gebot*. Ethos originated with custom. *Der Staat* creates and guarantees ethics. Odysseus, the clever individualist . . . Only the Israelites tied ethos to the eternal [*das Ewige*)] (HAS: why then do Greeks swear their oaths in temples?) (HAS: be holy because [*ki*] God is holy—the eternal enters?)

Thou shalt love thy neighbor as thyself, I am Yahweh—the second part of the sentence determines the validity of the first part. God's entry into the world is of a commanding significance: command is categorical. Significant is the difference between heathen cosmogony and Israelite creation.

Gebot is unconditional, creation, the internal cohesion of man— Idea is tension between the finite and the infinite in the *Gebot*. Thus, there is no transcendence problem in Israelite religion. Ethics and mysticism are one, mysticism of the *Gebot*, ethical mysticism, Grace [χάρις] and law are one, *Gnadenerwartung* "velut paralyticum" absolutely contradicts the ethical *Gebot*. The basic link has a revolutionary quality.

"To add a small excursus:" = Greek thought is aprioristic and prose, Jewish thought is poetic: Aristotle: *philosophoteron kai spoudaioteron historias poiesis 'estin* (Poetry is more philosophical and weightier than history). Faust, Hamlet, Prometheus: ultimate experiences can only be expressed in the medium of art [*das Künstlerische*]. The Bible is poetry, Plato's *Phaedros* is poetry . . .

Any single *Gebot* is determined by its time and was part of the constitution of Israelite theocracy.

(3—missing)

4. The unity of the eternal in the act of creation represents a *Gebot*, a commission [*Aufgabe*].

Paul thought that no *Gebot* should be imposed on man that he cannot fulfill. *Gebot* must not be the meaning of life; it must be capable of being obeyed, but since *Gebot* is always beyond complete fulfillment, man is born in sin. *Gebot* cannot redeem man. For Paul it is grace. Paul, being human, cannot satisfy the entire *Gebot*. He is sinful, a sinner.

In contrast, not being able to obey all the commandments [*das ganze Gebot*], Judaism does not consider sinful: each person [*der Einzelne*] can do no more than strive [*ein Strebender sein*]. *Lo alekha ligmor et hamelakha, velo rashai levatel mimena*—It is not up to you to complete the work, nor are you permitted to desist from it. Sin appears in hostility toward *Gebot* as such, only the denial of all morality being totally immoral. Man is on the way toward the *Gebot*. To complete only part is [the lot of] human[s].

There can be no creation without a consciousness of the *Gebot*. *Das Geheimnis ist Gebot* [mystery *is* the *Gebot*].

The Catholic Church, Calvin, Luther . . . Nihilism, Nietzsche— race was the last consequence—

The ethical monotheism of the Old Testament, the accent is on ethical, its monotheism was incomplete. *Gebot* is absolute because it comes from God, it is not created by the relativity of man. Monotheism is not a dogma, others had monotheism too. Xenophon . . . the

Bible knows subordinate gods, decisive is moving toward the one God. Theocentric thought is characteristic of Judaism: world and man are centered on God.

—

Mysticism is striving for immediacy with God through immersion in one's own self. . . . Plotinus . . .

Jewish mysticism is *Gebotsmystik*. In all cases where Jewish thought influenced Christian mysticism the *Gebot* comes through . . . Eckhart, Albertus, Thomas through Maimonides.

The mystic knows the place—not the way; Judaism shows the way. Being on the way is the decisive quality. Moses, Amos, Isaiah, Jeremiah.

—

Prophets are ecstatic but fulfilling the *Gebot* is the goal of their ecstasy, being on the mission is the goal, the *Gebot* of justice and love.—

The second characteristic of ethical monotheism is its teaching that the One enters from infinity into the finite. This differs from polytheism, Zoroastrianism, Holy Trinity. Its manifestations are one, not many. The unity of God corresponds to the oneness of man. The language of the Bible proved insufficient to express the concept of oneness. . . . If man fulfills the *unum necessarium*, he is the complete man—*tamim*.

5.

The unity of mankind is the goal. Language is tie between thought and word, one must struggle for the right expression. . . .

To let the One and Good enter into the Limited, Defective, implies a judgment on the world, the *Weltanschaung* of optimism.

The world has the task to be good, the best of all possible worlds . . . *Tov leolam shelo nivra*. It would have been better if the world had not been created. In the Bible, the world is not good, but since it has been created, man should be as good as he can.

Jewish optimism is not identical with Enlightenment optimism. . . . World has an ultimate meaning that will and must realize itself. Tragic optimism. . . . Two concepts of the tragic, the Greek . . . Jewish concept is struggle of the good and ideal with matter, like the artist and his marble. Good can be accomplished only through struggle, like Jacob's with the angel. You fought with God and prevailed. Suffering derives its meaning from being a partner in the struggle for the good. Being good does not happen or "be"; it can only be realized through struggle. Judaism contrasts with salvation religions like Christianity, where salvation, grace from above, liberates man for becoming good. Undeserved liberation through grace is absolutely unethical. Judaism is a religion of reconciliation; the idea of the kingdom of god, the total realization of life. . . .

Between 1939 and 1942 when the Hochschule was closed by the Gestapo, I had taken nine courses with Leo Baeck among the altogether forty-seven courses entered in my rollbook. Selecting what I remember as a totally immersing experience for a twenty-two-year-old does not reflect Baeck's immense breadth of learning in several fields of Jewish and classical or philosophical scholarship, or his, to me, fearless use of critical tools. His technique of associating widely diffused quotations from numerous texts with his interpretations resembled the methods by which the Talmud had been interpreted over the generations, but reached far beyond Jewish to Greek and medieval texts. His "Ideen des Judentums" had, of course, been long elaborated in his works, beginning with the seminal *The Essence of Judaism* of 1895, itself changed in subsequent editions. This may have been his most influential work, expanded here into the dialogue out of which his concepts of Judaism arose. His most precise literary criticism may have been reserved for the lectures on the Midrash, the collections of narrative, parable, morality tales, and philosophical polemics Baeck saw as a major source of post-biblical intellectual Jewish history, advanced by preachers over hundreds of years. To me, his critical history of ideas, however generalized and obviously *parti pris* it came across, tied in with my Würzburg base, but it approached it in a breathtakingly universal context, whose textual basis I could well accept, precisely because it was often couched in humanistic terms and was indefinite enough to allow one's own projections somewhere between the conflicts to be harmonized.

Thus, Leo Baeck became the focus of my involvement and my separation from the personal and communal chaos of growing up and serving communal needs under persecution. With Elbogen's and Täubler's emigration to the United States, Leo Baeck became the last overarching symbol of free Jewish thought, on whom all our dilemmas could be projected, as if, father-figure by style and choice, he could have transcended the iron limits imposed on the rest of us by the powerlessness that imprisoned him as well.

When I enrolled as a matriculated student in April 1939 with the encouragement and approval of the faculty, I was informed that Dr. Ernst Grumach would advise me on "general scholarship" and that it would be good if I took courses with him. Almost by default—historians dealing with Jewish history had dwindled in number and significance since Elbogen had left in the fall of 1938—in biblical criticism (Bibelwissenschaft) and ancient Jewish history Eugen Täubler became the most significant teacher I would have in these fields, which Elbogen, of course, had never represented. His work was in post-biblical literature. Eugen Täubler had much in common with Elbogen and Baeck. They were about the same age; like them, he was born and raised in the province of Posen (Poznań); and his Jewish roots had grown out of the meeting of an Eastern Jewish tradition with German Protestantism and cultural and political nationalism. This mixture had formed their "modern" German Judaism, their personalities, and their work. I felt it as more intense and ideological than what I had known from Würzburg: maybe the frontier quality of this province and the relationship of at least three national or ethnic minorities—German, Polish, Jewish—had faced their generation with dilemmas that effected stronger personal lines and commitments: all three had pursued Jewish studies as their profession, Baeck and Elbogen projected a serenity that appeared of one piece, the German and the Jewish fused harmoniously in a strong Jewish identity. Our experiences since 1933 did not seem to them to need recognition or to call their assumptions into question. Inflexibility was their strength, needed as grandfathers are needed when it storms outside.

Quite different from them, Eugen Täubler[13] had also had a most creative career not only in Jewish studies when I took my first course with him at the Hochschule in 1937. He was recognized as a major founder of Wissenschaft des Judentums in its modern, twentieth-century form and had revolutionized it since before the

---

[13] Herbert A. Strauss, "Das Ende der Wissenschaft des Judentums in Deutschland: Ismar Elbogen und Eugen Täubler," *Bibliographie und Berichte: Festschrift für Werner Schochow*, ed. Hartmut Walravens (Munich: K. G. Saur, 1990), pp. 280–98. David N. Myers, "Eugen Täubler: The Personification of Judaism as Tragic Existence," *Leo Baeck Institute Year Book*, 39 (1994), 131–50, includes relevant biographical references.

For Täubler on general history determinants in Jewish history, see "Die weltpolitische Stellung des jüdische Staates in der hellenistisch-römischen Zeit," *Jahresberichte, HWdJ* (1912): 71–92.

First World War. But Täubler had spent his professional life in Roman and Greek classical studies as well as Jewish, and had had a brilliant career and become innovative and productive in both fields. He had held professorships at Heidelberg and Zurich Universities and at the Hochschule long before the Third Reich, and he had directed major institutions of the Wissenschaft des Judentums and articulated the philosophy I heard from Elbogen and Baeck: from biblical times on, Jewish history will be properly understood only if it is seen in interdependence and cross-fertilization with the relevant structures and events of general history on local, regional, national, or universal and overreaching levels. At the end of this century it may be hard to appreciate the effect of the truism this had become since then.[14]

Thus, he came to the Hochschule with an awe-inspiring reputation. I waited a year before taking a course with him, and began to read some of his historic writings, leaving aside his Roman studies for which I had no preparation. He had laid down the direction of modern Jewish history in well-turned historiographic essays at the end of World War I, and had applied his concepts to Jewish history as early as 1913. I remember the revelations I found in an article of his analyzing the Maccabees from the perspective of Roman imperial military geopolitics in a frontier region (1912).[15]

He had been an early Zionist, but had also served in World War I and been wounded at the front; he had resigned from his Heidelberg professorship eighteen months before Nazi law prescribed his dismissal. His having been a "frontline soldier" at first exempted him from dismissal, but he let his personal and national pride prevail. In public demeanor, Professor Täubler appeared as the most professorial of our three most eminent scholars. But as time went on, I began to see him as more open to what I felt was "our" sense of life and our dilemmas. He did not let his character and his identity be determined exclusively by the Jewish world from which he and Baeck and Elbogen had come: he was shifting from Jewish to Roman history, and from Berlin University to the Hochschule and back to Zurich University. He had been the last assistant to

---

[14] For several overviews I have attempted on Eugen Täubler's significance for the Hochschule, see preceding note.

[15] See his "Die weltpolitische Stellung des jüdische Staates in der hellenistisch-römischen Zeit." (See note 13, above.)

Theodor Mommsen, the renowned historian of Rome, and had taken courses concurrently at the orthodox Berlin Rabbinical Seminary.

What projected his kind of openness and vulnerability in culture and politics was not the contents of his technical lectures on the Bible and ancient Jewish history; I took seven of his courses and seminars in the three terms remaining before he left for Cincinnati, and underwent two long examinations by him in biblical criticism and Jewish literature, both of which I left with the feeling that I had not yet acquired a grasp of his critical method. Consulting the class notes that accidentally survived, I have difficulties recreating in my memory most of his courses but recall others quite clearly. He had a convincing way of linking biblical history—for example, of the epochs of the Kings or the Babylonian exile and Ezra's and Nehemiah's Restoration—with foreign policy and the great-power *Realpolitik* small Judaea faced if it wanted to survive. The great prophets and their political and religious messages gained new life and light in his treatment. My notes also help me recall the shock I felt in his course on "Non-Monotheistic Cults in the Bible" ("Fremdkulte in der Bibel"): I do not know how much of the course was based on the scholarly literature he copiously cited, and how much on his own independent research, but it did not matter: understanding the religious development in Judea as a confusion of local forms of heathenism until they jelled into the cult of the temple and the control of the priests (Josiah's *Kultreform* of 621 B.C.E.) explained exactly what I needed to know to orient myself in my Würzburg world.

Täubler's methods and concepts did not differ in essentials from those of Elbogen, who with Täubler and Baeck appeared to form a triumvirate in Hochschule scholarship. But he spoke with a much sharper edge than gentle Elbogen. After the war had broken out, and after I had once seen him in his office about my future in 1939, he would encourage me to visit him and his wife, Selma, in their apartment, although I never quite overcame the slight self-consciousness his personality and his conversation would at times create. In the fall of 1938, Täubler delivered what he jokingly called his "inaugural lecture" (*Antrittsrede*) about three decades after his inauguration (*Antritt*). The historic role of the Jewish community was, at its core, "tragische Existenz," facing again and again the tensions of its mission and claim to truth in monotheism. The optimism of his and Selma's perceptions of their German Jewish fusion as one of the few great stellar cultures of Jewish history drowned in the almost prophetic gloom that the agony of German Jewry was impressing on him, his somewhat high lecture voice rising as he controlled his inner excitement. I know now that Eugen was often caught in bouts of depression and discouragement as his far-reaching innovations in scholarship and politics (for example, for the Hebrew University), so often ahead of the imagination of his listeners or readers, were not taken up when they were made. I have not pursued the historic subjects he taught us so well in his classes and do not know if the discipline has adequately examined and incorporated them into its canon. Our rare relationship broke off when he left in the summer of 1940.

Sometime in the late 1940s, the bell of my run-down immigrant apartment in New York rang: Eugen Täubler had found my address and wanted to see me. It was a good turn in the tough circumstances of a poor immigrant, and we saw him several times as a dinner guest at 8 Manhattan Avenue near 101st Street. In the 1950s, I would meet him in the New York Public Library's reading room, and we would walk uptown together after it closed at 9:45 P.M. I was treading my way into new interests in modern history and assembling the collection of "documents on American foreign policy seen through presidential messages" I would publish in Switzerland in 1957. He was working, he told me, on some aspects of the graphic work of Albrecht Dürer, the early sixteenth-century German master: two survivors and refugees from their time following their intellectual commitments wherever they may lead in the splendid isolation of that cavernous but sheltering reading room.

If the subjects taught by these three men challenged me in important ways, I cannot say the same of the Talmudic studies at the Hochschule. I had known that Talmud study took time and immersion in an endless literature, and dutifully took twelve semester-long courses in the subject, including one seminar with Leo Baeck. Alexander Guttmann, the lecturer who had succeeded some established experts in the field following their emigration, was a serious though bone-dry philologist. I cannot judge his significance in the field or whether his was an innovative approach bridging traditional Talmud learning with Wissenschaft des Judentums. I understand that, after his emigration to the United States, his method did not conquer the preoccupation of his more conservative colleagues, but I would not venture a judgment on this matter. I found his successor at the Hochschule, Rabbi Gescheit, considerably more accessible and informative on the subject. Both teachers coupled reading a Talmud tractate with reading the corresponding sections in a sixteenth-century digest of then current law and practice, the *Shulkhan Arukh*—a book stupidly maligned in antisemitic literature at the hands of people who could read neither the Talmud nor the digest.

In 1941–42, I began to pass a sequence of one-hour examinations on the "Dezisoren" (post-Talmudic rabbis or scholars handing down legal decisions often published in digests). They were administered by Rabbi Gescheit, a congenial and witty traditionalist who was well able to reproduce a semblance of the Eastern Jewish Talmudic spirit that had formed him. As I learned later from documents saved by Ernst Grumach, as late as the mid-1930s students had felt that even with the time given to the subject, the place for such studies in a Liberal-Reform institution like the Hochschule remained in question if measured by its later usefulness and the time needed to master it. One of the subjects I was examined in concerned the rules guiding an expert in the examination of ritually slaughtered animals—*kashruth*. I had never been to a slaughterhouse, and ritual slaughter had been outlawed by the Nazi government early in 1933. The near-ludicrous unreality of the examination must have been as clear to the professor as it was to the student, who once more saw the realities of centuries of tradition refusing to acknowledge a tradition suspended only temporarily, for this moment in time.

Alexander Guttmann would cross my path many years later in an embarrassing context. He had been asked by Dr. Hermann Veit-Simon, the chairman of the Board of Overseers of the Hochschule, to hide a small number of the rare books and incunabula from our library among the numerous books he would take with him to his new teaching position in Cincinnati, Ohio, in 1940. For the next forty years, Guttmann kept this treasure trove in his attic in Cincinnati. He did not mention it when I visited Cincinnati in the late 1970s to interview him and other German Jewish refugees in the

Midwest about their immigration experiences for our oral-history archives.[16]

Then, in June 1984, while teaching at the Technische Universität of Berlin, I was asked over the telephone by my friends in New York on behalf of the Jewish Restitution Successor Organization if I could identify a person who might have taken some Hochschule rare books with him to the United States. Remembering my conversation of November 1938 at the Hochschule, I named Alexander Guttmann as the only possible person to have done so. It turned out that the attorney general of the State of New York was investigating the well-known Sotheby auction house through which Guttmann had publicly sold the Hochschule books. The attorney general had agreed not to divulge the name of the consigner. Before the public auction, Yeshiva University Library and the Library of the Jewish Theological Seminary, both in New York, had bought some of the more valuable tomes. The matter had come to light because the auction catalogue issued by Sotheby duly noted that some books bore the Hochschule stamp, and an American philanthropist and bibliophile had called from Jerusalem to alert the designated institutional heirs of the Hochschule's properties salvaged from their Nazi despoilers. On February 27 and March 1, 1985, I went through the first and last cross-examination of my life at the New York State attorney's office, an event that did not increase my respect for the civility of American trial lawyers. The case was settled out of court. Guttmann received a substantial financial compensation for his expenses from a private philanthropist, later connected with Yeshiva University, New York. The books were recalled and turned over to Jewish theological institutions in the United States and to an Israeli library. At the time, some of the Jewish periodicals seriously considered the idea that, by Talmudic law, Guttmann had acquired title to this treasure because he had risked his life saving them, the Talmudic analogy to snatching prop-

---

[16] Interview of Alexander Guttmann by Herbert A. Strauss, Cincinnati, Ohio, June 13, 1972; see John C. Lessing, comp., "Guide to the Oral History Collection of the Research Foundation for Jewish Immigration," in *Jewish Immigrants of the Nazi Period in the USA*, vol. 3, part 1, ed. Herbert A. Strauss (Munich: K. G. Saur Verlag, 1982), p. 43, no. 79. The transcript is at the Archives of the Foundation in New York City.

erty from a burning house at the risk of one's life. I considered this moot for several reasons inherent in Talmudic lore, including the precedence given to the law of the land over such Talmudic prescriptions—*dinah demalkhuta dinah*—and found it a sad postscript to a respectable teaching career.

I never returned to Talmudic studies after my Hochschule years, but I never lost my respect for the accumulated efforts of centuries to adapt law traditions to the order needed at a given period for Judaism to be practicable, and I think with some nostalgia of the closed moral world encased in the literary portions of its great narrative tradition, the *Aggadah*. I recognize its intellectual culture which had formed the Eastern European personalities I appreciated, like Moses Sister, Nahum Goldman, Rabbi Gescheit, and many acquaintances whose names have gone with the Holocaust. My Hebrew studies had included Yiddish works in translation. One of my two graduation essays in 1941, suggested by Rabbi Gescheit, described a minute provision in Talmudic law that allowed respect for human dignity to suspend, at least for a limited time, an injunction, a "lo ta'asse," laid down by the Bible. It was this humanizing code that had created Jewish religious humanism, even if the same culture spawned the zealots among the ultra-orthodox in the United States and in Israel, and, in the 1920s and 1930s, catapulted the second generation, in a rebound, typologically considered, out of the ghetto into secular political creeds.

Basic to all teaching in Judaistic subjects was the thorough training in ancient Semitic languages that orchestrated my entire seven or eight semesters. For my then proficiency in modern Hebrew (*Neuhebräisch*, to set it apart from classical literature) I owed much to my Jewish primary school in Würzburg that had instilled the sense for grammatical forms in me, to religious instruction during the Gymnasium period, and to our youth movement which declared learning Hebrew a "*chalutzic* duty." From 1937 on, I benefited from the Hebrew atmosphere of all our work in Judaistics at the Hochschule even if we did not affect the *Neuhebräeisch* "Sephardic" vocalization over our accustomed "Ashkenazic" one. The teacher who challenged me most by making us read modern Hebrew prose and poetry and learn a new vocabulary was Dr. Gustav Ormann. I regret that I was never able to let him know how much his teaching advanced my understanding of modern Hebrew literature. I learned from documents only a few years ago that he had a desperately disappointing start after going to Palestine (in 1939–40?). He had helped to advance my Hebrew enough for me to pass an entrance examination in Hebrew (speech and writing) for the Beth Hakerem Seminar in Jerusalem. He had been working at Hebrew University.

A most joyful and in some ways cheerfully absurd source of learning modern Hebrew in Berlin was my (invited) membership in a "Circle of Hebrew Teachers"—*Chug Hamorim*. The circle was made up of about twenty or twenty-five mature men—I was by far the youngest; they must have been generally in their forties and fifties—all of whom were immigrants from Eastern Europe and worked in some capacity in the Jewish school system as language or Bible teachers. After the first exchanges they fell to treating me with subdued mockery and equally subdued respect—a German Jew, a *yekke*, among the experts, and when I returned their well-meaning Hebrew barbs with equally well-meaning counter-barbs, I was taken in and probably taken seriously as well. In the winter of 1937–38, they assigned a Hebrew lecture on Goethe to me, I believe in all seriousness, Goethe, besides the "more freedom-loving" Schiller, being a most respected German culture hero in pre-Hitler Eastern European Jewish civilization. I acquitted myself to their linguistic and literary satisfaction. Here, in a classroom of the Grosse-Hamburger-Strasse-Schule, probably in the spring or early summer of 1938, in the middle of Nazi-dominated Berlin—I still remember the stale after-class smell of the room—adult Jews were finding intellectual play and common ground in a Hebrew lecture on Goethe's youthful explorations of the Frankfurt ghetto. By the testimony of Eckermann's *Gespräche mit Goethe* (Conversations with Goethe), which I was beginning to discover at the time, Goethe might have appreciated the singular compliment we paid him, at that improbable juncture of history, in the language of the Bible and at the end of a Jewish place in Germany. Goethe had written about the life and manners of his Jewish neighbors in the ghetto in his autobiographical *Dichtung und Wahrheit* (Poetry and truth) (1811).

Hebrew literature was also the subject of the last Hebrew classes I took at the Hochschule, with Rabbi Gross, a young and knowledgeable Judaist and linguist who had graduated from the Hochschule a few years earlier. On May 6, 1941, he signed the protocol of the Semitic philology section of my final examination: grammar, a translation, and an essay in Hebrew for which he had chosen the topic "What does it mean to live as a Jew?" ("Mahu ze lichyot betor yehudi?"). The last two courses I took with him after the examination were "Targumim to Esther" (Aramaic commentaries to the Book of Esther) and "Legal Documents of the Ancient Orient" (Near East) (*Altorientalische Gesetze*). He remains in my memory as a well-knit, dark-haired, clean-shaven figure, a quick speaker and thinker, a careful and conscientious teacher, young enough to care for each student.

Manfred Gross's last signature in my roll book is dated February 28, 1942. I never saw him again.

Ismar Elbogen, Manfred Gross, Gustav Ormann, and the experiences I was privileged to share in core-Jewish Berlin at the Hochschule might well have made a Semitic philologist out of me, or so I thought. It was nothing short of a miraculous achievement that the Hochschule continued to offer quality and quantity instruction in these fields to the very end. Later on, I added three years of Arabic studies at the University of Bern and offered Semitic philology as a minor in my doctoral examination. My nemesis in Berlin was Assyrian cuneiform, which I began to study at the suggestion of Dr. Grumach. He was doing his own most basic research in Egyptian and pre-Greek writing (the Minoan script) and in Greek philology. There was no course given in this subject. I might have taken Grumach's courses on Egyptian hieroglyphics had he offered them in 1939–40. Instead, I took a large and continuous slice of time out of my weekly schedule and concentrated on the cuneiform textbook given to me, the author of which I have forgotten. As a language assignment, it did not go too badly, except for the rather monotonous vocalization of the vowels as compared to the more colorful Hebrew. The common Semitic roots were often recognizable. But I could not sustain the balance of the time and attention it was "taking out of my life" of involvement with humanistic and religious studies. Obviously, my transformation from a would-be kibbutznik and collective farmer to a serene Ancient Near East antiquarian was meeting its limits in my own temperament as much as in the narrowing time perspectives of our community under stress. Knowledge had to speak to an "existential need," as I would have called it at the time. I did not know yet that there would be a price to pay for such self-indulgence.

The historian of ideas Max Wiener emerges from my recollections and from my copies of a few letters written following his emigration as a lovable, unworldly man, whose overwhelming learning and overly sharp analytic mind far outdistanced the speed with which he was able to articulate his thoughts. It may or may not have been more than an isolated incident that, two days before their scheduled sailing date, he and Mrs. Wiener fell victims to a pickpocket on the London subway who lifted all their travel and immigration documents and their passports from their absent-minded pockets—a properly ironic letter to one of his colleagues written from a New York hotel address describes the happy ending of one more harrowing experience in the lives of émigrés. His knowledge of the history of medieval philosophy dominated the image I was able to form of him in his classes. It took me considerable time later on to understand how radically "out of season" he had been in his thinking on contemporary Jewish problems.

The most significant teacher I had the very good fortune of studying with until 1942 was Ernst Grumach,[17] a classical philologist, epigrapher, and historian of ancient philosophy and religion. He was Wiener's equal in analytic sharpness and in thinking against the conventional, but he had a personality that appeared more "modern" than Wiener's. He had studied with Heidegger, who no doubt had stimulated him to write his dissertation about the "Old Stoa" and their recourse to pre-Socratic philosophy. We spent two terms each on Heidegger's central opus *Being and Time* and on Kant's *Critique of Pure Reason*, without being proselytized for existentialism as the only contemporary philosophy. He was no system-builder and taught me to avoid the cheap victories of premature generalizations and global speculations, as had Elbogen and Täub-

---

[17] For Ernst Grumach's early years, see his *Physis und Agathon in der Alten Stoa*, Forschungen zur klassischen Philologie 6 (Berlin: Weidmann, 1932); "Früh-ägäische Schriftprobleme," *Orientalische Literaturzeitung*, 34 (1931): 1012ff.; "Zur Herkunft des Altsemitischen Alphabets," in *Festschrift für Leo Baeck*, pp. 161–74; "The Cretan Script and the Greek Alphabet" (London, 1967) (posthumous); Hellmuth Flashar, "Ernst Grumach°," *Gnomon* (1968), 221–22; Flashar, "Ernst Grumach, 1902–1967," *Eikasmos* (Bologna), 4 (1993): 191–93; Rudolf Kassel, "Ernst Grumach, 1902–1967," Berlin, 1967 (eulogy). References to his post-1945 scholarly activities are omitted.

ler. He confirmed their scholarly methods and, like Elbogen and Täubler, did not rest content with positivistic detail. I thought that he knew the value of a lifetime spent on scholarly work, as I myself became painfully aware that we may indeed have been living suspended in empty time. What he could teach me spoke to my own deepest convictions since I had left Würzburg. In more than one way, Grumach thought outside the liberal tradition of the Hochschule. He showed no interest in organized religion and was not identified with ideals like Zionism. Far from pursuing one cohesive scholarly or systematic interest, Grumach balanced a bundle of superficially conflicting research specializations whose systematic links were not immediately evident since they crossed several academic disciplines.

Grumach had been appointed to a position in the Allgemeinwissenschaftliche Abteilung at about the time I had entered as a non-matriculated student. His correspondence with a Reichsvertretung representative, the mathematician Otto Töplitz,[18] speaks of the extreme poverty from which the appointment had saved him. He had held a part-time position (*Lehrauftrag*) in the University of Königsberg, his hometown, from 1930 to 1933, had been dismissed by the new regime in 1933, and had eked out a minimal living by taking over his father's (?) small store specializing in "Jewish" books. In late 1936, the Berlin *Reichsschrifttumskammer* (sic) (Chamber for Literature), had notified him that his license was being revoked there, too. Thus, he was unable to pursue the several promising scholarly projects he had been working on, but the damage went far deeper: like many other scholars of his age group, he was prevented from accumulating a record of teaching and publications, and his research work was interrupted at a delicate point of maturation into intellectual autonomy. I do not know whether Grumach ever tried to obtain a position abroad during this time. The correspondence with the Hochschule speaks of the great respect in which he had been held by his peers and his teachers. Töplitz expressed his hope

---

[18] Otto Töplitz (b. Breslau, 1881; d. Jerusalem, 1940), a widely respected professor of mathematics at Bonn University (until 1933) and an ingenious innovator in teaching it, had made his thorough knowledge of German academic personnel available to the founders of the new Allgemeinwissenschaftliche Abteilung. See Fuchs's "Hochschule für die Wissenschaft des Judentums in the Period of Nazi Rule," p. 79, note 3.

that he would replace the university studies (a Dr. phil.) from which Jewish students were barred, and that he would find students majoring in Classical Greek studies, which he was appointed to teach.

Since Grumach failed in whatever attempts he made to secure an academic appointment in England or Sweden after November 1938, he was soon the only ranking major lecturer in the Division and developed it, during the short time of three years, into a veritable school of Greek and philosophical studies. From 1941 or 1942 on, he was forced to work as a cataloguer of the huge collection of books and manuscripts that the Nazis had looted ("confiscated as enemy property") in Eastern and Western Europe. The defeat of Holland and France had unleashed a race between several groups of "experts" and "collectors" in the German Army Command and the Nazi Party for the cultural treasures assembled over generations by Jewish institutions and prominent families (like the Rosenthals in Amsterdam or the French Rothschilds). While Goering and Hitler appropriated priceless paintings and objets d'art, representing all epochs of art history, Alfred Rosenberg, the would-be philosopher, now seized the opportunity of giving his as yet anemic "academy" ("*Hohen Schule*") for Nazi *Kultur und Weltanschauung* (culture and ideology) in Frankfurt am Main a foundation that would leave his competitors in the outfield: he would assemble the largest and greatest library on "World Jewry." In three separate decrees dated July 5, 1940, September 17, 1940, and March 1, 1942, Hitler empowered Rosenberg to "search out, safeguard, and ship to Germany materials found in libraries, archives, . . . or owned by Jews," and confiscate them to serve the "ideological purposes of the NSDAP or the scholarly research of the Hohen Schule" (March 1, 1942). It would form the core of his "Institute for Research on the Jewish Question." A file notice written by a member of his operational staff (*Einsatzstab*) dated July 12, 1943, and introduced in evidence at the Nuremberg Trial (PS-171), details some of the institutions from which his *Büchermassen* had been stolen. They included about 100,000 volumes "transferred to the Rosenberg Library by other agencies like the internal revenue services," that is, books left behind by deportees and processed by the tax office, like my own modest Judaica student library. A number of crates filled with this loot had been shipped to Rosenberg's "Reichsministerium" located in Berlin.

Dr. Grumach's cataloguing of these books represented another wager with time against fiercely competitive Nazi bureaus at cross purposes about Hitler's wartime priorities about the Jews: Grumach believed that he and his co-workers were firmly secured against being deported to the East by working for the chief Nazi ideologue, because he had no other experts to do this work. Little did they know that Rosenberg was already losing ground in the power jungle of Nazidom. Hitler, the chief criminal fanatic, and his SS-SD-Gestapo executioners, vitiated all rational considerations.

On November 14, 1945, Ernst Grumach wrote to Alexander Guttmann in Cincinnati:

Of the large circle of people who once frequented the Hochschule, almost no one is alive today. Drs. Lewkowitz, Alexander, Gross, Lehmann, and Stranz had worked under my direction as part of a group of Jewish scholars and librarians. They had been drafted for working in a government agency [*Behörde*] and were thus especially secure [against deportation]. I even succeeded in having the entire group, including all members of their families, placed on a list of exemptions [*Sonderliste*] and repeatedly obtained the release from detention centers of individuals or entire families [prior to their deportation] when they were caught in one of the many *Aktionen*, including the horrible mass sweep at the end of February when more than forty persons had been detained [out of this group]. Soon after, however, and in spite of this, fate caught up with them. My attempts to effect a delay, at least to urge that Theresienstadt be chosen as deportation goal, were in vain. Not even Lewkowitz was granted transportation to Theresienstadt, although his age would have entitled him to it. Only Stranz sent us word that he was in Auschwitz. We immediately sent him small parcels with food, but never heard from him again. Only Dr. Breslauer and I are still alive of this entire group: we owe this to our marriages [with Christian spouses]. My good friend Meyer Spanier for whom I had found a room in our (apartment) house—he had been driven from two other apartments previously—committed suicide together with his wife. It was one of the most shocking experiences I remember. . . . Dr. Gescheit attempted to flee to his brother in Hungary after the protection granted to Jews of foreign nationality had been ended. The attempt failed; he was taken to Buchenwald concentration camp where he met his end under terrible [*traurigen*] circumstances. Herbert Strauss . . . succeeded in escaping in the nick of time [*rechtzeitig*] and crossed the Swiss border after some months of living underground in Berlin. . . . If you are in touch with him, please transmit my greetings to him and let him know that I salvaged part of his books and papers from his room. Mrs. Dr. Dresel, too, lived in hiding for some time and often saw us furtively until her visits stopped one day. Only Dr. Fabian and Mrs. Wilde [of the Hochschule] have returned alive from Theresienstadt.

This is a terrifying report. I have had great difficulties writing it down but felt that I had to report the facts to you. Please pass them on to friends and relatives living there [in the USA] [my translation].

I also would have been on Grumach's list: sometime in the early summer of 1942 Grumach persuaded his handlers to draft me, too, for his group, but I was dismissed after one week, probably because of my lack of bibliophile experience and library science. After the war, Grumach and I corresponded about a plan of his to publish his catalogue of this supreme collection of Jewish books in Europe through a New York Jewish publisher or organization. It failed because Koppel S. Pinson, of Queens College, and Salo W. Baron, of Columbia University, for whom I worked at the time and who watched over Jewish cultural reconstruction, understood the moral and political defects of Grumach's and Breslauer's plans.

The books and cultural treasures the Nazis had stolen all over Europe would become a subject of controversy after the war. The bulk of the books were brought together in a depository in Offenbach/Main (near Frankfurt), possibly because it was close to Rosenberg's Institute, where at least 300,000 books had been taken. Books in the Berlin collection appear to have been stored by Rosenberg's office in Czech castles and similar locations considered safe from Allied air raids. For some time, a Mr. Pomeranz, later historian of the U.S. Army, and Koppel S. Pinson, professor of history at Queens College, New York, were put in charge of the Offenbach depository and presumably supervised the return of books to their rightful owners insofar as they had not been annihilated during the Holocaust and could be identified. The Jewish Restitution Successor Organization was given title to all "heirless property" by a decree of the U.S. War Department for the Occupation Authorities in Germany. (The political [lobbying] process that led to this purely administrative decision cannot be reconstructed.) This organization (JRSO) sold considerable real estate and other property that formerly belonged to German Jewish congregations and organizations, and distributed the books in the name of the Jewish people to libraries in Palestine and Jewish centers in Europe and the Western hemisphere. Gershom Sholem, the Jerusalem expert on Jewish mysticism, Grumach reported in a letter, traveled about Czechoslovakia and selected what he considered of value for Israeli libraries. JRSO had formally voted to distribute these books only to already existing libraries. This disinherited "the legitimate heirs," the former German Jews, then struggling in their new worldwide dispersion to rebuild a semblance of their destroyed religious and intellectual institutions. It created considerable resentment against a power play that allowed JRSO, led by Nahum Goldman and Israeli and American Jewish functionaries, to indulge in what many leaders of exiled German Jewry could understand only as a great *Unrecht* (miscarriage of justice).[19] This may have been the context in which Alexander Guttmann, with or without Leo Baeck's knowledge, preserved the Hochschule rare books valued at several million dollars, for a possible successor institution to the Hochschule.

I was a major beneficiary of Grumach's scholarly teaching and took fifteen courses and seminars with him between 1939 and 1942, one-third of my total load. My rollbook documents the intellectual reach of his mind, one of the sharpest and most retentive minds in Greek and Hellenistic studies I would ever meet. Different from Wiener, Grumach was an agile and witty conversationalist with a slight and inoffensively puckish provocativeness. He sought and enjoyed company, found me a furnished room on the third floor of his apartment house, Schlüterstrasse 53 in Charlottenburg, and initiated a personal relationship that went from informal teaching sessions to common meals, visits to the small wine restaurants that had a long tradition in Berlin, and extended walks in parks and in the near vicinity of the town. Our relationship gave Grumach a wider circle of friends to whom I introduced him and gave me an education in German learning and the literature of the classical and nineteenth-century periods, from the epigrammatic literature of

---

[19] Interview of Max Grunewald by Evelyn Ehrlich, November 7, 1984, p. 12. The transcript is in the Archives of the Research Foundation for Jewish Immigration in New York. For a somewhat selective insider account of the scramble for Guttmann's hoard, see Herbert C. Zafrin, "From the Hochschule to the Judaica Conservancy Foundation: The Guttmann Affair," *Jewish Book Annual*, 54 (1996–97): 46–55.

Goethe's old age (*Conversations with Eckermann, Conversations with Chancellor Müller*) to Kierkegaard (translated from the Danish, of course) and to Friedrich Nietzsche, Jacob Burckhardt, Johann Jakob Bachofen, and Franz Overbeck at the end of the century. Freud was not considered respectable, in spite of some links with Lou Andreas-Salomé, a patient and colleague of his and an emancipated intellectual woman in her own right who had been admired by Nietzsche, Rilke, and other avant-garde minds of her time. It seemed to me that this post-Nietzschean world coincided well with Grumach's many-sided mind and interests: he knew numerous continuities but acknowledged the general loss of cohesion and comprehensiveness. It was the ultimate contrast to Baeck's essentialist world.

Of Grumach's formal courses and seminars, some records have been preserved. Grumach took my lecture transcripts from the room the Gestapo had closed with a paper seal after my flight, and preserved them through the vicissitudes of the air war and the conquest of Berlin. In the 1980s, I also received important correspondence and part of Grumach's own preparations for a course on *Oracula Sybillina* from Drs. Renate Grumach (Berlin) and Irene Shiroun (Jerusalem), his widow and daughter, respectively. These notes reveal the painstaking preparations he had lavished on these lectures: I was his only student in the end. His philological, archaeological, and conceptual methods added up to mountains of detailed arguments—and all around us was barbarism! Some high points stand out. We read (in the Greek original) Book Lambda of Aristotle's *Metaphysics*, a course on pre-Socratic theories of motion. Aristotle was solving the problem of how our imperfect world of matter could be set in motion by a perfect prime mover who would, of course, lose his perfection by any contact with this imperfect world. This perfection consisted precisely in eternal self-contained motion, perfect because it was unchanging. It could be visualized only as circular motion—that is, motion undisturbed by contact with the imperfection of a changing world: change presupposed higher and lower states of being. Aristotle's solution avoided contacts between the perfect and the imperfect: the imperfect world was attracted by the perfection it was forever unable to reach.

I still remember how enthralled I was when I understood this elegant solution and the Greek values it implied. It was at the source of Maimonides's hints at how incompatibly Genesis and Aristotle co-existed in medieval scholasticism. The contrast between the Greek *primum movens* and the biblical God of Creation appeared glaring: Aristotle's prime mover lacked all interest in man and his history on earth.

A year-long immersion in the syncretistic absurdities of the Sibylline books centered on the origins of what were seen as their Greek or Jewish traditional components. The course turned into a seminar on the pre-Greek (primitive) foundations of the classical Greek religion, based on the literature, the inscriptions, and, most new to me, the archaeological evidence. Many years later when I visited the temple district of Delphi with my small family, the shock of recognizing what I had studied in photographs, engravings, and maps twenty years earlier in Grumach's seminar was as overwhelming as my first visit to old Jerusalem. Grumach's political views on Jews and Judaism emerged with grating clarity in his interpretation of Greek–Jewish relations and of ancient "antisemitism," as scholars had (incongruously) labeled Graeco-Roman anti-Jewish writings and riotous conflicts between Greeks and Jews, for example, in Hellenistic Alexandria. Like other scholars, Grumach held a major event in Jewish history responsible for the rejection of Jews by Greek philosophers and geographers: the revolt of the Maccabees (168–164 B.C.E.) had cut the promising cultural symbiosis of Jewish and Greek culture and had originated a fateful strain affecting many centuries. In a paper that was brought to Switzerland by a friend, I had analyzed the known and long compiled and -published Greek sources on Jews and Judaism[20] and had to agree with Grumach's timing of the negative turn—but I clearly articulated in my preface that I found projecting modern contexts (assimilation versus nationalism) into the remote past quite impermissible. I submitted this paper in 1941 as one requirement among others for the final graduation examination of the Hochschule.

Grumach's view of the place of Judaism and the Jewish community and people in European politics and culture emerged quite clearly in our talks on my paper: *as I understood his attitudes,* Judaism

---

[20] Theodore Reinach, *Textes des auteurs grecs et romains relatifs au judaisme* (Paris: Presses Universitaires de France, 1895; repr. Hildesheim: Georg Olms Verlag, 1963).

had lost its raison d'être when it met with the classical roots of universal civilization, the Greeks and Hellenism. Organized religion was a matter for Religiongeschichte (history of religion). It rested on the inescapable forlornness of existence in a universe whose Pascalian fright and Heideggerian loneliness could be endured only if they became "religion," from mythic rituals to sublime theological speculation. When the Maccabees and later the Pharisees turned Jewish history away from cultural fusion, they had started two thousand years of suffering. Grumach, a Jewish German, was attracted by the sophisticated despair of the existentialist revolution in modern philosophy, while I, a German Jew, confronting a vital Jewish tradition that reinvented itself in the image of Eastern European cultural nationalism, sought a deeply personal faith grappling with modernity. I felt quite invigorated by differences in orientation, as they emerged in seminars and my paper on "ancient antisemitism."

The topic inadvertently caused Grumach some anxiety: he had forgotten his own notes on the subject of ancient antisemitism in a Berlin subway car and lived in barely controlled fear for a few days until a finder returned it to the address on the cover.

This incident illustrates how thin the margins of security had worn for many in this community. The few documents surviving from the last Hochschule years document the arbitrary and unpredictable repression under which faculty and administration had to work even in the entirely nonpolitical field of Jewish scholarship. When it was founded in 1936, the entire Division of General Scholarship had to be camouflaged against Gestapo controllers intent on finding fault.[21] Articles and scholarly journals were confiscated following publication, because historians like Selma Täubler-Stern or editors like E. G. Lowenthal did not sufficiently stress the Nazi exclusionary and separatist line that Jews never co-existed fruitfully with Germans in history or culture. At times, the official tactical Nazi line was their separate and unequal *Nebeneinander* (side by side) until Germany would be cleansed of Jews. Grumach made fun of these culture policemen by naming his Heidegger seminar "Zeit und Ewigkeit" (time and eternity), a persiflage of the title of Heidegger's main work *Sein und Zeit*, or by calling a Kant seminar

---

[21] See above, p. 79, note 3.

"Foundations of the Philosophy of Hermann Cohen"—the Marburg Jewish neo-Kantian philosopher. Using veiled language of different provenance, from biblical symbols to subtle analogies in sophisticated historic contexts, was quite commonplace.

The Hochschule had to cool its heels for years before the Gestapo granted it permission to publish books of purely Jewish-scholarly contents—the last one appeared as late as mid-1941 but was confiscated before it could be distributed (*Monatsschrift für Geschichte und Wissenschaft des Judentums*, vol. 47). I had helped a scientific secretary, Miss Johanna Nathan, to read proof for its index a year earlier. It was reissued from a surviving copy by the Leo Baeck Institute, New York, in 1963.[22]

I never learned what happened to Miss Nathan, the administrator of the Gesellschaft für die Wissenschaft des Judentums, after the *Hochschule* was closed.

Grumach's attitudes on the fusion of Judaism with Greek civilization and on ancient antisemitism happened to be part of his broader view on cultural fusions and cross-fertilizations in the ancient world. It may have been one of the threads that ran through his diverse scholarly interests, binding them together with his methodology into an unforgettable intellectual profile. Nothing shows this better than his lifelong preoccupation with one of the more esoteric issues of ancient history: the transformation, accomplished over hundreds of years by Semitic people, of an Eastern Mediterranean hieroglyphic script into the phonetic Ur-Semitic alphabet, the acknowledged model of the Greek, and thus of all European alphabets. One problem was whether the hieroglyphic model had been Egyptian or Minoan (Crete). Grumach had started his scholarly career with an article on the "Problems of Aegean Script" in 1931. He died of a heart attack in London in 1967 after he had delivered a series of lectures on "The Cretan Script and the Greek Alphabet." About fifteen years earlier, he had returned to the topic after a scholarly career that reflected the discontinuities of his life since 1933 as much as his many-sided creative genius. Grumach held a lifelong conviction that the as yet undeciphered script of the tablets found in the palace excavated (and somewhat fancifully recon-

---

[22] *Monatsschrift für Geschichte und Wissenschaft des Judentums*, 83, No. 47 (1939), reissued in 1963.

structed) by Sir Arthur Evans in Knossos on the island of Crete represented hieroglyphics for a Minoan language. He also argued from early on that its more complex form, Evans's Linear B, not Egyptian hieroglyphics, had served as models for the evolution of the Semitic scripts. It contributed to a lasting scholarly controversy. With time, the argument moved from hieroglyphics to history encompassing a millennium of Eastern Mediterranean linguistics, archaeological remains, religion, demography, and migration. It offered a complex interlocking re-creation of a region where Semites traded with their neighbors over large distances and received and passed on cultural stimuli to what would become one of the roots of the high civilizations of Europe.

During his Hochschule tenure, Grumach offered a lecture to a festive Hochschule convocation "On the Origin of Ancient Semitic Alphabets." It was subsequently printed in a jubilee volume for Leo Baeck celebrating the twenty-fifth anniversary of his association with the Hochschule.[23] I remember being overawed by Grumach's sophisticated epigraphic argument and by the multilingual sources and extensive international literature at his command. It would culminate in the masterly comprehensive argument he would present in his 1967 posthumously published London lecture which I read as a lifelong student and college teacher of "general" history long after I had turned to the nineteenth and twentieth centuries. By 1967, the epigraphic argument seemed to have been clinched by the sensational discovery that Linear B was a phonetic and syllabar script—in a Greek dialect. Two English scholars, John Chadwick and Michael Ventris, advanced what became the broadly accepted solution.[24] They applied cryptographic techniques developed by wartime British intelligence. But they failed to convince Grumach and other skeptics in the epigraphic community. He published several comprehensive critiques of their work and, with like-minded friends, founded a new scholarly periodical devoted to the epigraphy of the ancient world, *Kadmos*. It was generally acknowledged as

---

[23] See above, note 17.

[24] Michael Ventris and John Chadwick, "Evidence for Greek Dialect in the Mycenean Archives," *Journal of Hellenistic Studies*, 73 (1953): 84–103; Ventris and Chadwick, *Documents in Mycenean Greek*, 2nd ed. (Cambridge: Cambridge University Press, 1973); Chadwick, *The Decipherment of Linear B*, 1st ed. (Cambridge: Cambridge University Press, 1959), 2nd ed. (Cambridge: Cambridge University Press, 1967).

open-minded and quite objective. Grumach died before the inconsistencies he pinpointed persuaded many respected scholars to consider this issue unresolved.

Grumach's (Heidegger-influenced?) regression to pre-Greek culture endowed the lectures and seminars I attended with him at the Hochschule with depth and breadth that may have been rare among the classicists of his generation. He had worked hard to anchor his insights in the history and archaeology of the Ancient Near East, and in his lectures drew upon his precise knowledge of the region.

The Ancient Near East, until then a blank spot on my historical map, was coming alive, and classical Greek literature and history acquired a new depth. The "Nordic Greeks" of the Nazi *Kulturpropaganda* (cultural propaganda) had built on a substratum of pre-Greek peoples and cultures; their achievements were born of migrations and cross-fertilizations, not mystically pure blood. Greece, like ancient Israel, gave and took in a wide cross-ethnic field of forces made up of temples and priests, kings and conquerors, migrants, seafarers, and traders. Greek religion, too—not an original Grumach insight, of course, but brilliantly documented across the disciplines—regained its raw and primitive basis, its chthonic darkness, its primeval threats and mysteries from the traces that led from the "noble simplicity and serene greatness" of Schliemann's period to Friedrich Nietzsche, Johann Jakob Bachofen, Rudolf Otto, and the English historians of Greek religion. The Jewish religion, even in its ultimately canonized practices, had been shaped just as much by the dialectic contrasts of its prophetic heights to the nativist substrata of its region—Täubler had demonstrated it in his earlier lectures on "Non-Monotheistic Cults in the Bible" ("Fremdkulte in der Bibel"). Now in Grumach's equally critical philological argumentation, it was acquiring the dignity of a law of history waiting to be conceptualized, the religious and cultural lines connecting the classics with preclassical and precanonical myth and ritual.

Even Grumach's postwar work in classical German literature appeared to follow this model—his encyclopedic *Goethe und die Antike* (Goethe and antiquity) was acknowledged as a masterly presentation of the continued presence of classical antiquity in German thought and literature.

I do not know whether my later work in the migrations and acculturation of Jews fleeing Germany during the Nazi period had
any connection with Grumach's re-creation of cultural change fer-
tilized—cross-fertilized—in international population movements.
Too much had happened since I sat in his seminars and smaller and
smaller classes. At the time, I related my work on *Wissenstransfer*
(the transfer of knowledge) through migration to my own experience. It was a source of deep satisfaction to me that he survived and
I was able to express my intellectual debt to him after 1945. I still
think that he was one of the most endearing and alive personalities
I met among my teachers, and that he was the most innovative and
comprehensive "classical philologist" I would meet, uniquely
poised between the Judaic and the Greek worlds in the openness
that our situation in wartime Berlin impressed upon us—in our determined dissent.

If the intellectual world I was privileged to participate in emerges
in my memory as an unlikely oasis of civilized discourse isolated
from the barbarisms around us, so was the small circle that grew
out of our informal "walking and talking society" during joint leisure hours. I introduced Grumach to my friends, both younger and
older. Thus, he met and liked Lotte and my friends Ruth Basinski
and Anneliese Levy. I also introduced him to Ernst Maass and his
family, with whom I was connected through Ursula von Hielmcrone, a friend of Dörte's sister: her Jewish stepfather had married
her mother, the widow of a Danish officer who had been killed in
World War I fighting on the German side as a volunteer. He lived
with two of his own daughters by this marriage in a Dahlem villa
(Auf dem Grat 44), but was prevented from leaving his room by
debilitating heart disease. Grumach and I would spend many precious hours at his house. We were soon joined by one of Grumach's
acquaintances, Richard Schaefer, whose *Bildung* interests also
ranged over Jewish learning, classical education, and German literature. He had moved to Berlin from Stettin after he was deprived of
his law practice and had shifted his emphasis to work for the Jewish
community. In 1933, he was asked to direct the education department of the Berlin Jüdische Gemeinde. I treasure the memory of
these rare hours: we differed in age, education, political and religious views, wealth, character, and family background. Had the
threats we were facing stopped at the door, or were they present in
the sympathy that made our bond alive?

Ernst Maass died in his bed in 1940 or 1941. I conducted the traditional Hebrew services Mrs. Maass requested, at his grave, in one of the eighteenth-century inner-city Jewish cemeteries in North or Central Old Berlin. The mourners whom I spoke to after the ceremony were almost exclusively Lutherans.

Ulla von Hielmcrone would become an active supporter of the academic resistance group around Professor Kurt Huber and Hans and Sophie Scholl in Munich, who would be caught, tried, and executed for dropping anti-Nazi leaflets from balconies into the central inner courtyard of Munich University. Luckily, her links with the group were not detected by the Gestapo. Ulla proved a steady friend to both Lotte and me until we left Berlin. I especially appreciated her cheerful matter-of-fact way of dealing with our frequent attacks of doubts about the ultimate outcome of the war and our chances of survival. Mother Maass and her two other daughters by her marriage with Mr. Maass survived the war; a third daughter had gone to England and entered a social work career. I saw them on my infrequent trips to Europe and stayed in close touch with Ulla. She fell seriously ill following her emigration to the United States in the late 1950s and lingered on for long years in a New York mental hospital, incapacitated by a stroke. She regained some of her physical mobility, and we saw her several times there before she died. The kindly nurses she had befriended in her upstate New York state hospital proved to be exceptionally thoughtful and caring. We had looked forward to helping her to build up a new life and to reminiscing together as we got older.

Richard Schaefer died in Auschwitz, where he outlived his family for about a year. He had explored opportunities for emigrating and had been urged by his friends to stay abroad, but returned to Germany in 1937, married, and had had two young children, who were sent to the gas chambers with their mother upon arrival in Auschwitz.

Grumach's wife and daughter survived the bombing and conquest of Berlin. Irene teaches Egyptology at Hebrew University. She and Mr. Shiroun, her husband, have kindly assisted me with copies of Grumach's *Nachlass* (papers) and have helped to clarify some aspects of his life. I did not meet again Irene's mother, Grumach's first wife, who had shared economic hardship and persecution with him and, being non-Jewish, had indirectly saved his life. Ernst Grumach and I corresponded for some time after the war.

He had learned about my studies and the doctorate I received in 1946 at Bern University from a fellow Königsberg classicist on the Bern faculty, Professor Willy Theiler, who had "sat in" on my doctoral examination. My reports on our initial distress and on academic employment conditions for "refugees" confirmed his resolve to reject the American immigration option for himself. He had begun to give central place in his research and writing to the influence of Greek and Roman culture—*die Klassik*—on modern German culture, especially on Goethe's works. They had been an intense avocational scholarly interest of his for many years. His *Goethe und die Antike* was about to be completed. The high-school–level survey courses I had to teach as the lowest man on the academic totem pole did not sound encouraging for his academic needs—as they had not been for mine. In 1949, he accepted an appointment at the East German Humboldt Universität and took charge of parts of a new Goethe edition for the Deutsche (formerly Prussian?) Akademie der Wissenschaften (Academy of Science), once a most prestigious scholarly organization in Germany. Not surprisingly, the political climate of the German Democratic Republic made him write, in comments in a new edition of Goethe's *Conversations*, that "Goethe's spirit reaches us, admonishing, counseling, clarifying, comforting us in our dark time, in which 'confusing dogma spurs the world into confused action.' " (The last words are verbatim quotations from a Goethe text.) He had given a fundamentally new direction to "Goethe philology" in German scholarship. Did he consider the invitation to direct a final "standard" edition of Goethe's work as a unique scholarly opportunity that would be beyond his grasp if conditions were normal, not having been trained as a "Germanist"? He relinquished his position at the East German University in 1957, his Akademie position in 1959, a time of intensified re-Stalinization *après* Stalin in Communist East Germany. The rumor persists that colleagues, administrators, or Communist education functionaries in the German Democratic Republic had discovered his wartime involuntary impressment into ordering the looted Jewish libraries held by Rosenberg in Berlin, and that he left to avoid another mindless persecution.

As it was, Grumach's release from the Hochschule sometime in 1941 was followed by my being forced to work as a streetcleaner in January 1942. Already in the fall of 1941, I had been given a partial release from course requirements. Our short and intensive intellectual relationship, the most exciting if not the smoothest of teacher–student contacts I enjoyed during my studies, declined to occasional conversations and meetings.

After the war ended, and letters began once again to move across borders and oceans, we began exchanging reports on our survival. Lotte and I were able to send the inveterate smoker some cigarettes and food, a drop in the bucket of scarcity that was postwar Germany. I realized that the unique circumstances that had made a relationship possible had changed, and, I presume, so had I. He indicated that his scholarly interests were shifting away from classical philology in parallel to my own changing to nineteenth- and twentieth-century European history, which he noted with relish. Our contacts ended when he obtained his glamorous appointment to the Berlin Akademie der Wissenschaften of the German Democratic Republic, and to the East German Humboldt University. Since I had become active in émigré politics in Switzerland, my first such experience, I had few illusions about the lack of freedom of thought and the absence of personal autonomy in Communist parties or systems. I had written some seminar papers on the precise moment in German intellectual history when the concepts of democracy and liberalism had become irreconcilable in Marx's development. I presumed that the singular opportunity of pursuing his avocational interest in Goethe on a professional level was as irresistible as his career needs were pressing.

It did not diminish my gratitude for the privilege of having been introduced to the world I had missed in the Würzburg Gymnasium by a complex man, a scholar, who had been formed by the challenge of being Jewish and by superb humanistic scholarship in the German tradition, even as he denied one pole of the tension. Grumach spoke to the very subject matter that concerned me at the time and to which Elbogen, Täubler, or Baeck, each in his own way, had spoken, too. I observed them and my other teachers as they did their work, swimming free of conventions and concentrating on what seemed central, "essential," or "existential" to them, whichever term would fit in their own language what they conveyed best. Grumach appeared to me as most congenial to my personal involvements and the experiences that seemed to replace the coherence of my youth with a scholarly methodology that carried its precise if limited "system of meaning" in itself.

6

Abitur:
Berlin, March 1942

By THE SUMMER OF 1941, I had advanced sufficiently through the numerous stages of the final examination for graduation at the Hochschule. It covered considerable ground even in wartime. The stiff upper lip, in the best of Leo Baeck's Jewish tradition and Prussian duty *à l'outrance*, which had maintained the Hochschule curriculum until its last day, also gave teachers and students a center to integrate their lives. Nobody faced the deportations of Jews from Berlin with anything but "deep concern, anxiety, despondency, terror." A report I wrote in October 1941 reflects the inner turmoil that I, and surely not I alone, felt as chaos infringed on self-discipline and the wish to give others courage. I believe it was Baeck's personal traits, his iron self-discipline, and his uncompromising refusal to acknowledge defeat or disorder, the minority rabbi from the province of Posen (Poznań) pacing the army chaplain of World War I, that kept the traditions alive as intellectual resources diminished.

Nobody let us know, if anybody knew it, that with the invasion of Poland in 1939 and Russia in 1941 the mass murder of Jews had begun, while we were protected by razor-thin walls built on the cynicism of the Nazi government and our wager against time. The war of 1914–18 appeared to repeat itself: the two-front war; Russian space; America's late entry into the war; the failed invasion (courtesy BBC of the winter of 1940; it was, of course, never tried); the Battle of Britain, and other facts and fictions we encouraged ourselves with. The word *holocaust* was as yet another entry in my *Concise Oxford Dictionary*.

In October 1941, I entered the last remaining Jewish high school in Berlin on the urgent advice of my mentors Baeck and Grumach. It seemed one further step in the removal of my academic deficiencies. While Berlin began to burn, my grades for the Hochschule examination series were quite good. In a reversal of Hochschule statutes, the faculty requested that I obtain the Gymnasium Abitur they had waived when they admitted me as a matriculated student in 1939. I was expected to enroll in the final form of the high school curriculum. (At that time, if I was correct in deducing it, all German high schools would offer Abitur at the end of eight years of attendance.) The first page of the Certificate of (Final) Examination I was awarded states, in the language of the educational bureaucracy, that

—I had "attended the Lehranstalt (Hochschule) from October 1936 on and passed its final examinations (*sic*) during the summer term of 1941." (Presumably, the Hochschule administration had so informed the school.)

—I was "admitted by the authorization of the *Prüfungskommissar* for qualifying examinations dated January 8, 1942, installed by the Reichsvereinigung der Juden in Deutschland, to take the final examination as Nicht-Schüler [nonmatriculated student], and was directed to the board of examiners as undersigned for the examination."

When I entered, I knew nothing of this school or its history. It bore the title "Private Jüdische Höhere Schule, Reichsvereinigung der Juden in Deutschland," and probably had a minuscule number of pupils. The class I entered, the last form, had about fifteen boys and girls in their late teens. I was twenty-fours years old and the senior, but had no trouble liking and respecting them. My class was located on the upper floors of an administrative building that had originally belonged to the German Jewish Reform congregation of Berlin, whose synagogue was on the ground floor of the rear building. I understood that this high school was part of the network of schools the Berlin Gemeinde had been permitted to maintain by the Gestapo right into the war years: Jewish pupils had increasingly been barred from entering public schools after 1933.

Like the Hochschule, this school system was allowed or forced to stay open until a decree originating with the central SS security office directed the Ministry of Education to dissolve all Jewish educational institutions effective July 1, 1942, "in view of the recent development of the resettlement of the Jews." The motives for keeping Jewish children in school were probably mixed: education officials in the ministries followed their rules about *Schulpflicht* (compulsory schooling) and supervisory mandates; the police and the Nazi authorities wanted to forestall the pauperization and criminalization of Jewish children that would result if they were neglected and abandoned to the streets; it would have created political problems with the population if the pseudotranquillity of the bourgeois order would have been pierced by disorder (*Unordnung*) defying authority. It also would be noticed by the foreign press, whose correspondents were concentrated in Berlin. The Jewish community itself had no choice; educating children was a religious duty and the only responsible course to take.

Page 3 of my graduation certificate, dated March 31, 1942, describes the proper procedure: "The Board of Examiners installed by the Reichsvereinigung der Juden in Deutschland with the permission of the Herr Reichminister für Wissenschaft, Erziehung, and Volksbildung" signed the document. Here are the names of the members of the board: Dr. Hugo Israel Theodor, Studienrat a.D., Kommissar der Reichsvereinigung der Juden in Deutschland, Director of the School; Jacques Israel Rabau; Dr. Kurt Israel Lewinstein, Oberstudienrat a.D.; Dr. Therese Sara Jacobius, Studienrätin a.D.; Dr. Oskar Israel Beer, Studienrat a.D.; Salomon Birnbaum, Studienrat a.D.; Arthur Israel Heckscher, Studienrat a.D.; Gertrude Sara Rosendorn, Studierätin a.D.; Fritz Israel Wachower, Studienrat a.D.

The first names of all teachers except two include the biblical Sara and Israel. A Nazi decree of July 25, 1938, had ordered Jews who bore "non-Jewish" names to adopt these surnames; I had become Herbert Israel. The list of "Jewish" names appearing in the text of this decree includes biblical names laced with Yiddish language names, including names of endearment and diminutive forms. These, of course, were derived to a large extent from the medieval German that Jewish settlers had spoken when they migrated eastward from the fourteenth century on. Very few Jews born or raised even as immigrant children in Germany had been given Yiddish first names at birth: the list was meant to demean and stamp their bearers as outsiders and pariahs. Joseph, Michael, Johann, and the like had long been assimilated to Christian folk culture from their Hebrew roots, and become "German" names.

The titles affixed to the signatures, except for that of the mathematician Jacques Rabau, indicate that the entire examination commission held tenured positions—Studienrat/rätin—in the educational hierarchies of the Weimar Republic. If I recall correctly, Dr. Rabau did not have the German nationality and may thus have been prevented from teaching in the public school system. He was an imaginative teacher—in general, the pedagogical skills I experienced in the classrooms of this school struck me as intellectually more flexible and less routinized than at the Würzburg Gymnasium, exceptions granted on both sides. I also met the first women teachers I had had since first and second grade in primary school, and appreciated them greatly as both professionals and in their humanity and for their feminine qualities. I had taken only one course with one of the few women who taught at the Hochschule, mainly languages, and during my three years of study at the University of Bern, Switzerland, I was taught only by men—the faculties of history and government seemed not to employ women, and I am not sure if other departments had employed them on any level. My first co-educational experience was, in fact, at this high school in 1941–42, when I was twenty-three years old!

Two of the teachers stand out in my memory for the three months I was able to attend the school, October 1941 to mid-January 1942. Dr. Lewinstein taught German literature as our homeroom teacher, and represented a venerable scholarly tradition in Germanistics: he had studied with Erich Schmidt, a legendary figure in literary history and criticism at the University of Berlin. Lewinstein taught me the first lessons in the history of motifs in German literature. Since he knew of my Hochschule background, he introduced me to the opera texts of Richard Wagner, seen as literature and religious myth, which I read matter-of-factly as he expected. No word of Wagner's bigotry and antisemitism, and this at a Jewish school in Berlin at the end of 1941! We also did *Faust* in class. I tried out for the part of Faust, thinking myself a great romantic lover-scholar who knew much about the human heart. The work was to be read with a role allotted to each pupil, and we competed for them. Alas, I could not take Würzburg out of my style, even if I had long ago left Würzburg behind, and was disqualified as a sentimental provincial. Instead, I landed the role of the earth spirit, but here, too, my success was limited since I saw a *golem* in him, not the subtle force of nature Goethe had conceived. I also disappointed Lewinstein in the written German examination, an essay for which the candidate was given four hours. Since Lewinstein knew that I had been preoccupied with the late poetry of the symbolist, Prague-born poet Rainer Maria Rilke, he assigned a Rilke topic to me when I was locked up in the examination room. When he returned four hours later, however, I had written an extensive introduction to the topic, and Lewinstein, a stickler for balanced form, marked my piece as failing. I redeemed myself in a rather uncompromising oral examination before the board, and squeezed through with the equivalent of "C" as the final mark in German literature.

Lewinstein was an impressive and intellectual teacher whose sad face and provocative and unorthodox delivery veiled his vast knowledge and projected trust and excitement. His brilliant career as a teacher, scholar, and school administrator at one of the two or three most respected private high schools in Berlin, the Französische Gymnasium, was cut short by the Third Reich. In the 1980s, the then director of the Gymnasium was preparing a history of his school and interviewed me several times about my recollections of Lewinstein. Lewinstein survived the war, possibly protected by his Christian wife and children.

These literature classes had one feature in common with the other classes: they were integrated into the prescribed German curriculum, as if the deportation of Jews from Berlin had not already begun, the Nazis had not already murdered Jewish hostages in Berlin, and our living space had not been turning into a mine field and a prison. In October 1941, the German army faced its first massive setback, and while we only dimly perceived from the daily army bulletins what is known today from history, that they collected winter clothing from the population was one more sign that something was amiss. Only our geography teacher, Mrs. Gertrud Rosendorn (or Dr. Therese Jacobius), matter-of-factly taught in her economic geography class that the Soviets had rebuilt their armaments industry in the Ural Mountains and east of the several north–south river systems she pointed out on the map. No informer, if there was any, could fault her for presenting the facts. I retain the fondest memory of her refreshing personality and her teaching, as I do, less distinctly, those of the other teachers. My young fellow pupils were a quick-witted and very gifted lot, with fields of interest like chemistry or mathematics already clearly emerging.

That we all hoped against hope and lost makes the pretended normality of our hours together one more simile of the sense of absurdity that deepened when I understood our situation afterward. I believe that only a few of the teachers and students survived the war, among them the later American orchestra conductor Franz Bibo.

7

Forced Labor: Berlin, January 10–October 24, 1942

IN JANUARY 1942, my formal education in Berlin Jewish institutions ended abruptly. I was caught by the Berlin Labor Exchange for Jewish Labor and impressed into forced labor, as were nearly all Berlin Jews still able to work. Deportations to East European destinations had begun in October 1941, just about the time I had enrolled in the Oberschule. They strengthened the illusion among us that doing "war work" would postpone or even prevent being selected for the East. I had been called twice before to this office, and twice had been exempted as a student of the Hochschule. This time the routine letter on Hochschule stationery, bearing Leo Baeck's signature, was disregarded, despite my protests to the man in charge, known to be a rabid Party hack. He was universally feared and despised among Jews in Berlin for sending elderly Jews to work details that overtaxed their strength and produced sickness and death in their wake. Soon after he had sent me streetcleaning, he was denounced to the Gestapo for smuggling large quantities of silk from occupied France to Berlin. A report from a military detention camp I wrote shortly after entering Switzerland in June 1943 described the details of his murder. Our streetcleaning foreman, Party member Pomerening, told us that his jailers had placed a rope in his cell, suggesting suicide as a favor to an old Party member, but he "was too cowardly or too clumsy" (Pomerening), and "they had to help him along."

I was to report to the City Hall of the district of Lankwitz, a subdivision of the municipal administration of Steglitz, in South-West Berlin, for my assignment as a streetcleaner. My rollbook indicates that on April 24 and 26 and on May 31, 1942, I was still able to enroll in three courses at the Hochschule: Talmud Pessachim

(Gross), Advanced Hebrew (Mrs. Rotbart), and a seminar on Philo Alexandrinus (Grumach). I also retain some memories of classes attended in the Oberschule, but I cannot reconstruct in any detail how I should have been able to do so, unless classes were held after work (7:30–12:30, 1:00–5:00) or on Saturday afternoons and Sundays (Saturday hours 7:30–12:30). As a consequence of this turn, I had to interrupt my final examinations at the Hochschule with about one-tenth incomplete.

As forced labor went, my job was not especially onerous. During the early weeks, it was snow and ice removal; then, with less inclement weather, I joined two elderly fellow Jews who had already worked there for some time, most of the time shoveling our little heaps into a wheelbarrow and unloading the full barrow at spots where the municipal garbage trucks could pick up the dirt. Our foreman, Mr. Pomerening, I was told immediately, was a Nazi and wore a streetcleaner's uniform. As time went on and my Christian fellow workers on other assignments would gain confidence, they would identify themselves and their colleagues by the names of the political parties of the Weimar Republic, although the parties had been dissolved by the regime ten years earlier! It was a somewhat weird situation among these men, whose service records probably reached back into the Republic: they would not resist the Nazi regime, which had raised their wages and probably provided increased job security, except for the threat of being inducted into the army and shipped to the battle fronts. Our broom-and-shovel team ranked lowest in job status, because our equipment was not mechanized and the job involved direct exposure to dirt, the public, and the weather. The top of the ladder was occupied by drivers and skilled mechanics. The office staff ranked higher, white-collar workers snaked up the status-and-salary ladder through the municipal *Ordnung* for employees and tenured officials. For the administrators in the City Hall, Jewish forced labor posed no problem. They were paid according to the municipal tariff at the lowest level as *Hilfsarbeiter*——"auxiliary worker"—and had a weekly contribution to the German social security system deducted from their salaries! At the beginning of March, I saw the division chief at the Rathaus and asked for three days of special leave for the end of March. It was clear from the conversation that I had met an "old Social Democrat" who had worked his way up through the ranks and felt quite apprehensive about the catastrophe he saw brewing in parallel to World War I. He also cautiously hinted at his consternation about forced labor and antisemitism. Soon after, I received written notification, copy to the local administrator, that I had been granted a special leave of three days: *"Zweck: Ablegung der Reifeprüfung"*—purpose, standing for the matura examination. It may have been an historic first in more than one respect, the absurdity of which I would not quite appreciate at the time.

The area we had to clean was a well-to-do quarter of mostly single-family houses opening on tree-shaded cobblestone streets and leaving little doubt that order and cleanliness were next to godliness here, too. We worked wearing our yellow stars with the word *Jude* in phonily Hebraized German lettering. Most people ignored us as the better part of wisdom, hatred, or sympathy. I remember only one serious altercation with a labor-front official, wearing a polished uniform and highly polished jackboots, on his way to his nearby office: he claimed I had soiled him with a watering can. I also remember about half-a-dozen friendly encounters during this time: passersby would deposit paper bags containing cigarettes or fruit: we could not buy fresh fruit on our ration coupons, because we were forced to go shopping primarily after hours when all fresh produce or fruit had already been sold. Once an officer wearing the red stripes of the general staff stopped our foreman and inquired about us. He should do everything he could to keep us here; terrible things were happening in the East, Pomerening reported to us later. The well-meaning man had talked to a Party official who may well have denounced him for a few brownie points soon after. We were not the only "slave laborers" in Steglitz: an electronics factory employed large contingents of Polish women who looked quite emaciated, and at a construction site in nearby Zehlendorf West, we could observe concentration camp inmates in striped pants and jackets working under SS supervision. The guards toted carbines at the ready. I also met a few young men and women who had been detailed to do forced labor for a vegetable gardener in our as yet partly rural district.

My two fellow Jewish streetcleaners were elderly men, a commercial employee and a café-house violinist of Eastern European parentage. As the youngest by far, I did the work considered more strenuous, but their work, too, was affected by the seasons: the only

winter I worked there was rather harsh and demanding, and in the
fall we had to manage the leaves falling from trees in gardens or
from trees lining the streets. Our conversations were somewhat
guarded, since one of my fellow workers was too friendly with the
foreman and the two of us did not trust him. None of us knew
anything of the Holocaust, then in full swing in Eastern Europe. In
the spring, Levinson, the commercial employee, was called up for
deportation and mused aloud about going into hiding. I did not
encourage him, because I estimated his chances of not being discovered as small, for several reasons. He chose deportation. I never
heard from him again. I understood only later that the chances of
surviving in the East were nil. I do not know what happened to
our other colleague, because I went into hiding while he was still
employed by the borough.

My reaction to my new condition was shaped by my determina-
tion to hold on to my "normal" life. In the evenings I returned to
my room and my friends and teachers in Charlottenburg, the West.
The hours with Lotte became more precious because she, too, had
been drafted for forced labor in an electronics factory. Without her
help and the food we received from her parents and my mother
(via food parcels from Würzburg), I would have lost weight more
radically and quickly than I actually did, the fresh air and the physical labor working up appetites beyond the weekly food rations. My
age as yet protected me from the deep exhaustion that would have
come with the years.

Weekends and evenings were still filled with friendship, classical
records, visiting, reading, outings to parks and lakes, the growing
intimacy with Lotte, the sociability of the young. I presumed then
that forcing a student of the Hochschule to clean the streets of
Berlin was meant to be degrading: streetcleaners ranged on the
lower end of the status system, unskilled work with dirt. I held up
my symbolic end by dressing as usual, by wearing gloves while
pushing the wheelbarrow, even in the summer, by finding corners
where we could stop and talk with each other, including the foreman Mr. Pomerening, by chatting with the other workers—in
short, by turning the degradation into a normal work situation, for-
getting that our weekly pay bought just about 250 grams of butter
on the black market and that we survived in style only because we
had help. It helped that the people in the streets ignored us com-

pletely, with the few exceptions noted. No clergyman ever expressed his sympathy, or helped with food, but no rowdies ganged up on us either in this prosperous residential area. Parvenus learn to avoid commitments and extremes, and protect themselves against being visible, yet similar attitudes prevailed in workers' quarters, too.

It might well have been our need to push the horrors and threats to the margins of our attention and out of our minds that allowed us to maintain these exhausting dual lives. If I "already" had to work for them, at least I did no war work. At least I learned that working hard helps only the boss. At least the work was not overly exhausting, even if I slimmed down and went hungry. At least there was no incident against the yellow Jewish badge when I boarded the streetcars every day at 6:30 A.M. and 5:00 P.M.

With the onset of mass deportations in October 1941, the contrasts and conflicts between emotions thickened, deepened, blackened; the abstract had turned concrete and come close. Bodies tensed more as deportations became almost weekly occurrences; stomachs contracted through the effort to maintain self-control and loosened up more slowly. What we felt was that our wager on "our" victory, on winning the race with time, became less and less plausible; we were losing wager and race, and all this in full ignorance of the comprehensive death they had imposed on us in a typically ostentatious lakeside villa across town at the "Wannsee Conference" of January 20, 1942. Its *"Protokoll,"*[1] Eichmann's prettified and expurgated official version of the execution plan, would, of course, emerge only in the Allied Trials of Major War Criminals in the Nuremberg Justizpalast in 1945–46 and in Eichmann's trial in Jerusalem in 1962.

My small working group of streetcleaners, including me, reacted in ways that I believe resembled more general attitudes held by Jews during this last agony of Berlin Jewry. Nobody in Jewish office or authority whose words we might believe ever spoke in public or

---

[1] On the "Wannsee Conference" informing the ministerial bureaucracy of the mass murder of European Jewry already in progress on January 20, 1942, see Summary of the Conference on the "Final Solution," Trial of Major War Criminals, Doc. NG 2586-E (Eichmann). For Eichmann's testimony at his trial in Jerusalem on his smoothing over of the language of the *"Protokoll,"* see 78th Session, June 23, 1961; 79th Session, June 26, 1961; 107th Session, July 24, 1961.

private about the mass murders in the East. Even the rumors did not convey the frightful and unbelievable truth, the truly absolute horror of which needed time to sink in and be emotionally accepted by opinion in the Western world, including many Jews. From October 1941 on, deportations happened so fast and so frequently that they dulled emotions. Their pain cut to the bone when they tore away friends, relatives, and families from inside our own emotional space.

In May 1942, the Gestapo arrested 500 men and women, Jewish communal officials and members of their families. Of these, 250 were shot immediately without trial in a nearby concentration camp, probably Sachsenhausen. They died in reprisal for a fire set by a group of young Jewish Communists/radical Leftists/Zionists in an exhibition set up by the Propaganda Ministry in a central Berlin square, the Lustgarten near the Schloss. It aimed to show the "Soviet paradise" (its title) in the usual Nazi defamatory and antisemitic style. Nearly all members of this group, the "Baum Gruppe," were soon caught and, after brutal tortures, tried and beheaded. The names of the executed were made public through blood-red, black-framed, small posters affixed to the large, round or flat advertising columns dotting Berlin at that time. I had known some of the Gemeinde and Reichsvereinigung functionaries among those killed (their families were deported to Theresienstadt and other camps in Eastern Europe). Baeck never as much as mentioned this crime against humanity.

There had been some treatises in German international law and in some respected textbooks in the 1920s justifying the execution of *Repressalgeiseln* (hostage killing used as a deterrent) in ratios as high as one to one hundred.[2] The tragedy of the resistance group was compounded by the near-total futility of their sacrifice. Paul Eppstein told me at the time that the Reichsvereinigung had known of the group's plan and had urgently asked that they weigh the possible consequences for the larger community. That the act was directed against an anti-Communist propaganda target rather than an ammunition plant or a military object suggests that political calcu-

---

[2] For international law opinion justifying hostage killing, see Herbert A. Strauss, "Hostages of World Jewry: On the Origin of the Idea of Genocide in German History," *Holocaust and Genocide Studies*, 2 (1988): 125–26, 135, 139.

lations among German exile Communists or Comintern function-aries may have influenced timing and choice of target. This does not diminish the respect we pay to the Baum Gruppe in the history of German resistance to Nazism, and to their self-sacrifice.

In May 1942 I saw my father for the last time. He had been arrested by the Potsdam Gestapo which controlled the agricultural center Radinkendorf, where Jews did forced labor under the nomi-nal jurisdiction of the Reichsvereinigung der Juden in Deutschland. My mother and I were permitted to speak with him for a few pre-cious minutes after he had been re-arrested and brought to the Lev-etzowstrasse collection point, a farewell forever burnished into my memory. Obeying our family tradition, we maintained our calm, not to burden father with our grief and our fears. After mother went home, I broke down and did not leave my bed for a week.

On October 24, 1942, Lotte's parents were deported to an un-known destination in Eastern Europe, probably in Riga (Latvia). She had failed to persuade them to go into hiding. We saw them disappear in deep sorrow and despair, once again opting for the life-giving illusion that we would be reunited after the war.

Sometime in late 1941 or early 1942, a woman of my age, Anne-liese Levy, was caught in a dragnet of the Gestapo. She was a won-derfully spirited and intelligent woman whom I had met when she needed a Hebrew teacher. We became friends and shared many attitudes toward self-assertion in the face of the lurking danger around us. She walked into a Gestapo trap when she used the ele-vated city railroad, leaving from her parents' house in Westend to ride to the city without wearing the obligatory yellow Jew badge. A few days after I lost contact with her, a uniformed policeman re-quested to see me, shocking my landlady, Mrs. Neumann. Anne-liese Levy was being held at Levetzowstrasse Synagogue before being placed on a deportation train to Riga. The officer brought cordial greetings and word that she wanted to keep a pullover I had lent her, as a souvenir.

I did not know then that these would be the last signs of life from her, a vital and bubbling life filled with hope and expectations. A memorial volume issued by the German Bundesarchiv has the entry "Anneliese Levy, 07.19.1922, Riga, presumed dead [*verschollen*)]."[3]

---

[3] *Gedenkbuch für die Opfer der Verfolgung der Juden durch die nationalsozialistische Gewaltherrschaft in Deutschland, 1933–1945* (Koblenz: Bundesarchiv, 1986), s.v. Anneliese Levy.

Robert M. W. Kempner, in *Gegenwart im Rückblick* (The present in past perspective), has identified four transports taking Jews from Berlin to Riga for this period: November 27, 1941; January 13, 1942; January 19, 1942 (Welle IX); and January 19, 1942 (Welle X).[4] There are no other traces of Anneliese Levy's murder.

Sometime after she was taken prisoner, her father, a gynecologist, and his wife were caught when they sought to cross into Switzerland over mountain paths they had been familiar with from previous summer vacations. I did not know them in person but had heard from Anneliese about their self-confidence and their courage.

In 1941 or 1942 also, two very dear neighbors of mine were fetched and deported by the *Abholers*. Mrs. Stern, already on in years, was of Würzburg origin; we both had that slight Southern softness in our high German speech that set us apart from the aggressive brash Berlin speech and had brought us together for many precious hours. Mrs. Stern cared for an invalid gentleman, Mr. Baruch, and accompanied him when the deportation order came. Another subtle friendship had sprung up with a frail old lady living in my house. She spent her days sitting in a leather-backed captain's chair in front of a round table on which she had arranged photographs and two or three framed handwritten letters by the German-Czech symbolist poet Rainer Maria Rilke. They commemorated a short love affair with the poet which had dominated her emotional life from then on. We met over our common interest in Rilke's life and works from his (and my) romantic beginnings to his mature late metaphysical and symbolist poetry. I am ashamed that I cannot recall her name any longer: I see her gentle person vividly before my eyes, an island of inner strength protected against reality. I hope that strength also veiled from her the degradation visited upon her when she was deported, I believe to Theresienstadt, the "old-age ghetto" camp in Czechoslovakia.

My landlady, Mrs. Neumann, and a fellow tenant, Mrs. Levy, took their lives when the deportation order arrived. I retain the fondest memories of these two brave and gentle women. Our rela-

---

[4] Robert M. W. Kempner, "Die Ermordung von 35,000 Berliner Juden: Der Judenmordprozess in Berlin schreibt Geschichte," in *Gegenwart im Rückblick: Festgabe für die Jüdische Gemeinde zu Berlin, 25 Jahre nach dem Neubeginn*, ed. Herbert A. Strauss and Kurt R. Grossmann (Heidelberg: Lothar Stiehm Verlag, 1970), pp. 184–87.

tionship had been mutually respectful and supportive, and I presume that Mrs. Levy knew some truths about the mean death that would await us in Eastern camps, although she never mentioned a word to me: she was employed by the Jüdische Gemeinde administration. It was a rational act then to take your own life. The two women took an overdose of Veronal, a sleeping pill, after swallowing a preparation that would keep the poison in. I heard that every tenth person called up for deportation took this way out, primarily old and sick people or people who may have known what awaited them at the end of their railroad journey to a then-unknown last stop.

Did I have any grief left as so many were taken away, men and women close to me, close to Lotte, my fellow students, my teachers, the Gemeinde officials, the professional contacts in the Reichsvereinigung—Dörte's lovely Greifenhagen aunt who volunteered to accompany the old and sick she cared for in the Gemeinde home Grosse Hamburger (or August?) Strasse, Steffi Guttmann and her colleagues in the kindergarten of the Gemeinde, Lotte's aunt and uncle Bildesheim, the remaining Würzburg Gemeinde, Paul Eppstein, the congregations I served? Learning to mourn for these and many other friends and members of the community would become more difficult the more the accumulating evidence of the historical record broke down my defenses: few of the men and women whose lives had touched mine ever returned. The images I can recall are fixed like photographs frozen in time. While it happened, our very ignorance or disbelief, that we suppressed the worst as unthinkable, and it was unthinkable, helped to take the future—their lives, our lives—enough for granted to suppress panic and allow rational action for survival. I remember only one instance where the hatred and rage I also felt spilled over into a public event. On the eve of the joyous holiday Simchat Thora—probably in 1942—I had been assigned to an orphanage in the Pankow district whose prayer room held about 150–200 persons. Before the service began, the director whispered to me that the home had been informed that day that children and faculty would be deported to Eastern Europe in a few days' time. I do not believe that the children had been told. The cantor carried out his duties—especially geared to the joys of youth—as if he did not know that the end had come for the institution and its accumulated services to children in distress. I did not

Pre-war prosperity: the Strauss family, c. 1910. The author's grandmother Ernestine, seated second from right, and her six children, including the author's father, Benno Strauss, at left.

The author's mother and father, Magdalena and Benno Strauss, 1915.

Jewish public school (Moritz Hellmann's class), Würzburg, c. 1927

Above: encampment of Jewish youth groups, Black Forest, early 1930s; author in center. Below: soccer team of Jewish sports club, Würzburg, c. 1935.

Würzburg Neues Gymnasium school outing, c. 1932. Author at bottom.

Walther (1916–1928), the author's brother, at right

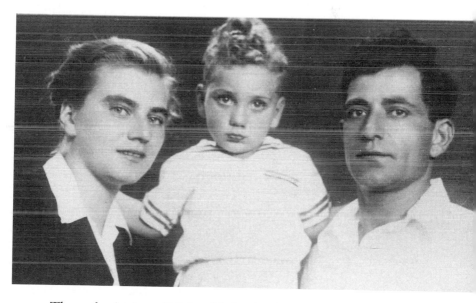

The author's sister, Edith, with her husband, Shimon Nisanov, and their first child, Assaf, at Kibbutz Chulatha

Lotte Strauss (née Schloss), the author's wife, 1940s

Annalora Ehrenbacher, the
author's first love

Dorothy Greifenhagen, who
moved to England in 1939

Herbert Strauss, c. 1940

Dina Meyer Ehrenreich, Berlin,
c. 1938–39

have the strength, disregarded the prepared outline of my sermon, and cursed the regime and the fate that let the children suffer. In the first ten minutes, to preserve my intellectual integrity, I offered arguments from the meaning of Jewish history and its age-old experience with the redemption that would follow suffering in a new personal and national rebirth. This time Baeck's lecture of 1940 sounded hollow. The moral chasm it opened between tradition and reality had deepened further. The children received their traditional chocolate and candy presents. The director and I silently embraced after the service. As far as I was able to establish after the war, nobody who worshiped that evening at the orphanage was ever heard from again.

In May 1942, the Berlin Polizeipräsident (chief of police) closed the Jüdische Oberschule with whose final matriculation class I had graduated two months earlier. I do not think I understood, as Baeck did at the time, the implications of this act. As long as the Nazis (and their by no means all-nazified education authorities) let Jewish children be educated, he had counted on some future for Jews in Germany. I was too drained of emotional responses to grasp that having been among the very last half-dozen students of the Hochschule had involved me in seventy years of the most innovative intellectual and religious history of German Jewry.

There was no other choice but to pluck on in dull efforts for daily strength and use the evenings and the weekends to reassert your emotional life, your intellectual interests, the comforts derived from friends offering news about the course of the war. America had entered the war a month before I had to start cleaning streets. The German armies had failed to take Moscow or Leningrad. The invasion of England was out of the news (since we had celebrated its failure—on false information—in late 1940). The beginning of 1942 had brought a noticeable decline of public optimism about the war, but until the end of that year the Nazi government appeared to have had some success with its "everything looks good as usual" propaganda lines. In Berlin, air raids were becoming more frequent and buoyed our spirits, even if the damage we could see (and I went looking when I could!) was slight. The biggest disturbance air raids created for the population at that stage may well have been loss of sleep. In my memory 1942 forms one gray mass between the bogged-down winter campaign in Russia and the turning points at the end of the year.

Still, there were friends of ours who succeeded in overcoming the beginning exhaustion. Herbert Marcuse and his wife, Gerda Berlowitz, a close friend of ours, succeeded in piercing the wall around us and fled to Sweden. Herbert had done his forced labor in a lumber yard exporting wood products and had built a hollow space for himself and Gerda in a railroad car destined for Sweden. They arrived safely and were granted asylum. Herbert later received government permission to settle in Sweden; Gerda divorced him, remarried, and settled in Kiryat Bialik near Haifa. I knew of no other successful escape abroad at that time, even though our fantasies circled around such hopes and wishes. Lotte, who had moved to a furnished room in my neighborhood, did forced labor at an electrical equipment factory. As our atmosphere grew heavier and the daily cares increased, our support for each other created a new seriousness and closeness.

8

Underground in Berlin: October 24, 1942–June 9, 1943

DURING THE NIGHT OF OCTOBER 24, 1942, Lotte and I were forced to flee from our furnished rooms to avoid being picked up by the Berlin Gestapo. We were to be brought to the synagogue that served as an assembly and staging point for Berlin Jews before they were put on the trains and deported to Eastern Europe.

The circumstances of this arrest were unusual and did not conform to the bureaucratic procedures that were generally being followed in rounding up Jews in Berlin, or, for that matter, in other cities. Lotte, the initial target of the arrest, had not been informed by the Jewish Gemeinde well ahead of time to prepare herself and pack a prescribed list of personal belongings. Police and Gestapo men were usually accompanied by a Jewish helper they had forced the Gemeinde to provide. Usually, daytime or evening hours prior to midnight were fixed for the deportees to hold themselves ready.

The transport we escaped is listed as the twenty-second "Ost-transport," without designating the camp or ghetto to which it would be directed. October 24 was almost a precise anniversary: the first mass transport of Jews from Berlin had occurred on October 18, 1941. Altogether, about 35,000 men, women, and children were still to be deported from Berlin to Eastern Europe, mostly to death camps, between February 27 and June 1943, and about 14,900 Jews of advanced age to the camp of Theresienstadt, including persons of very advanced age and the sick. Most would soon be killed by the hardships of the camps, or shipped from Theresienstadt to extermination camps, primarily Auschwitz.

Our arrests were ordered by the Berlin Gestapo office, whose *Judenreferat* was located in the Burgstrasse, near the government district. It, and the other local Gestapo offices, were executive agencies for the Main Reich Security Office (RSHA) controlled by Himmler and Heydrich. When defeat and the conquest of Germany became certain, these offices were ordered to destroy all vestiges of their crimes. Consequently, the Gestapo everywhere in Germany shredded the substantial files they had been assembling since 1933 on the heinous persecutions, murders, tortures, extortions, and so forth they were guilty of. Only three sets of files survived for some technical reason (such as being worked on elsewhere) in Würzburg, Dortmund, and Wiesbaden.

The *Leitstelle* (executive office) of the Berlin Gestapo employed at least one hundred agents and drew upon the regular ("criminal" and "order") police for additional power. Berlin, after all, had been the center of the Weimar Republic; it had had a left-wing majority electorate and city government; its 4,000,000 citizens had included up to 176,000 Jews. Its very size allowed political dissidents and resistance groups to operate, once the Third Reich was in place. The destroyed files would have documented in a central way the extent and the forms of dissidence and refusals of assent and cooperation during the Third Reich.

The Berlin Gestapo did not succeed in destroying all their records, however, for a typically bureaucratic reason. Before being deported to their deaths, Jews were forced to sign legal papers transferring all they owned to the Reich. They were told that the transfer would pay for their future upkeep in the East (*sic*), as stated in the forms they were required to complete. The new owner of their property was the Reich, specifically the treasury, the Reichsfinanzministerium, not known to be an accessory to murder until this time. Its local branch was the Oberfinanzpräsident Berlin-Brandenburg. Its accountants needed proper documentation to process the property transfer in legally prescribed ways, and the Gestapo sent them not only the transfer documents (of 40,000 Jews and "enemies of the Reich") but also the so-called *Transportlisten* for 35,000 Berlin Jews: names, dates of birth, last Berlin address, and so on. A friend of mine, the late Robert M. W. Kempner, from whose essay on the subject these data are abstracted,[1] called them "a ghostly gravestone" for Berlin Jewry: "*einen gespenstischen Grabstein.*"

---

[1] See above, chap. 7, note 4.

Beginning in 1969, after years of preparation, eight of the officials of the Berlin Gestapo office were brought to justice in a jury trial in Berlin. The largest number of persons implicated in their crimes went scot free, presumably for lack of documentation and evidence. In 1970, I visited Berlin-Moabit, where the trial was held, to search for information. Like many other postwar trials of Nazi war criminals before German courts, it was in slow motion and mired in the procedural issues that jurists love and call justice. Neither trial nor punishment, twenty-eight years after the event, fitted the crime. German legal and political culture after 1945 missed setting an example for the future.

The two or three police agents whom we eluded in October 1942 may have been Gestapo men or Kriminalpolizei, as was usual in the composition of such groups. "They just did their duty," as the phrase went. They looked standard enough, and given their bland faces, I would not have recognized them in a police lineup even at the time.

The transport we eluded was identified—I presume in the Gestapo's own count—as "Osten," that is, the precise location was not given. More than 12,000 persons had been deported to varying destinations in the Baltic countries, Ukraine, and Byelorussia before this date. German witnesses, in war-crimes trials after the war, deposited heart-wrenching accounts of how these persons perished.

The contrast between the vile death that would have been ours and the tranquilizing routines we would have been going through in Berlin, while being fed by a helpful and benevolent Jüdische Gemeinde before entering the trains, was designed by the Gestapo as a malevolent mockery imposed upon German Jewry in its final agony.

The Berlin Secret Police office—Gestapo—would inform the Jüdische Gemeinde that a transport of Jews, usually about a thousand persons, was scheduled to leave Berlin on a given day. They were to be "resettled"—*umgesiedelt*—in Eastern Europe, or if the goal was Theresienstadt (Terezin), in occupied Czechoslovakia, they were to be transferred to "an old-age home." The Gemeinde received lists of these victims from the Gestapo. The victims themselves were informed well in advance by mail to prepare themselves for "resettlement," and were supplied with mimeographed lists of items they were allowed to take with them within a weight limit of,

I believe, 110 pounds. The Gemeinde usually had to call up more than the requested number because of the high suicide rate. On the specified day, a van manned by Nazi police, and the Jewish helpers the Gemeinde had been forced to supply, would pick up the victims waiting in their apartments, and take them to a collection point. There they were given food prepared by the Jüdische Gemeinde and forced to sign the legal documents transferring their (remaining) property to the state "to cover the costs of their upkeep in the resettlement location." When this farce was completed, they had to march or were driven in trucks to a railroad yard, Grunewald or Moabit, and loaded into trains for the journey east. The routine quality of this procedure, the presence of Jewish helpers, and the use of routine legal formalities to initiate mass murder on a genocidal scale had the effect of minimizing impulses to flee or resist—and made the risk of refusal or flight seem greater than falling in with the law-and-order procedure and the bureaucratic calm in which it was practiced. Resistance was not likely in any event, given the advanced age of most Berlin Jews at that time, their ignorance of what awaited them, and the absence of preconditions (arms, organization, leaders, communication, plan of action) that would have made resistance possible.

Lotte was to be taken by car—it was waiting before her house where I saw it—to the former Levetzowstrasse Synagogue, in the Hansa quarter of Berlin. Lotte's parents had been picked up a day earlier, on October 23, and were already confined there.

Louis and Johanna Schloss had lived in a house in a suburb, Berlin-Kladow, that belonged to Lotte's uncle, where they had cared for their last remaining parent, Lotte's grandmother, until her death. The uncle had emigrated and had acquired Argentinian citizenship. At the time, he lived in Lausanne in retirement, and had tried in vain to obtain Swiss visas for his sister's family. The Swiss authorities had turned him down. An attempt of his to secure a visa to Switzerland for Lotte failed as well, because cantonal authorities in Vaud had "already admitted many Jews."[2]

---

[2] Confederate Alien Police, Office for Emigrants (Eidgenössische Fremdenpolizei, Emigrantenbüro) to Dr. Willhelm Abegg, Solicitor, February 16, 1943: "the Canton [Vaud] has refused to tolerate [dulden] the petitioner on its territory. Even if the Canton had arrived at a positive decision, we would not have been able to admit Mrs. Lotte Kahle. The number of persons of Jewish descent who wish to

The house in Kladow, built in English country-house style in the 1920s, was surrounded by a well-designed garden, and had a small pier for swimming and boating in the River Havel and the Wannsee. It was a tasteful jewel of a house, and allowed a view of the Havel River, the Wannsee, and the Pfaueninsel. During World War II, you still had to pass through open fields to reach the bus station on the main road to the village.

Father and Mother Schloss were the most gentle and hospitable people in the style of their small-town Jewish community in Wolfenbüttel near Braunschweig. This town had been their home until rampant antisemitism, the rude provocations of the Hitler Youth, and the destruction of their livelihood in 1938 drove them away to Berlin. In Berlin's impersonal anonymity Jews could escape the police-informer mentality the Nazis had fostered among the German people.

Their lives in Berlin-Kladow had an almost remote quality, and they felt themselves protected by the Argentinian citizenship of their brother and brother-in-law in Switzerland. It had been Nazi policy to avoid incidents with foreign nationals which might produce adverse publicity abroad and lead to diplomatic démarches.

In the fall of 1942, a highly decorated flying ace of the German Luftwaffe—he had been awarded the *Ritterkreuz* (knight's cross)—discovered the house in Kladow which until then had drawn no attention to itself as "foreign property." He had been transferred to the neighboring airfield—Gatow—and set about to commandeer the property as his residence. Mr. Schuermann, the real estate agent administering the property for the absent owner, with offices at Friedrichstrasse at the corner of Unter den Linden, had sent a member of his firm, Mr. Schmidt, to show the house to the officer. Lotte, expecting the worst, had urged her parents to move out forthwith, to forestall the deportation that would follow an eviction of Jewish tenants. Louis and Johanna Schloss moved to an apartment in Berlin's Westend. Not long after, Louis received notice

enter Switzerland from Germany or from the areas occupied by Germany continues to be large. We cannot grant residency permits to all petitioners; only those related in the first degree to Swiss citizens or residents in Switzerland may obtain permission. Petitioner has not demonstrated such special relations to Switzerland. We had asked the Cantonal authorities to investigate but received a negative reply" (Schöneberg papers, in my possession; translated by the author).

that he would be "resettled" in "the East." Johanna may have been spared a formal notice because Lotte's employer had put her on his payroll to protect her as long as possible from precisely that fate.

Lotte spent feverish days with her parents trying to persuade them to hide with friends in Berlin. But, for complex reasons, they could not see themselves taking the step into illegality. On October 23, 1942, the "helpers" came and picked them up. The questionnaires that Louis and Johanna Schloss had to fill out as deportees while they were interned in Synagogue Levetzowstrasse included a reference to their daughter, Lotte; there was no other source from which the police could have obtained her identity. In June 1994, I obtained copies of these declarations; they consisted of sixteen printed pages, each containing detailed, intrusive questions about their families and their property. They also had to list Lotte's address in Berlin. She had long before left her parent's home and was going under the name of her former husband. The principle on which Lotte was to be included in this transport was *Sippenhaft*; that is, the entire extended family (*Sippe*) was included in punitive actions against single members. All persons who knew of the *Ritterkreuzträger*'s intended theft of the Kladow property were to be eliminated as inconvenient eyewitnesses.

The Luftwaffe officer who was responsible for their eviction and murder never knew the Schloss family, but he could not have been unaware that he had driven the legitimate tenants away. Sometimes I speculate that he may well have been young enough to be one of those ex–Hitler Youth in a branch of the German armed services that rewarded merit more generously when it rested on fanatical Hitlerism. Or he may well have been inoculated with hatred for Jews from his cradle on. Or he may have long been brutalized and did not care if others were killed for his convenience. In the end, he did not take the house at all, presumably because he found one more to his liking.

On October 24, at 3:30 A.M., a Gestapo team rang the doorbell of the boardinghouse where Lotte rented a furnished room around the corner from my room, in the same large city block. The address was Niebuhrstrasse 76, 3rd floor. They roused the tenants by their noise, entered Lotte's room, and woke her with the announcement that they would take her to her parents in Levetzowstrasse Synagogue. They would give her only enough time to have a tenant help sew the "Jewish Star" badge on her overcoat, and amused themselves meanwhile with inspecting the apartment and frightening the aroused and fearful tenants. This gave Lotte the opportunity to slip out of her room through the apartment door and the unlocked door of the house without being detected; the driver of the police car parked in front had probably joined his colleagues upstairs.

A series of frantic moves followed her flight from the apartment. She reported that she first had gone around the corner to wake me, but nobody answered the bell—she had a key only to the entrance gate. The landlady, Mrs. Neumann, saw her leave across the courtyard and roused me out of my deep sleep. We had had to unload potatoes in a railyard for ten hours that day. Lotte then went to the Lietzenburgerstrasse post office, about four blocks away, and telephoned a friend with the request to come to warn me. Christl Simon, the friend, properly considered this a futile move that would draw additional persons into danger. I dressed meanwhile, went over to Lotte's house, and climbed the three flights to her apartment, passing a car parked in front of the entrance. The door was ajar, and I caught a glimpse of two young men inside, berating the assembled tenants in loud and vulgar voices. Lotte was not among them. She had paid a second visit to my apartment while I was looking for her, and told Mrs. Neumann what had happened. I tiptoed downstairs, and when I returned home, my first impulse was to pack my knapsack and put on my coat. I had barely finished when Lotte returned, recounted in staccato what had happened, and suggested that we catch our breath. She was quite exhausted from her flight, the fear, the danger. Instead, we took off immediately. My apartment would have been the logical place to search for Lotte. Her fellow tenants knew me well. While we were halfway down the staircase, the phased light in the hallway went off. We did not dare relight it and entered the courtyard of the Gartenhaus-complex. Somewhere in front of his ground-floor apartment we could make out the janitor, Carlsson. From the main entrance door, locked at night, we heard loud voices identifying themselves as Gestapo and requesting entrance. Carlsson delayed opening the door long enough for us to dive into the air raid shelter in the cellar and hide in one of its upper bunk beds.

About thirty very tense minutes went by while we stayed in those beds, listening for every noise that might signal discovery and cap-

ture. Then we heard steps down the staircase of the Gartenhaus—
the air raid shelter's recesses where we were hiding adjoined its
entrance to the stairwell. A door fell shut. We heard steps across
the courtyard; the entrance door closed with a thud, the sound of
keys in the lock. It must have been Carlsson locking it from within.
After a while, we went above ground again. The courtyard was still
fairly dark. It was probably around 5:00 or 5:30 A.M. Sunday morning, October 24. Carlsson and his wife could be made out dimly in
their apartment door entrance. We saw Mrs. Neumann, my landlady, waving to us from the second floor, out of the small toilet
window. I waved the Carlssons and Mrs. Neumann good-bye. We
carefully opened the front door; the street was empty, no one was
visible, no suspicious black car was parked in the vicinity. The tension gave way to a moment of jubilant relief. We had outwitted
them, we were free—*Goldene Freiheit*, the potboiler verbiage of colloquial popular literature. The raw, jubilant sentiment escaped me
involuntarily as we walked away from the house and the good people who had been with me as I had been with them for over two
years: Mr. Carlsson, of Swedish descent; Mrs. Neumann, the lady I
respected for her style and her human qualities; the neighbors.
Bonds born of years of distress endured in common had been broken. Lotte and I were thrown together into a new closeness we had
not known before.

We never learned if Johanna and Louis Schloss ever knew or felt
certain that we had escaped. Lotte had frequently spoken of her
hope of doing so. There was nobody who would have been able to
tell them and comfort them with information about the events of
the night. Given the Gestapo's malignant glee and mockery of their
prey, they may have told the Schlosses about their mission before
we eluded them, and expressed their ironic gratitude to them for
letting them have Lotte's address. I hope against hope that when
we failed to be brought in, her parents sensed that Lotte had taken
her own advice and gone into hiding, the advice they had not dared
to take themselves.

On October 26, two trains with 791 Berlin Jews left for the East.
Until the Soviet political withdrawal from the Baltic States in 1991,
I made many unsuccessful attempts to find the destination of these
transports. The Gestapo lists—bureaucratic pedantry as usual in
recording their mass murders—offered only "Osttransport" as des-

tination, that is, no information. In 1970, I enlisted the help of a Berlin state attorney general, Dr. Günther Sczostak, and of Robert M. W. Kempner, a Nuremberg Trial prosecutor and law professor at the University of Pennsylvania, to search the documents they had assembled to try the Berlin Gestapo heads for war crimes. They revealed nothing definite. Nor did an advertisement we placed in Berlin newspapers at that time, offering a reward for information. I got only phony replies. Logic pointed to Riga as a possible destination. I searched the hellish, hair-raising documentation on the murder of Jews in Riga, and the murder of Jews reaching the town in transports from Germany. Once again, no record of October 26 transports from Berlin. In 1993, Professor Wolfgang Benz, the director of the Berlin Zentrum für Antisemitismusforschung (Center for Research on Antisemitism), sent me an autobiographical report on the Riga ghetto published by a Latvian eyewitness-survivor.

In the early 1990s Margers Vestermanis, who directs the Riga Jewish Museum and Documentation Center, thought that the absence of any records suggested strongly that this transport had been halted before it reached town and that its prisoners were murdered. Finally, in mid-July 1999, after I had readied the manuscript for Fordham University Press, Dr. Gertrud Schneider, a survivor of the Riga ghetto and a colleague at the City University of New York, shared with me the research she had been conducting in Latvian archives. The horrible truth was that Osttransport 22 had been diverted to the forest of Salaspils, an SS killing ground near Riga, and its prisoners exterminated upon arrival, with the exception of 50 to 100 younger men who had been selected for work in a factory and on the construction of a concentration camp, Kaiserwald. The mostly older men and women were forced to shed all their clothing and to lie down at the bottom of a large pit excavated in the forest on top of whoever had been executed previously. They were killed by machine-gun fire from the rim of the pit, layer after layer, by SS troops and Latvian mercenaries under their command. Only a few not seriously wounded managed at some locations to feign death and escape after night fell.

I believe this apocalyptic scene—it recurred elsewhere in Nazi-occupied Eastern Europe—belongs to the most infernal acts perpetrated by Nazi troops and their local (ethnic) helpers in World War II. I pray that Louis's and Johanna's suffering may have been made easier by the extreme emotional exhaustion and the panic they must have felt after days of travel without rest that must have dimmed their senses. If we had been caught in Berlin and placed on this transport, we would have been unable to assist anybody in any way, or to ease anyone's discomfort. I had sought to learn the concrete truth about their deaths, to find peace in certainty, in knowing where they, my father, our friends had ended their lives, to accept the challenge of turning mourning into an affirmation of life. Even fifty years later, today, I bridle at the memory.

Louis was sixty-one years old in 1942; Johanna, fifty-seven. My father was sixty-six years of age when he had vanished in mid-1942 from the Warsaw ghetto. We would have wanted them to share our lives in the United States, in New York.

The entire sequence of events in Berlin that had ended in our escape had taken about two and a half hours and seemed both shorter and longer while our situations changed. Neither Lotte nor I had any choice. We had talked about going into hiding should we be selected and taken to one of the collection points. Since October 1941, twenty or more trains had taken thousands of Jews from Berlin into a void that returned no signs of life. I had lost my own father and some wonderful friends to be "resettled further east." At most, I believed we would face a harsh Darwinian struggle to maintain ourselves. Earlier on, Baeck had discouraged me when I told him that I would be ready to go east with the Gemeinde and help, if help was needed, to Lotte's immense relief.

Now, when our loose talk about "going underground" was put to the test, nothing had been prepared, except a backpack waiting to be filled and a suitcase with clothing and personal documents that had been taken across the Swiss border in the summer of 1942 and left with "an address" there by Ursula von Hielmcrone. We should have known that our turn could come at any moment, but I did not *feel* that my life would be threatened: the danger did not penetrate and trigger an alarm.

I have long since puzzled about this condition of avoiding to appropriate emotionally what one knows or should have known. It was characteristic of many others among us. Getting used to living on the slope of a volcano? Being deceived by the very ordinariness of the deportation process? Tranquilized by the quietism of Jewish authority figures, by their lack of candor if they knew the truth about the Holocaust? Theirs had been a humane decision to involve Jewish helpers in picking up the victims from their apartments, assisting them in filling out the preposterous legal documents. Had the preachers and rabbis, myself included, not tried to project a spiritual world of history or theology that spoke to the inward needs but left the external realities unmentioned? Did all this prepare us for submission where rebellion might have moved more of us to save ourselves and those we loved and cared for? That our culture had determined the reactions of the community makes the dilemmas of perception and moral action no less unbearable in retrospect.

Once we were out of our district and the sun broke on that Sunday, food, shelter, clothing, the elementary needs, had to be faced. Lotte and I at the earliest "decent" hour called a number of friends who might give help or advice and the bed for the night we needed most. The friends we called were overwhelmed and unprepared to face our problem. By noon, we had found our first host, August Sapandowski, in the Schmargendorf district of the western section of Berlin, an acquaintance of Lotte's mother. He put us up in a cellar a few blocks away from his apartment, in Laubacherstrasse 39, where he used to store paints and the gear he needed for his occupation as a master house painter.

The cellar had a separate entrance, and contacts with tenants of this apartment house and the superintendent of the building could be avoided. Into a niche, Mr. Sapandowski had built two alcoves containing a bedlike contraption and a mattress to sleep on, even a makeshift night table with a candleholder. Being close to the heating and warm-water plant, the room was reasonably warm. A water closet (toilet) and a small sink could be reached over a long board covering some holes in the floor; there were two small windows opening to the sidewalk from basement levels, and one door. We were greatly relieved by his offer and most grateful. This cellar was our first home "underground" for about six weeks, probably through November 1942.

Mr. Sapandowski, even by the standards of that "time out of joint," appeared to us to be a rather unusual and unorthodox person. By an unlikely coincidence—another unlikely coincidence— Christoph Hamann, a Berlin schoolteacher, wrote to me in March 1999 that he had interviewed Mr. Sapandowski's daughter, Vera

Ipczynski, seven years earlier for an oral history project and offered to share his knowledge with me. August's living room had been decorated with a large oil depicting Hitler, but the reverse showed an equally gaudy portrait of Stalin which August had displayed proudly during our first visit to him a few months earlier.

His parents had destined him for the Catholic priesthood. Instead, he learned the trade of house-and-church painting and, in 1921, joined the German Communist party (as evidenced by his surviving membership card). Samples of his poetry in his daughter's possession sent to me by Mr. Hamann reveal a streak of emotion-tinged "Christian humanism" linked with almost sectarian social protest and anti-Nazi and anti-war sentiment. This background may help to explain his deviation from the party line of the Weimar period which depicted Jews and Jewish political or cultural ideologies like Zionism as hopelessly mired in reactionary nationalism, backward religion, or capitalist exploitation. His helping Jews against Nazi persecution may also have been linked to an intimate friendship with a Jewish companion, Elsbeth Orgler, whom he had met following the death of his wife. It was through her that Lotte's mother had met him in Kladow.

Three weeks after we succeeded in leaving his cellar behind, a woman tenant living above us informed the Gestapo of the goings-on in the basement. The fugitives following us were arrested. August and Else themselves went into hiding in South Germany. Unbeknownst to us, August had stored his anti-Nazi writings under a heap of garbage in a corner and feared discovery. After three months he felt safe enough to return "above ground," was arrested a few weeks later and grilled for three months in a Berlin Gestapo prison (Burgstrasse prison on Kaiserdamm). Else was deported to Auschwitz with the 40th Osttransport (and 98 other victims). She did not return. August, after release from prison—his fifteen-year-old daughter, arrested with him, had not betrayed him in prison—continued to help Jews and anti-Nazi oppositionals in his apartment, and was informed upon allegedly by a Jewish woman, Emmy Brandt, who was herself deported to camp Ravensbrück as late as November 24, 1944. August was re-arrested and murdered by mistreatment in the Bergen-Belsen camp. The SS physician there certified "circulatory failure" as the cause of his death on March 11, 1945. His dream that a "Communist regime" would replace the

Third Reich ultimately failed. I do not know how he reconciled his "Christian humanism" with what he must have known about Soviet crimes against their own people. We remember him not only as our first helper in need but as a man who acted on his convictions, religious or atheist, with exemplary courage.

Our new quarters—the first ones Lotte and I occupied jointly after three years of close friendship—had to be used with great care, lest the concièrge—a concièrge was often a V-man (*Verbindungs-mann*, informant) for the Nazi Party—inform on us. We could enter only after complete darkness had fallen, and had to avoid any noise that might give us away. At night, the two small windows had to be covered tightly with thick cloth to avoid light's being seen from the street, the only light besides a candle being a naked bulb in front of the toilet. We also had to suppress all noise and speak in whispers, but could not entirely avoid the creaking of the board leading to the toilet or that of some places on the floor. After several weeks, our host gave refuge to another couple, an elderly retired jurist and his wife, Mr. and Mrs. Flatow, who had also met him through Lotte's mother. They stayed only a few days and moved to a more adequate shelter. After them, he let a mother and her teenage son stay in the cellar. They were less adapted to noiseless behavior and care with light. Soon after, we succeeded in leaving the cellar and finding other shelters. A few weeks later, mother and son were denounced by a tenant and arrested by the Gestapo. We never heard of either couple again.

In the early weeks with Mr. Sapandowski, we solved Lotte's and my clothing problem. Lotte had retained the keys to her apartment but not to her room. The tenants were at their forced labor jobs during the day. This allowed us to enter the apartment. We peeled off the paper seal the Gestapo had affixed so that it covered both door jamb and door. I experimented with a picklock key like those used in break-ins for simple locks, and the lock yielded in spite of my lack of experience with stealing someone's own belongings from her own apartment. It was simpler to remove some of *my* clothing from my room at Schlüterstrasse 53: Dr. Grumach had entered it earlier with Mrs. Neumann's agreement and saved some documents relating to my studies at the Hochschule and, possibly, the high school graduation certificate I had acquired only a few months earlier. He, too, had peeled off the paper seal; loosening it a second time was easy. At least we had solved our clothing problem. Nobody stopped us or noticed us with our suitcases when we left our old homes, this time for good.

The next pressing problem was to obtain funds. Lotte and Lotte's parents had drawn compensation for taking care of the house belonging to Ludwig Schöneberg in Kladow, and Ludwig had instructed his (Christian) business manager, Henriette Schneider (nominally his "Aryan" successor), who had at first refused help in a fairly self-righteous manner, to advance whatever would be needed to save us and ease our possible escape. Letters from Ludwig, who lived in Lausanne with his wife, reached Berlin through a diplomatic mail pouch that was not subject to censorship and went by courier. A Berlin delegate of the International Red Cross, with its seat in Geneva, Jean Friedrich, was an acquaintance of the Schönebergs. He had previously helped Ludwig and Ilse stay in touch with Ilse's parents and Ludwig's business contacts. Another channel we did not use that early in our flight was a courier of the German Foreign Office attached to the German Embassy in Switzerland, Mr. Jankowiak, a fervent anti-Nazi. His only son (who lived with his divorced mother) shot himself after he had deserted from the army and the Gestapo found leaflets of the Scholl resistance group in his apartment. Until the early 1930s, Mr. Jankowiak had worked as Ludwig Schöneberg's private driver.

My own student scholarships had ceased with the dissolution of the Hochschule, and my mother's small stipend would be insufficient for whatever lay ahead. A few days after we had "dived under," as the colloquialism went, Lotte was asked to meet with Ludwig's accountants and his business manager. She also contacted Ilse's parents, the Voigts. Ilse's father had retired from his civil service position as postmaster in a middling Saxon-Anhalt town (Wittenberg) shortly before. The meeting took place in the accountants' office in Friedrichstrasse or Unter den Linden. It did not go well. They would, of course, follow instructions from their client, but could not see how we would manage to stay alive for the duration of the war. This was November 1942. German defeats in El Alamein or at Stalingrad and the American invasion in North Africa would occur soon after. They said the Luftwaffe and the submarines would keep the Americans away. The submarine "wolfpacks" reported high tonnage figures of sunk convoys in the Battle of the Atlantic.

The police were ubiquitous; I was of draft age and not in uniform; Lotte looked too "Jewish" for them; the money needed and the risks taken were prohibitive.

Around this time, my mother visited us. She had been alerted by telephone by my good friend Ruth Basinski, in whose room she stayed during this visit. Mother, too, urged us to throw ourselves on the mercy of the police, whom she had been brought up to fear as close to omnipotent. Most difficult for us to take was that, in her desperation, she berated Lotte for bringing about my downfall ("*ins Unglück stürzen*"), touching a vein of guilt Lotte spoke of after we had escaped. My mother left Berlin convinced that she had seen me for the last time in our lives. Yet, she proceeded to give us all the support she could. She continued to send the weekly food parcels to Berlin that had helped to sustain me, first to Ruth Basinski's address, then to another friend, Wanda Dombrowski, the Protestant wife of a Jewish émigré, who had visited her in Würzburg and struck up a friendship with her. The parcels usually included a half pound of *Fränkische Landbutter* (country butter) which she owed to her longstanding connections with peasant women who would come to our house or apartment, be made welcome, and sell their produce. Wartime rationing had not interrupted this old, acquired right, the peasant wife's pin money.

We both understood the occupational rationale that had produced the accountants' advice. But were they ignorant of the mass murders that had been going on in Eastern Europe at least since the S.D. Einsatzgruppen (Security Service operational groups) had begun their unspeakable atrocities behind the advancing German army, in Poland in September 1939, and in Russia in June 1941? We also understood what had shaped my mother's fears from early on, and the emotions that needed a scapegoat.

With these exceptions, our life in hiding, which was to last for more than seven months, was borne along by the sympathy and help of quite a few people, Jewish as well as Christian. In October 1942, Berlin still harbored about 35,000 Jews, in addition to about 20,000 persons living in "mixed marriages" with Christian spouses and of the Christian religion. Jewish institutions like the Gemeinde or the Reichsvereinigung continued to function with some strength at least until mid-1943. This was our community; private relations continued, even if they changed in quality. Visits or common lunches or dinners acquired a restless edge; being found with us meant being charged with harboring a fugitive and would probably have been punished by imprisonment and deportation, preceded by torture and interrogation to extract information on a "network" and on links with political dissidents. These were the rules of survival we had to follow: Don't outstay your welcome, because it is safer for you and your host, and avoid repetition and regularity in social schedules; do not eat lunch with a friend at the same place at regular intervals; choose hours when a restaurant is crowded; don't linger after meals. We had lived in the middle-class, western sections of Berlin, and we presumed that the police had not built a web of informers like café owners or bar keepers or its own detective system there to patrol the streets for criminals, as, we presumed, they had done in what they considered high-crime and proletarian areas. On New Year's Eve, 1943, we traveled with a group of young German Quakers to a restaurant located outside of Berlin at Castle Rheinsberg, an eighteenth-century country house that had served Frederick the Great as playground and escape. Lotte was asked to carry an Italian newspaper, but nobody asked any questions. Lotte and I met regularly in the Berlin Zoo, about middle distance between the two main entrances, varying the animal habitats we pretended to inspect as we moved from the elephant house, the regular starting point. It was advisable and necessary to move about during the day: an unknown guest in an apartment spending the day by himself or with the host's wife would be noticed or gossiped about; any move he would make in an apartment, while the owners were at work, could be heard on the floor below in most of these homes. And I needed to meet friends and a variety of people to exchange information, find food or ration cards, look for an overnight stay on the very few occasions when I had not secured a bed by noontime. I convinced myself that finding us among four million Berliners was unlikely and that the police did not have the manpower for systematic identity checks. Being stopped by military police looking for deserters or AWOLs would have been equally treacherous. I ran into neither during my more than seven months of hiding, which was just as well, since for a long time, I owned no identity card—*Ausweis*—and would have been done in. After several months, a friend—I've forgotten who it might have been—used some business stationery for an informal substitute, but I lost it when I ran out of a Gestapo trap. I also had to abandon the respectable briefcase "one carried" at the time like a lady's handbag, together with a much missed pound of butter from Würzburg. Only by March or April did I finally have a foolproof "authentic" Ausweis in my breast pocket.

We would not have lasted and survived if friends, acquaintances, and strangers had not helped us in large and small ways. With the end of our "above ground" life all but one contact with fellow students of the Hochschule had come to an end, except with close friends like Ruth Basinski or Lutz Ehrlich. If it ever was a community, it broke apart as each coped with the dangers. Contacts also ceased with the faculty of the Hochschule except Ernst Grumach. Leo Baeck I last saw in early January 1943 when I received a request of his to see him in his apartment at the Schöneberger Park. By the end of January he had been deported to Theresienstadt. I learned of only three faculty members besides Baeck and Grumach, and four students including myself, who were still alive on May 8, 1945. That Grumach had removed my Hochschule and the Jewish high school certificates would prove of utmost importance when I enrolled at the University of Bern after our flight to Switzerland.

Among the friends and acquaintances who took the risks we brought into their already precarious lives as a matter of course, none survived more extreme and life-threatening situations and came out undiminished in body and soul than Ruth Basinski, a longtime friend and fellow student at the Hochschule. Ruth was born a few years before I was in Rawitsch (Rawicz), a town in the (then Prussian) province of Posen (Poznań), and had worked her way out of the poverty of her family by way of a teachers' seminary. She combined an extremely sharp and quick intelligence with a solid talent for music (she played the recorder) and a wary distance from an environment that had burdened her from early on, without losing the capacity for trust and strong emotions. She enrolled in the Hochschule in 1940, and took introductory Talmud lessons with me. I had met her earlier through Günther Aron, a mutual friend, in whose parents' apartment (Gervinusstrasse) I had rented a furnished room.

When we had to flee into homelessness, my relationship with Ruth shifted focus, the emotional ties remaining undiminished, but our previous easy give-and-take in daily matters became one-sided for a time: she still had her room and a mailing address, could be in touch with my mother, found room for me for a night when I had no place to sleep, and helped out with ration cards she would collect from friends and acquaintances. Her landlords in Halensee were Otto Bernstein and Jenny Schaffer Bernstein,[3] each well known in his or her own right for an acting career on first-rank German stages in Dresden and Berlin that had spanned twenty-five years. I had experienced Otto Bernstein as an impeccable *Rezitator* already on the Würzburg Jüdischer Kulturbund stage. (He recited litera-ture written by Jewish authors in German, or German literature like Lessing's *Nathan der Weise*, the classic eighteenth-century plea for religious tolerance, which the Nazis had conceded to the Jewish theater they had permitted after 1933.) From 1939 on, he had taught Speech at the Hochschule. The Bernsteins proved quite helpful now, and invited me to take an occasional bath in their apartment.

Early in 1943, they were deported to Auschwitz and "selected" for the gas chambers upon arrival. This of course made Ruth home-less. She had suffered a schizophrenic episode and was treated in the Jewish hospital, Iranische Strasse, by a psychiatrist, Hermann Pineas, with optimal success. (Dr. Pineas and his wife survived the last two years of the war on forged papers in South Germany, work-ing for a medical supply company. We met again in New York after 1945.) But when she returned from the hospital sometime early in 1943, she had to move into a Gemeinde shelter in Grosse Ham-burgerstrasse and thus expose herself to the threat of early deporta-tion. She had to be helped urgently to get away.

In December 1942, my mother sent a young woman from Würz-burg to Ruth who, she thought, might be able to help us cross the border to Switzerland. She had met Ilse Sonja Totzke[4] through a friend of hers, Mrs. Schwabacher, who had been forced by the Ge-stapo to move into a "mixed marriage house," as had mother after

[3] Ulrich Liebe, *Verehrt, verfolgt, vergessen: Schauspieler als Naziopfer* (Weinheim/ Berlin: Beltz Quadriga, 1992), pp. 219–44, with limited data from *Bühnenjahrbuch*.

[4] For Ilse Sonja Totzke, 1913–1943 (?), see "Würzburg im Dritten Reich: Kata-log der Ausstellung 30. Januar bis 28. Februar 1983," arranged by Bruno Fries, Paul Pagel, Christian Röding, and Kurt Scheidenberger. This unpublished listing includes short biographies and documents preserved in the former Gestapo Ar-chives in Würzburg. See also Robert Gellately, *The Gestapo and German Society: Enforcing Racial Policies, 1933–1945* (New York: Oxford University Press, 1990).

father had left Würzburg. We met Ilse together with Ruth: Ilse's father, an orchestra leader in the Alsace, had been forced to flee when the province reverted to France in 1918–19. Ilse had retained links with the area and knew the border section adjoining Switzerland well enough to attempt a crossing. After we discussed Ilse's generous offer for quite some time, we had to agree that it was premature to risk a relatively vague and unprepared trip without support from a native of the region acquainted with the guard system. As yet, none of us had identity papers to pass safely through the controls we would meet traveling south. Lotte had hopes that the connection with her uncle through Jean Friedrich would result in a better-prepared plan. Ilse stayed some days with Ruth and returned home, but came back to Berlin in January and persuaded Ruth and a friend of ours, Toni Boronow, to go with her. We said a tense and triste farewell to them in mid-February, with forebodings about the desperate risks they were taking without proper preparation.

We never heard from them again, and had to presume that they had been caught by the police on their way to the border, or by the customs and Gestapo details we thought would be guarding it. From Ruth's postwar story and from Ilse's Gestapo file preserved in Wurzburg their incredibly bad luck emerges as follows:

On February 12–13, Ilse, Toni, and Ruth left Berlin to reach an area Ilse had known from a vacation stay earlier in 1942. But, early into their journey, Toni separated from her companions because she lost confidence in Ilse Totzke and wrote a letter warning us about it addressed to Hella G., the young woman who had been sheltering Lotte after our "cellar" life with Mr. Sapandowski. Hella turned this letter over to Lotte or me three weeks after it arrived, too late to make any difference, part of the dangerous irrationality that had crept into our relationship with her. Toni returned to Berlin subsequently, but there was no opportunity to meet her any longer. She survived in Berlin. We met again after the war during our first visit there. Ilse and Ruth spent a week in Heidelberg, changing rooms every night to avoid being registered and investigated by the police, and crossed the border during the night of February 26–27, 1943, by "climbing over a [barbed?] wire obstacle." Swiss customs officials arrested them on the spot and returned them the following night to Germany after detaining them during the day in their post. The women made another attempt at a nearby unguarded spot the next night, walked "for two or three hours" away from the border but were once again spotted and arrested by Swiss customs men. This time, the Swiss turned them over to a German custom post (identified as GAST [*Grenzabwehrstelle*], that is, border counterespionage agency, in the Gestapo protocol of Mrs. Totzke's deposition). Ruth was brought back to Berlin and deported to Auschwitz; Ilse, to Würzburg and imprisoned in the Konzentrationslager Ravensbrück. The Gestapo file sent with her identified her as an "open enemy of National Socialism who feels unhappy under the Hitler government and finds the Nuremberg Laws incomprehensible . . . an obstinate person and philosemite . . . a *Judenweiss*. . . ."

Ilse Totzke's story was reconstructed from the surviving archives of the Würzburg Gestapo office for the first time in an exhibition on "Würzburg in the Third Reich" in the Stadtarchiv Würzburg (Greilinghäuser) in 1983. The exhibition was assembled by Bruno Fries, Paul Pagel, Christian Rödig, and Kurt Scheidenberger, German teachers shouldering the burden of their fathers. In 1993, Robert Gellately reconstructed in detail Ilse Totzske's *via dolorosa* in Nazi Germany from the same archival materials.[5] Ilse had been persecuted for many years by the Würzburg Gestapo and again and again informed upon by neighbors egged on by women or wives who told the Gestapo that they felt scandalized by her free lifestyle: she was seen as having lesbian relations with young Jewish women in Würzburg where she had studied music until a motorcycle accident ended her career. She had inherited a small fortune from her mother after fighting her father's control over her legacy in the courts. Her Gestapo file reveals the suspicion she aroused in women—whatever its psychological basis—who wrote to the Gestapo at times anonymously, or sent friends or husbands to do "their patriotic duty" by denouncing her for her "suspicious behavior," her unorthodox hours, her being seen near military installations. Worse still, she was perceived as "flaunting" lesbian tendencies and as making no secret of her contempt for Nazism and its hatred for the French and for Jews. Accordingly, the Gestapo had read her mail and possibly set an informer on her as early as

---

[5] See Gellately, *Gestapo and German Society*.

1936. In December 1942, she evaded an order to appear at the Gestapo office: she had been friendly with three Jewish women. From
October 24, 1941, on, the Central Security Administration in Berlin (RSHA) had instructed its local branches to intern the "Jewish
part" of homoerotic friendships in a concentration camp "for deter-
rence."[6]

I do not know how much my mother knew of Ilse's involvement
with the Gestapo—she was singularly free of the standard prejudice
against homosexuality. She knew Mrs. Schwabacher, who had introduced her to Ilse Totzske, and trusted her, and she had been told
by Ilse that she had already taken two Jewish girls from Würzburg
across the border to Switzerland and safety. This may have created
an image of the professional *Emigrantenschlepperin* (literally, an
"emigrant dragger," one who led emigrants across the border) in
Swiss records and led Swiss customs officials to their harsh decision
to apply the letter of Swiss law, with fatal consequences.

Her Gestapo file details the mean behavior respectable postwar
Würzburg hates to be reminded of. It also documents Ilse's extraordinary—in fact, suicidal—courage in speaking her mind to all and
sundry. Rage and contempt must have paced her reckless urge for
self-destruction.

Ilse did not return from Ravensbrück. Emaciated and near death
at the end, Ruth did return from Auschwitz, where, with incredible
luck, she was chosen to play the recorder in the inmates' orchestra.
We spent many happy hours with her and her daughter after she
had emigrated to New York in the 1950s. She was one of the few
survivors with whom we shared the precious gift of not having to
explain.

Through Ruth, we met a teacher in a kindergarten maintained
by the Jüdische Gemeinde in Berlin Nord (North Berlin), Steffi
Guttmann, and her Christian lover. Steffi did not return from the
camp she was deported to.

Of other Jewish neighbors and friends I met during the first four
months of underground life I have no distinct recollection any
longer and no documents to consult, but I remember well that the
continued presence of Jews living their "normal" lives in their
apartments or houses was of immense importance to me, not only

---

[6] Ibid.

because we continued our relations "as if" all had been normal, but also for the encouragement and warmth that flowed between the mostly older men and women who had remained behind after their children had left for Palestine or overseas, and a person their children's age. On occasion, I would meet an acquaintance wearing a Jewish star in the street or on public transportation like a streetcar, and would acknowledge him or her through carefully disguised greetings, glances, smiles, eyebrows. On other occasions, I would be invited for supper and to stay the night by a physician, a friend of the Schloss family in Kladow. I had become friends with Dr. Steinitz earlier, after he treated me for a wound I had inflicted upon myself while cutting logs with an axe. He had married a Christian woman and lived a happy life in semiretirement in a house overgrown with ivy and fronting the river. His two children were about my age. Another Jewish acquaintance of Lotte's I kept contact with was Willy Meyer, who did forced labor with Lotte in an electronics company in North-Central Berlin (Kreuzberg). On one occasion, I visited his third-floor apartment in Leibnizstrasse 48, a large turn-of-the-century sequence of rooms arranged in a rectangular design centered on the "Berliner Zimmer," the large drawing and music room, open to both flights of rooms and large enough for the status-symbol piano. I had hoped that he would have a bed for the night for me, but instead of Willy Meyer two young men opened the door and guided me inside. I had walked into the Gestapo arresting Willy Meyer for helping fellow Jews acquire forged identity papers. Willy had apparently been informed upon, or somebody he had helped broke down under Gestapo interrogation. At the back of the apartment, in the kitchen, where they took me first, I faced about half a dozen dejected-looking men and women sitting around the table. But when they took me back to the Berliner Zimmer and began asking questions about my identity, I was able to distract their attention for a second by placing my briefcase on the piano, and racing through the front entrance. They had neglected to lock the door, and never caught up with me as I more vaulted than ran down the winding staircase into the blacked-out Leibnizstrasse, colliding with a tree and breaking my eyeglasses. I knew that my eyesight was poor at night. We lacked vitamin A in our diets.

Willy's friends, the Einzigs, who owned this apartment, went into a prepared hiding place when their time came. Genia Einzig followed us in crossing "illegally" into Switzerland, making use of the contacts Lotte's uncle had opened, but her husband had given himself away and was arrested on a train shortly before reaching the border. Genia wrote us later that Willy had been deported following his arrest that night. Neither man returned from deportation. She also told the Schönebergs and us in Lausanne after the war that a fellow-tenant in her house claimed to have heard shots in the stairwell that night.

Between October 26, 1942, and February 27–28 1943, the small band of Jews surviving until then rapidly diminished. Gestapo statistics list about 6,000 Jews forced into "Osttransporte." During the final days of February, in unannounced raids, the police tried to arrest all Jewish workers at the factories—for example, the Siemens Werke in Berlin-Spandau—where they had to work on war-related production. Estimates speak of as many as 5,000 persons who managed to flee during these two days and go into hiding. After Berlin fell in 1945, about 1,200 survivors from among them were found among those registering with U.S. Jewish aid agencies in Berlin (Jewish survivors received American food parcels there and were unlikely not to claim them). Several of my closer friends, including the mother of my good friend and fellow student Lutz Ehrlich, were deported to Auschwitz, the destination of all transports from Berlin until October 1944, when only few Jews still remained or were caught.

Thus, after four months of my being with my own, of being carried by feelings of connectedness and last resort, the community was finally wiped out. It was "finally," because my life since 1933 in Würzburg and in Berlin had been punctuated by forced separations from friends, from family, from community. Losing them by leaving town, by their emigration, and now by their deportations, the true nature of which I refused to accept and knew only in the abstract, had patterned my emotional reactions. I believe "something" had hardened, since being forced apart from friends and family had become embedded in daily life. That it did not become overwhelming but had merely turned into a slow-burning rage instead of mourning or dejection may well have been because I denied that the losses were final. This was not the *anésthésie affective* noted first by a French psychiatrist as a defense mechanism in concentration camp inmates.[7] Getting used to facing loss limited emotions; survival demanded all attention and adequate reactions. I coped with the need of being alert without letting signs of tensions penetrate the cover.

Paradoxical as it appears, living "underground" had won us new friends among Berliners. Both Lotte and I had Christian friends before October 1941. They were friends of friends, friends of children of Christian-Jewish couples, or friends Lotte had retained from a previous marriage to a Christian husband, the son of a Berlin Social Democratic politician with numerous connections to Jews. Weimar culture, after all, was only a decade away. Now isolated anti-Nazis across the political and cultural spectrum found each other everywhere. Links with Jews had become badges of rebellion. Our grocery store lady provided us with food she was not supposed to sell to Jews. A Polish woman, Lydia, working as a maid in a villa owned by the family of the architect Erich Mendelsohn who had emigrated to Palestine in 1933 sought out Lotte in December 1942 and gave us a "Polish Christmas goose," while she spoke of her hatred for "*Die Deutschen*." While I had to clean the streets of Steglitz and Lankwitz still wearing a star, some passersby left paper bags in my handcart containing cigarettes or fresh fruit. The Schloss family was served by the village tradespeople and provided with scarce items they were not supposed to sell them. Our janitor in Schlüterstrasse 53, Mr. Carlsson, and his wife, saved our lives that night. I did not dare to maintain some contacts after turning "illegal," but one sensed that the skepticism about the government and the war appeared to rise to the surface of faces, gestures, doggedness more frequently and among more people than before. In 1940, when Paris fell, the euphoria, feigned or real, was palpable. In the winter of 1942–43 the news was all grim, the signs that serious setbacks had occurred at Stalingrad, at El Alamein, with the Allied landing in North Africa, could not be suppressed. Also in 1943, the first serious damage was inflicted by air raids on Berlin, though it was still limited and local. Even if some of these observations were based on wishful thinking at the time, there was a shift in mood

---

[7] E. Minkowsky, "Observations on the Psychological and Psychopathological Consequences of War and Nazism," *OSE-Review*, 6 (1949), 3–10; Paul Friedman, "Some Aspects of Concentration Camp Psychology," *American Journal of Psychiatry*, 105 (1949), 601–605.

supported by rumors heard from the British Broadcasting Company (BBC). The obvious discomfort was apparent in official propaganda efforts to put a spin on the accumulating defeats. It was reflected in tortured verbiage used in the High Command's daily bulletins like "victorious retreat," "shortening the frontline." It helped our self-esteem. Being hunted and hiding was contrary to my self-image and my Würzburg disdain for the brown uniforms, and at times I resented it badly. Lotte neither understood nor shared such moods. She had grown up surrounded by the political controversies of late Weimar. My pride and spite had been reinforced by knowing more comprehensively about our intellectual and moral refinement and their barbarisms. Now I was on the run.

As long as we lived in Berlin, the food problem was solvable. There was rationing, of course; NS Welfare Offices were in charge of distributing the "Food Cards" (*Lebensmittelkarten*) and vouchers for buying shoes, textiles, cigarettes, or chocolate. To register for them, an identity card and a permanent address were needed. We had neither. Jews received much lower rations but as yet did not starve, and those who needed to eat less would share cards or food with big eaters or persons doing hard labor. The problem of being homeless was much more serious: the local police precinct had to register the personal and occupational data of any person moving into a room, apartment, or house within twenty-four hours of arrival. The registration sheet also asked about religion and nationality, and all data had to be documented once again by an identity card. Penalties for harboring unregistered visitors were severe. Jews hiding illegal ("submerged," *untergetauchte*) persons faced deportation without the trial non-Jews would face for an identical transgression, without the civil trial protections still provided by law.

For eight or nine months, Lotte and I found shelter hiding with Christian friends, most of whom we had not known previously. Nor had they all known one another. Some of them had talked with each other previously in person or by telephone, or had known and were able to trust each other with disclosing their rejection of the Nazi regime. With one near-fatal exception, they were also able to trust one another's discretion and rationality in case we would be discovered, and they had to rely on our not breaking under the pressures of interrogations that might include extreme physical mistreatment if the Gestapo believed that they would find pockets of resistance against the regime in this way.

The relatively few people who protected and sheltered Lotte belonged to the silent and inactive political opposition. They were socialists or from socialist families, Communists, left-wing intellectuals, or Quakers. I was saved by a more diverse group that was not politically homogeneous like Lotte's and did not know one another. They included the daughter of a Westphalian industrialist who was acquainted with Ilse Schöneberg; a journalist of Swedish nationality; a former Berlin trade-union leader; and a factory worker employed by the locomotive factory concern of Borsig Machine Works in Berlin-Tegel.

Lotte's "network" originated with a chance fellow tenant in her apartment in Charlottenburg, Ilse Kassel, a physician practicing in a proletarian Berlin district. (It distinguished a number of Jewish physicians in Berlin before 1933 that they had been motivated by their social conscience and political conviction to practice "social medicine" and pressure the government for health legislation through Social Democratic political and professional organizations.) In the mid-1930s, Ilse Kassel was arrested and tried for joining the relatively numerous local Communist cells in their information-and-propaganda efforts and drew a three-year prison term for "safe-keeping a Communist typewriter." After her prison-born daughter's and her release, she was hunted down, her medical degree routinely rescinded ("for high treason") and she was pushed into utter destitution. When her family in Israel failed to obtain an immigration certificate for her, she went "underground" but was denounced by an informer and committed suicide. Her seven-year-old daughter, Edith, died in the gas chambers in Auschwitz soon after.[8]

The night the Gestapo looked for Lotte, Dr. Kassel was luckily not in the apartment. Her sister, alerted, put me in touch with one of her political friends, Mr. Rieger. We met at a given street corner in the Hansaviertel, a residential quarter adjoining the central Berlin park, the Tiergarten, in October and November 1942, and talked a good deal before touching our situation. I remember him as the kind of white-haired trade-union official whose self-education

---

[8] Cf. Bettina Goldberg, *Schulgeschichte als Gesellschaftsgeschichte* (Berlin: Edition Hentrich, 1994), pp. 182–86. Reference courtesy Christoph Hamann, Berlin.

had not destroyed the warm humanity he projected. German Social Democracy and years of organizational work for labor had molded his outlook and made it easy to trust him. When we met the third time, he had secured a shelter for Lotte with Mr. and Mrs. Weiner, a small grocer in Berlin North, Niederschöneweide. The Weiners turned out to be linked with a group of Social Democrats and Communists who may or may not have formed a formal cell. It had been exceptional, for some time, for Communist activists to take a political interest in Jews. Since the mid-1930s, the Communist Party or the Communist International had ordered the separation of Jews from non-Jewish resistance groups, because joint organizations would have involved double risks. I have no information on whether this policy was continued into the war years, but the most spectacular act of defiance carried out in wartime Berlin by Zionist–left youths and Communists—setting fire to an anti-Soviet exhibition in the Lustgarten (a square adjoining the royal palace) was carried out by a group that included only one non Jew.

This liberated Lotte from the cellar we had come to feel uncomfortable about, but she soon began to worry about the safety of her new shelter. The tiny grocery store had a door to the living room where Lotte was hiding during the day, but the door was inlaid with a large oval glass window through which the owners could observe customers entering the store.

This, of course, worked both ways. When her hosts introduced her to a small barber salon whose owner, Mr. Kottke, seemed to talk too much and too freely about his expectations for a Russian conquest of Berlin, and about his political views, and showed her the guns he had hidden under his floorboards for *The Day*, it was Lotte's turn to feel an extra risk she refused to share.

By mid-December, I was able to follow up another connection that Mr. Rieger had suggested: I was encouraged to visit the home of a former Social Democratic leader and former member of the Prussian state parliament, Ernst Heilmann, whom the Nazis hated with a passion for his outspoken and fearless polemics against them.[9] He was arrested immediately in 1933, incarcerated, and years later tortured to death in the Sachsenhausen concentration

---

[9] Horst Möller, "Ernst Heilmann: Ein Sozialdemokrat in der Weimarer Republik," *Jahrbuch des Instituts für deutsche Geschichte*, 11 (1988), 261–94.

camp. (His strongly national policies during the Weimar years, on the right of the Social Democratic Party, would tarnish his reputation among post-1945 left intellectuals.) During my first visit to see his sister (-in-law?), I was made to wait until a visitor had left: a young French woman who, I learned later, was a contact with the French resistance. I was received in a slightly Victorian, plush setting, the Heilmanns' living room, the center table lighted by the prestige lamp of pre-1914, a tassle-fringed cloche in rosé. Once again, I met with a warm, almost serene woman in her best years, who understood very quickly what needed to be done. They were ready to help Lotte, and introduced me to Ernst Heilmann's son Peter, probably in his late teens at the time. He introduced Lotte to his girlfriend, Hella G., who had Quaker sympathies and belonged to the Berlin branch of the English Society of Friends. She worked in a second, part-time job as companion to an artillery general of World War I, Marcks, who lived alone in another of those cavernous Berlin apartments. He apparently suffered from agoraphobia, reinforced by his disgust about Nazi antisemitic policies: I was told that he had lived with a Jewish woman and that, some years earlier, while strolling along Olivaer Platz near his apartment, Bregenzer Strasse (16?), he had read on park benches inscriptions barring Jews from using them. Since then, he rarely left his room. His maid/cook was politically "*in Ordnung*" (correctly anti-Nazi), and Lotte would have a good-sized room across from the entrance. She would be camouflaged as a cousin of Hella's seeking refuge with her relative in Berlin after being bombed out in another town (Munich) by Allied air raids. Even in 1942–43 such displacements were common occurrences and thus a plausible cover. We met, and Hella liked Lotte enough to issue an invitation. This turned out to be an incredible stroke of luck: Hella, about my age, and Lotte related well enough for Hella to keep Lotte in the apartment until she left Germany, about four and a half months later. Regrettably and from early on, Hella turned against me and acted dangerously irrational.

I presumed at the time that, being of draft age and healthy-looking, I would have more difficulties than a woman in finding shelter, but to my surprise was proven wrong. I was able to leave August Sapandowski's cellar when Lotte left, to our everlasting luck: we beat being discovered by the police by about two weeks. For the next six and a half months, I stayed with five individuals or families, until I too succeeded in leaving Berlin.

My first host was Friedrich Strindberg,[10] whom I had met several times previously at the Schlosses in Kladow. We met in mid-October over lunch, and when he heard about what had happened to Louis and Johanna and to us, he invited me to stay with him "whenever I had no other place to go." Now I had to take him up on his generous offer. He and his Dutch (second) wife, an intellectual in her own right, lived in a small house surrounded by greenery and well protected from the curiosity of the neighbors. They put a pleasant small room at my disposal, and we soon were engaged in the favorite Berlin pastime of the war, analyzing information on the course of the war from the available sources. Strindberg's politics were determinedly anti-Nazi, and since he was accredited as a correspondent for Swedish papers, he was able to provide perspectives from sources not available to me or others in an outsider position. This was the time of German distress at El Alamein, the Allied landing in North Africa, Stalingrad. The United States had been in the war for almost twelve months already; it was a heady time of hope. Strindberg and I differed considerably in our political views: his tilted toward a then fashionable conservative view in Germany that the postwar world would be dominated by a vigorous Soviet Union and by the Communist system, while Western democracies had become decadent and too soft to wield power properly. It was a variant of Goebbels's propaganda line. When we met again in the 1950s in Munich, the United States had been sentenced to similar decadence in Strindberg's short course in world politics.

In the 1930s, Strindberg had reported for a popular Berlin picture weekly, *Berliner Illustrirte Zeitung*, presumably in addition to his foreign press assignments, from the Franco and fascist side of the Spanish Civil War. His view of English and French foreign policy was clearly based on their nonintervention policy and their inability to prevent German and Italian aggression in time. The Spanish Civil War also had involved him in a conflict with Arthur Koestler, an Hungarian-born English journalist and writer popular

---

[10] A late son of Frank Wedekind's and Frieda Strindberg's, Friedrich was born before the formal divorce proceedings between August and Frieda Strindberg had become finalized in law. Friedrich retained his mother's then name (Information Monica Strauss, New York, 1998).

at the time. Because of one of his reports on Spain, Strindberg was blamed by Koestler for his capture by Falange forces and his subsequent imprisonment and death sentence (he was released later following the intervention of the British government). Strindberg apparently was haunted by the story, insisted on being blameless for the incident, and urged me repeatedly to "tell the Jewish world" that he had "saved a rabbi from death in Poland."

He told the story before I was able to. In 1945, Bonnier, in Stockholm, published a novel Strindberg had written under a pseudonym about a Jewish couple living in hiding from deportation in wartime Berlin.[11] When we met up with Strindberg again after the war, in 1958, he mentioned his book but was more than reluctant to let me have a copy of the German original, from which the Swedish translation had been made. He was unusually uncomfortable and apologetic about it, and hinted at his fear of a lawsuit. I bought the soon-out-of-print book on Madison Avenue from Bonnier, New York, subsequently, and I asked a friend to read it for me. On the blurb, the hero was identified as Herbert Staus (*sic*), the heroine as Lotte; it was an adventure story about a self-sacrificing hero and a self-centered and scheming woman, and bore no relationship to the human realities the thinly disguised pseudonyms suggested to us.

I fondly remember Friedrich and Utje Strindberg as the warm friends they became during my stay with them, as my first Western European–style intellectuals, however confused Strindberg's populist-authoritarian political philosophy may have been. They took the risk of sheltering me, although Friedrich was a somewhat nervous and fearful person, and must have suffered because of my presence. He had a touch of the misogyny and high-strung sexuality that August Strindberg transformed so memorably into world literature. In fact, I became aware that Utje and he lived in an undercurrent of tension that, I learned later, ended in their divorce. It is possible that my living with them distracted them at least temporarily from whatever vexed their marriage. We had agreed from the beginning that my idea of not staying too long at one place and not endangering my hosts was the right one. By late February, I had found another shelter for four weeks after staying for a few nights with Dr. Steinitz and with Wanda Dombrowski. Still, the Strind-

---

[11] Fredrik Uhlson, *Under Jorden i Berlin* (Stockholm: Bonnier, 1945).

bergs received me once more when I had no place to sleep and had run away from that Gestapo trap into homelessness, and at the end of my stay in Berlin.

I felt very well at the Strindbergs'; our continued political debates and our amateur analysis of the course of the war and of Germany's impending defeat reinforced the perspectives of my Hochschule years and kept me from despairing about my future. But Strindberg was also the first person I had met who told me with the insider's authority that the Nazis systematically murdered not only Polish and Russian Jews but also all Jews, and that the deportees from Berlin and from the rest of Europe were slaughtered. The version I had heard and believed up to that point was that they would force us into labor camps of such severity that it would amount to a Darwinian selection. (It was part, but only part, of the genocide agreed upon at the Wannsee Conference Heydrich had called in January 1942 to "legitimize" the extermination of European Jewry already in progress at that time.) Strindberg had heard concrete facts at a meeting of foreign correspondents. Lotte was present on this occasion. We had met after dark at the Berlin Zoo station to take the streetcar–bus connection that would get us to Kladow where we were invited for supper with Utje and him. Strindberg entered the bus at a later point, the transfer from the elevated train, but we stayed separate from each other and walked different ways to his house. It was Lotte's old home district, she had to avoid being seen and recognized, and we had no identification papers. When Strindberg detailed the news after supper, I was unable to believe it, although over the radio I had heard Hitler's speech of January 30, 1939, which included his first public threat to "exterminate the Jewish race in Europe" ("Vernichtung der jüdischen Rasse in Europa") if another World War would erupt, and I had read some of the subsequent threats repeating his first one. Lotte said that she believed Strindberg's story. Unlike Lotte, I had not been able to "accept" what I had heard: I was inured to shrill Nazi propaganda, to Hitler's lies, to the outrageous idiocies of their race theories. I had learned to not let it get to me, to dig in, not to "hear" it. It was just too unbelievable and fantastic that innocent people would be "exterminated" by those they passed on the streets every day and experienced as "average" or "normal" in their behavior. I do not recall when the ambiguities of "knowing" gave way, piece by piece, to panic and defeat in "accepting" what would be forever unacceptable, the final loss of the people to whom our dead belonged, and to find a way of mourning adequate to their unlived lives. I also remember that with the clarity of angst I heard over Strindberg's radio the infamous speech Goebbels delivered on February 18, 1943, at the Berlin Sportpalast to a ferally raucous crowd of political functionaries of the Nazi Party. We were stunned into silence by his hysterical calls for total war and total ruthlessness, and by the equally hysterical responses of his audience. It was his version of blood, sweat, and tears, and we could console ourselves only by inferring from his response the depth of the crisis the Wehrmacht was facing. Strindberg's strategic analysis at the time was of great help, but I stiffened at the thought of what "total war" would mean in new difficulties for us.

From late February on, I was sheltered by a woman who offered me a place through Christl Simon, an acquaintance of Ilse Schöneberg's and Lotte's from Westphalia. Christl had been close to a Jewish woman doctor, Dr. Friedenthal, for some time and had taken her into her apartment when she was to be deported. Christl had sturdy anti-Nazi attitudes and equally sturdy British sympathies and liberal opinions. I believed, or was told at the time, that she was linked with British Intelligence, and found it plausible, but, of course, never asked her if it was true. She did have substantial international connections and was our link to Jean Friedrich, whose mail pouch connected us with the Schönebergs. They had put Christl in touch with Friedrich. Christl and Dr. Friedenthal survived the war in Berlin. We met quite some time later at Christl's residence in Rheda, Westphalia, almost a living-happily-ever-after meeting of veterans of the same battles. Christl came to a lecture I gave before a Jewish-Christian Association in Bielefeld, a Westphalian town, in the mid-1980s.

My new host, Felicia Pauselius, lived in a tastefully furnished, book-lined apartment in late Victorian style of some size close to the Berlin airport, Tempelhof (Schulenburgring 5). Since she worked (as I learned later) as an executive for Lufthansa, or as an assistant to a Berlin dentist, Dr. Mehlhose, I had the apartment to myself during the day. But even walking around the apartment in socks, she feared, would create suspicions in her downstairs neighbors—the old parquet floor did creak—and the fear allowed me, to my entire satisfaction, to pick and choose from her library, lie on a couch, and read. The book I remember best was a two-volume English paperback, Aldous Huxley's *Point Counter Point*, a welcome change of pace in human relations: Huxley's were fictional. Also serious was that the apartment was on or near the top floor of a large apartment house whose tenants had to descend to the air-raid cellar I could not use, having no identity papers, once the alarm was sounded. In February 1943, the night raids flown by the Royal Air Force with a few airplanes still inflicted only limited material damage and their nuisance and, I presume, political, effects seemed still small to me, as far as I was able to notice. But each raid called forth a mighty racket of the AA guns ringing the airport, and, on occasion, the upper floors seemed to sway from the air pressure of guns or bombs. Schulenburgring 5 would not be safe if the air raids increased with time.

Mrs. Pauselius was most kind and matter-of-fact. Relations stayed on a formal plane; we did not venture into personal matters. It was only in the late 1980s that a grand-nephew contacted me in New York when he had heard me mention the name Felicitas Pauselius (wrong first name) in an interview on German radio or TV. He wrote that she had led an independent professional life after her marriage had dissolved, without contact with her husband and his family. She survived the war.

The only person I ever met in her house was a middle-aged infantry officer who served as a dentist with the German army in Finland and was visiting her. I presume he knew about my circumstances when we entered into a long conversation about the war. He voiced Protestant conservative cultural and political dissent about Nazism, but when I insisted that the war was already lost and that it was a Christian officer's duty to remove the Nazi Party from power, he said somewhat wearily that they had sworn an oath to the Führer, and one does not break one's oath. I did not pursue this any further then, because I felt that it made him uncomfortable, but I presumed that Mrs. Pauselius would not have introduced me to him if he was an enemy. Still, it all fitted neatly into what I learned after the war about the moral agonies of conservative nationalists about this and other conflicts of loyalty, and it reminded me of the (staff) officer who had spoken on our behalf to our Nazi street-cleaner foreman in Steglitz about a year earlier.

After the month Mrs. Pauselius had agreed to shelter me was over, I found my last and longest asylum with a worker in the Borsig Machine Works, which had produced locomotives in peacetime. I owed his address to Mr. Rieger, whom I could reach through the Heilmanns. My host, Ossi—I never learned his family name— occupied a one-room apartment on the ground floor, near his factory in the Tegel district of Berlin-North, that included a kitchen and a bathroom sink plus water closet. The room was filled with an enormous double bed Ossi shared with me. While I stayed with him, his work schedule fitted well with my needs. He worked the early shift of the three-shift day, and left the room long before daybreak. Since it had a separate entrance, out of sight of the janitor, in a huge low-income apartment house built around several courts, accessible through doorways on the ground floor, Ossi saw no problem in my coming and going without fear of being informed on. Ossi returned home in the afternoon and took his nap. In the evening, we ate a cold supper, or cooked the kind of meals men would cook without a woman's help. It was the most perfect arrangement for me, and, I believe, it did not upset his routine. It was understood that I would not be his guest but his tenant, and I provided for my breakfast, whatever food we needed for supper, and the rent. We never had to talk about it after I got him to hint at what he would consider equitable in terms of his perception of my relationship to him, and his to me.

Ossi had a distinct dislike of the Nazi regime and of the Labor Front and its functionaries who, he said, extorted money from workers for all sorts of distant causes instead of representing their interests. He also disliked their giving themselves airs and their "strutting around like peacocks" (his words). His was clearly a labor union tradition, not a political party ideology. It had not muted his sensitivity to what people would do to each other if left unchecked—a reflection of the intrinsically moral basis of German Social Democracy and its humanization of the class struggle. He included Jews—he had grown up with some—in his circle of sympathy, but the compassion he showed had no condescension about it, because he was able to relate what they suffered to his own deprivations, and he understood the years of poverty and occasional hunger I had been through as a student. I don't believe there was another house in Tegel at that time where a Jew and a socialist were debating the kibbutz in Palestine. To be sure, Ossi was no revolutionary and would never have taken action to resist the regime. The Nazis, recalling workers' unrest in World War I, paid top salaries to skilled workers in armament factories and made them into a labor elite. As Ossi showed, all they bought in this manner was limited acquiescence in the status quo as long as it served the workers' interest. Ossi's superb realism had not destroyed his loyalty to the democratic rules he was educated by before Hitler, or his sensitivity for the utter brutality of Nazi persecution.

The freedom of movement I thus had gained more fully than before was essential for the success of our plan to cross the Swiss border. After the care I had taken at Schulenburgring 5, I was now free to travel by public conveyance to Berlin West. As I sauntered forth from Ossi's place in the morning and took the elevated railway or the subway to Charlottenburg, the day was usually filled with numerous tasks that had to be taken care of. Until Lotte left Hella G.'s apartment, I would place a telephone call from a public phone booth and talk in hints about what I had to do and where we might meet. Everybody was convinced at the time that telephones were tapped, probably a useful but exaggerated precaution for those among the few million Berliners who had not come to the attention of the Gestapo. *Wie üblich* ("the usual") meant our date in the zoo. To buy food, ration cards were needed. If you were not given such cards by acquaintances or friends or by former maids of Jewish households, you met friends who had access to people who obtained them on the black market, sometimes from officials in card distribution centers out for the easy *Mark*. In addition, large families of modest means found that they could not use all the cards they were entitled to and would sell them to acquaintances. The non-Jewish household help of Jewish families, mostly of advanced age and long service records, were among the unsung heroines of this period, as they assisted the former *"Herrschaft"* they had worked for when times were good beyond any call of duty and certainly without monetary interests, and at great risk. One example was Emma—her real name—who carried the funds my colleague Lutz Ehrlich needed under layers of petticoats and (I presume) underwear, and produced the required amount by retiring into a corner and hitching up the layers. Hella G. had a stable and reliable household aide,

Alma, in General Marcks's apartment. She was also well paid by Lotte. There were others.

To keep contact and be informed of contacts for what was needed at the moment, one would meet with some of the men (no women!) who had gone underground as we had. One was Lutz Ehrlich. We had been friends at the Hochschule and somewhat complementary if quite diverse persons. In 1942, probably before we had to "dive below," Lotte and I were involved with him in saving his mother's life by helping her fake a suicide when the helpers would come to fetch her for the collection point, Levetzowstrasse, in whose vicinity she lived. The (carefully measured) overdose of sleeping pills she took was pumped out of her stomach in the Jewish hospital in Iranische Strasse to which she was taken after the Gestapo had left. After considerable pain she survived this risky procedure and returned home safe, alas only for the moment. On February 27–28 1943, she was arrested at her forced labor job and brought directly to the collection point for deportation. I believe that she had stayed unmolested until then because the lines of communication among the possibly collaborationist Jewish hospital administration, the police precinct, and the Gestapo were not geared to this contingency, fake suicide. Of my former teachers, only Ernst Grumach was still at our old address, and he was properly reluctant to be with me for any length of time. Visiting him in his apartment, on the ground floor of the same back-courts house I had lived in, would have been suicidal. At one of the few occasions we agreed to meet for a few minutes at a square or a street address, he turned some documents over to me which he had taken from my room. They included my high-school-leaving certificate of June 1942 and my certificate for the intermediate examination of the Hochschule of 1940. Jean Friedrich, to whom I took them, did me the inestimable good turn of sending them to Switzerland. Without them, even the very understanding dean of the Philosophische Fakultät I, the widely known and respected literary scholar Fritz Strich, would have had great difficulties admitting me to "immatriculation" at Bern University five months after I had left Ossi's room. Strich himself had left his academic position in Germany for Bern in 1929.[12] For rea-

---

[12] One of the grand old ladies of the intellectual life of Weimar Germany, Ricarda Huch, asked a friend in 1928–29 to support Fritz Strich's efforts to leave the antisemitic atmosphere among literary scholars (*Germanisten*) in German behind,

sons of security, however, contacts with Jean Friedrich at his Red Cross office were kept to a minimum. His help was essential to our plans for Switzerland, since he mailed our letters outside censorship channels. He also sent photographs of Lotte to Lausanne to be given to the German border contact who would expect her at the agreed border railroad terminal.

As long as I did not have a foolproof identity card, most of my time was spent in seeking contacts to a source, but without success. I found a connection to a graphic artist, I believe through Lutz Ehrlich, who would produce authentic-looking stamps on passports or identity cards. But until Lotte's more or less accidental connection with State Attorney (Staatsanwalt) Rudolf Caspary quite fortuitously helped solve this basic problem, my efforts had resulted only in a business letter identifying me as company-employed. It would not have stood up to police inspection.

Lotte, by a lucky coincidence, had less difficulty in finding an identity paper than I: 1943 was a moment of Third Reich history when they tried to make up their huge losses at Stalingrad and the Russian front by a maximum mobilization of manpower; until then, it had been less thorough than, for example, the Allied manpower mobilization or the recruitment of women for war work in England. I expected that now it would increase manhunts through identity checks and multiply the danger of being discovered. Hella G., who was privy to our plans, offered Lotte a (just expired) passport of hers whose personal data fitted Lotte and whose passport photo (in black and white) could be mistaken for a picture of Lotte. The passport could be reported as lost which would minimize the risk of being found out. After we had met, Hella, for reasons of very personal emotions, had tried to separate Lotte and me. She claimed that I looked exactly like a boyfriend who had just given her short shrift in a brutal and hurtful manner. It may have been a cover-up for acknowledged or unacknowledged emotional difficulties, a likely condition in view of Hella's behavior toward Lotte. When

---

because he felt held back in his academic career by their prejudice. A two-term lecture on "Goethe and World Literature" he delivered at Bern University probably in 1944–45 remains in my memory as one of the most moving—"European"—experiences of my years at Bern University, as he re-created an intellectual universe German culture appeared to have lost forever. See Ricarda Huch, *Briefe an die Freunde*, ed. Maria Bauer (Tübingen: Rainer Wunderlich, 1955), p. 122.

Lotte had offered to leave the apartment, she threatened what was ugliest in our situation, to inform the Gestapo if she did leave. Lotte stayed, and during her last few weeks in Berlin, I did not enter her apartment, and we had to meet without Hella's knowledge. But, after she gave her passport to Lotte, and Lotte was about to leave soon after, she called "Klix," a friend of Lotte's who had been connected with Intelligence, to inform on me and have me stopped by the Gestapo before I would reach the border. He, of course, refused to do her bidding. He told me of her request before I left in June 1943.

Hella G. and Peter Heilmann later married and settled in the German Democratic Republic, the part of divided Germany the Communists controlled until 1990. She died of cancer at a relatively early age. Peter returned to West Berlin after allegedly serving time for a drug conviction in East Germany, and functioned as a study director for the Protestant Evangelische Akademie (Goethe Strasse), a politically progressive adult education center. After the fall of the Berlin Wall, he was identified in the archives of the East German Staatspolizei (Stasi) as one of their informers in West Berlin. In April 1999, the Kammergericht Berlin found Peter Heilmann and his (second) wife guilty of many years of informing on West German public figures and professionals for the Stasi, and sentenced them to probation of 20 months and 12 months, respectively. Peter was 76 years old at the time.

The incident brought about by Hella G.'s irrationality touches upon the relationship of host and hunted on a plane deeper than the story of flight and survival. Taking an additional person into your household and your daily life would change an accustomed web of relations between men and women under even most peaceful and stress-free circumstances. In our situation, hosts were put under extreme tensions and exposed to extreme risks. They delivered their own safety, even their freedom and their lives, themselves, to persons who might at any time be stopped at a police checkpoint or by a military police patrol and betray them under the pressures of interrogation or torture. The hunted entered into webs of relationships their hosts had been part of before taking them in, and into the history of the hosts' own emotional states. Not every host would remain detached enough not to expect behavior from the hunted that would gratify his or her personal expectations or needs. Most persons taking fugitives in did not know them intimately or in person before—most people who knew them in good times found the risk too great in bad ones. Fugitives were practically coming from an emotional nowhere, and lived in a social vacuum in a strange household (unless they were with friends); they had none of the traditional ways of showing gratitude and understanding for what their hosts were risking—except a show of maximum normality, the brave front, the measured good cheer, understanding what was needed at the moment and giving it as much as they understood how and were able to. In this isolated cocoon of relations between host and hunted, you felt at times the presence of sexual tensions or frustrations structuring expectations, a variety of emotions intensified by the social void surrounding the hunted. And you made sure that you withdrew into whatever isolation you could find not to "get on your host's nerves," not to "outstay your welcome," not to "loaf around the house" while your host worked and left his wife behind with you, and to observe the thin line made up of respect, friendship, concern, distance, caution, noncommitment, loyalty to your emotional ties.

"Research" into our hosts' motives for helping us hunted Jews, from this point of view, becomes a lovable but oversimplified exercise in the researcher's favorite designs of the moment. Each relationship rested on a personal history and formed its articulation, an intense hidden history of relationships and emotions, morality and political convictions, fears, and hopes.

Yet, my memory has stored many situations that exclude the charity the survivor owes to himself. Many men and many women played a fateful role in destroying the lives of the hunted. Given Nazi practices, my father might have survived the war protected by mother or, at worst, might have died on a cot in Theresienstadt. His agony and murder were "caused" by a web of denouncers, Party hacks, Gestapo men acting in consort with them, a vicious woman driving her husband to use his Party connections to have an alleged smart on her "Aryan womanhood" revenged. Louis and Johanna Schloss were deported to remove witnesses to a *Ritterkreuzträger*'s robbery of Jewish property. Our successors in Sapandowski's cellar lost their lives because somebody saw "something suspicious" and informed on them. Ilse Totzke was spied and informed upon by her respectable neighbors disturbed in their sense of propriety by her behavior and attitudes. The American writer Peter Wyden unfolded the horror story of a Jewish woman ("Stella," 1992[13]) coerced by the Gestapo Berlin to catch Jews hidden in the Berlin underground and to deliver them to the police, like a dogcatcher taking stray dogs into the pound. (We had never heard of her before Wyden visited my Berlin university office in the mid-1980s in search of information: her victims centered in the Jewish high school she had attended in the 1930s, and she began after we left.) Upright conservative German business people in Berlin, believing in *Endsieg* (ultimate victory) and accepting the *Endlösung* (Final Solution) as pre-ordained, advised Lotte to turn herself in forthwith, because it would also be prohibitively expensive for their client, Lotte's uncle in Lausanne, to help us to stay alive underground in wartime Berlin. You were aware that now, during the war years more than ever before, informing and spying became patriotic duties done for the Führer and his imagined approval of your loyalty. Was it ultimately the need to "put everything in order" that produced all that vindictiveness?

Yet, my honor roll includes also numerous bystanders whom postwar German historiography in search of a usable past has relegated to the "non-conspirators." They were authentic counterweights to the bad taste legions of informers and self-righteous fellow travelers leave in your mouth. Carlsson saw us hide that night and delayed opening the door to the Gestapo pounding away at it. Mrs. Voigt brought toothbrush, toiletries, and underwear for Lotte. The Christian maids of Jewish households did not desert their employers when they had become homeless. The Polish maid in Kladow (Lydia), Toni Boronow, Wanda Dombrowski, and Steffi Guttmann helped with food and occasional shelter. The anonymous passersby who left brown bags in my streetcleaner's wheelbarrow. The lady in the grocery store who kept supplying us with food she was not supposed to let us have. "Klix" who tried to balance his conservative sense of decency against the horrors of the regime he was serving. "Putto" whose intentions to help were frustrated by the institutional rigors of a Protestant pastor opting for the letter of the law against man in need. Then there was the bookdealer's saleslady—Irma Schöller (?) in Buchholz's Leipziger Strasse store—

---

[13] Peter Wyden, *Stella* (New York: Simon & Schuster, 1992).

who invited you to the back and sat you down to read at your heart's desire. Or the men or women whose names and stations in life I have forgotten who went to a concert with me, gave me a ticket to a Bach concert, a Lieder recital?

But then, where were the German priests and pastors? The Quakers and the Swedish church ran underground railways for Jewish persecutees. German churches preserved their structures intact: at best they planned for the post-Hitler future, at worst they prayed for Hitler's victory. Meanwhile, some gave separate pews in church to Jews who had converted to their faith when they became distinct through the yellow star inscribed *Jude*. I met no university teacher, no social worker, no psychoanalyst, no lawyer. I know of no German doctor involved in rescuing Jews.

It meant much to me that in the depth of my flight I heard a soloist singing the Jesus score sing the last seven words of Christ in a performance of Bach's *Passion According to St. Matthew* in the very same Potsdam church where, ten years earlier, conservative German Protestants had solemnly legitimized Hitler as their savior. Incongruously standing out from the anti-Jewish invective of the passion, these Aramaic words measured my being forlorn and severed from whence I had traveled, yet at home in the deep humanity the music projected as Bach transcended this time and space.

This is my honor roll:

Alma, Berlin
Ruth Basinski, Berlin-Auschwitz, returned 1945
Otto Bernstein, Jenny Schaffner-Bernstein, Berlin-Auschwitz
Walter Blank, Susi Blank née Hammerstein, Berlin-Auschwitz
Ernst and Hedi Bildesheim, Berlin-Auschwitz
Brütsch-Mäder, Cantonal Police, Schaffhausen, Switzerland
Mr. and Mrs. Carlsson, Berlin
Rudolf Caspary, Berlin-Auschwitz
Wanda Dombrowski, Berlin
Ernst-Ludwig Ehrlich, Berlin
Emma, Berlin
Paul and Hedwig Eppstein, Berlin-Theresienstadt,
  "Auschwitz"
Mrs. Friedeberg, Berlin
Jean Friedrich, La-Chaux-de-Fonds (Switzerland)—Berlin

Hella G., Berlin
Steffi Guttmann, Berlin
Peter Heilmann and family of Ernst Heilmann, Berlin
Ursula von Hielmcrone, Berlin-Munich
Josef and Mrs. Höfler, Gottmadingen
Willy Jankowiak, Berlin
Ilse Kassel, Berlin (suicide)
Werner Keller, Berlin
"Klix" (Dr. Kurt Klietmann), Berlin
"Putto" (Metalotte von Klöten, Mrs. Margaret), Berlin
Mr. and Mrs. Kottke, Berlin
Lydia, Berlin-Kladow
Ernst (?) Maass, Berlin-Dahlem
General Marcks, Berlin
Louise Meier, Berlin
Willy Meyer, Berlin-Auschwitz (?)
"Ossi," Berlin-Tegel
Felicia Pauselius, Berlin
Mr. Rieger, Berlin
August Sapandowski, Berlin-Bergen Belsen, and Else (Elsbeth
    Orgler), Berlin-Auschwitz
Ludwig and Ilse Schöneberg, Berlin-Lausanne
Dr. Schürholz, Wangen (Lake Constance)
Christl Simon, Rheda-Berlin
Dr. Steinitz and family, Berlin-Kladow
Friedrich and Utje Strindberg, Berlin-Kladow
Ilse Sonja Totzke, Würzburg-Ravensbrück
Hermann and Gertrud Voigt, Wittenberg-Berlin
Mr. and Mrs. Weiner, Berlin-Niederschönhausen
Nathan Wolff, Stein am Rhein-Wangen.

9

Escape to Switzerland: June 12–13, 1943

MERCIFULLY, we did not have to test our resolve to prevail against the inferno of collapsing wartime Berlin. On May 1, 1943, Lotte succeeded in crossing the border to Switzerland; six weeks later I followed her, accompanied by Lutz Ehrlich.

Our escape on October 24, 1942, had been an unpremeditated act of self-assertion against the physical confinement of being arrested and imprisoned. Whatever mental testing we had done of such a possibility, even the one attempt I had made to get an uncle of mine—an amateur mountaineer—to show me the way across the Austrian Alps was more desperate pastime than serious resolve.

Yet, soon after we had vanished from civil life we were able to exchange messages and letters with Lausanne through Jean Friedrich that would not be read by the mail censor. In fall–winter 1942–43, Swiss newspapers were openly reporting on the mass murder of Jews in German-occupied Eastern Europe. From these published and from unpublished sources, some of which I was shown later in Lausanne, the Schönebergs understood the extreme danger of the Jewish situation in Germany.

Shortly after we were underground, Lotte wrote a detailed letter to Ludwig, on Jean Friedrich's insistence, reporting on Johanna and Louis and our own story. They mentioned later that it had turned their concern for the catastrophe inflicted on European Jews into intense emotional involvement with family and regrets over lost opportunities to save sister and brother-in-law. Jean Friedrich's analysis of what crimes would be perpetrated if the war were to be lost also impressed them deeply, coming as it did from a Swiss professional they respected. It was our impression that he was explaining to the Schönebergs in peaceful Lausanne what it meant to be homeless and hunted in Nazi Berlin, and how precarious it was to walk the streets without identification papers in the worsening hysteria produced by Nazi propaganda. While we were in hiding, the military defeats of El Alamein and Stalingrad, even though papered over by propaganda minister Goebbels, had affected many families and killed many young people. Many knew that they had brought this upon themselves and there was no way back, even if police terror would not have kept all such doubts below the surface.

Out of all this came a reversal of Ludwig's Berlin manager's lack of empathy; she returned to her customary correctness. We would not have to live on our own meager resources. Ludwig and Ilse must have contacted numerous acquaintances in their circle for practical advice. The result was a plan for Lotte to cross the "green frontier" between Germany and Switzerland. For me, they proposed swimming the Rhine River near Stein-am-Rhein, where it flowed rapidly but was not too broad as yet. They had been told that I was good at swimming and diving.

For us, trying to reach Switzerland narrowed the focus on getting to the border undetected, a long train ride from Berlin; on finding secure identity papers to pass through Gestapo and military police controls; and on connecting with German natives in the border region whose knowledge of the local custom and security systems could not be replaced by courage and bravura or good disguise. When Ilse and Ruth had given not a single sign of life since they had left in February, we were sure that they had been trapped by a Nazi net at the border or on their way down south. We would work in Berlin to prepare what was needed for the trip. But we would fail as Ilse and Ruth did unless we got precise instructions and were guided on the spot.

Ludwig and his Swiss friends appeared to agree that the best area for us to attempt the deed lay in the canton of Schaffhausen (of Rhine-Fall fame), because part of its territory jutted across the Rhine and formed enclaves whose borders zigzagged for no apparent reason through fields and wooded areas. They would be hard to seal off completely. These borders guarded jealously defended remnants of ancient territorial divisions or jurisdictions bulging northward beyond the Rhine in irregular formations. Ludwig and Ilse would work on finding reliable people nearby who, for whatever motives, would be willing to take us through.

It bespeaks the isolation of our near-ghetto life in Berlin that we were unaware of what happened to Jewish émigrés from Germany after they had crossed the border and became "immigrants," "refugees," abroad. We knew the "emigration emergency" as personal problems of finding a country that would take Jews in. I was knowledgeable about Great Britain's mandate policies and their immigration rules and restrictions; we thought we knew something about affidavits and quotas in U.S. immigration law. I also was aware of the cynical jockeying among immigration countries at the Evian conference which had been reported in the German-Jewish press in the summer of 1938, shortly before the Nazis ended its publication in November. But I had been unprepared for the problems we would face being accepted—tolerated—in Switzerland as escapees from a murderous threat. In fact, I had given it surprisingly little thought, so pervasive were the images and associations the name *Swiss* and the symbols connected with them would call up in my mind, from the chocolate in those violet Suchard wrappers father would bring home from his trips, to the Red Cross and the League of Nations, democracy, and William Tell. It was nothing to be proud of in political sophistication, but, then, my preoccupations had been rather demanding and isolating for many years: Jerusalem, Athens, Alexandria. We could not anticipate and overcome the dangers that would make us particles of the "refugee problem," the *"Emigrantenproblem,"* the "migration emergency" that had preoccupied social policies in major countries since 1933 and restrained me when I was unable to pierce the fences around Palestine and the United States.

Ludwig and Ilse knew about the difficulty of gaining admittance to Switzerland as Jewish refugees after residing in Lausanne for half a decade, not so much for their own persons as for their numerous acquaintances and friends. Ilse had worked effectively through her (Lutheran) church and as a one-woman committee in aid of refugees. They noted antisemitic stereotypes and hostilities just below the surface. Residence permits would have to be granted by a canton as well as by the federal government in Bern, and by the local community in which the petitioners would wish to live. As elsewhere, public attitudes and government policies toward admitting foreigners to the country were the outcome of balances of forces organized in social, political, bureaucratic, economic, or religious groups. Their political contests resulted in restrictive government policies on immigration.[1]

At about the time we slid into hiding in Berlin, these policies reached a peak among Swiss conservative bureaucrats and politicians controlling executive decisions on refugees. After April 1942, when the Nazi occupiers began to round up Jews in Belgium, Holland, Vichy and occupied France, and send them to their death, pressure had been building at Swiss borders in the Jura, the cantons Geneva, Vaud, and Valais, as refugees trekked across Western Europe and through France to reach the Swiss haven. Previously, Swiss policies were probably somewhat parallel to those of other Western nations and the United States in balancing their economic protectionism and social conservatism with pressures from liberal or left-wing constituencies for humane immigration provisions. Now, against their humanitarian ideals, the government tried to close the border. Between August and December 1942, the authorities granted asylum to 8,146 men, women, and children who had entered without visas, doubling the number of such refugees residing in the country. Government documents published after 1945 imply ugly thought on top of ugly bureaucratic prejudice and the petty fear of strangers. Previously, the tourist haven had no difficulty in accommodating large numbers of paying guests. Now they felt that the "boat was full," and strangers would dilute the national substance (*Überfremdung*). In August–September 1942, Swiss police registers listed 2,589 persons returned to Nazi-occupied territory, primarily France. In 1943, their numbers rose by an additional 3,344 persons, compared to 8,054 persons granted temporary asy-

---

[1] For an impeccably balanced government-commissioned report on Swiss *Asylpolitik*, see Carl Ludwig, *Die Flüchtlingspolitik der Schweiz seit 1933 bis zur Gegenwart (1957): Beilage zum Bericht des Bundesrates an die Bundesversammlung über die Flüchtlingspolitik der Schweiz seit 1933 bis zur Gegenwart (zu 7347)* (Bern: Verlag Herbert Lang, 1966).

A recent critical-historical analysis based on a wide range of relevant sources, including Jewish archives is Jacques Picard's *Die Schweiz und die Juden, 1933–1945: Schweizerischer Antisemitismus, jüdische Abwehr, und internationale Migration—und Flüchtlingspolitik*, 2nd ed. (Zurich: Chronos Verlag, 1994). The first political-historical overview prepared for the Swiss public by the "Federal Commission Against Racism," established in 1997, represents an up-to-date scholarly response to public opinion shifts in reaction in international criticisms of Swiss wartime policies on Jews and escapees from Nazi Germany. My recollections of my years in Switzerland, 1943–46 (in preparation), expect to touch on these issues.

Prof. Ernst Grumach and his
daughter, Irene Shiroun

Ernst Ludwig ("Lutz") Ehrlich,
who fled with the author to
Switzerland in 1943

Walter Reis (left), the author's friend from Würzburg, and the author

Institute (Hochschule) for Advanced Jewish Studies, Artilleriestrasse 14, Berlin. Courtesy of the Leo Baeck Institute, New York.

Dr. Ismar Elbogen's seminar at the Institute (Hochschule) for Advanced
Jewish Studies, Berlin, 1930s. Courtesy of the Leo Baeck Institute, New
York.

Faculty and students in the library of the Institute (Hochschule) for
Advanced Jewish Studies, Berlin, late 1930s. Dr. Leo Baeck is seated at
right. Courtesy of the Leo Baeck Institute, New York.

Rabbi Leo Baeck in conversation with former Hochschule students Ernst-Ludwig Ehrlich, the author, and Rabbi Eugen Maessinger in London, July 1946.

The first post-war meeting of the International Conference of Christians and Jews, Oxford, England, August 1946. From left: the author; Rabbi Chayim Zwi Taubes; Ernst-Ludwig Ehrlich; a Swiss delegate; Dr. Leo Baeck. Courtesy of the Leo Baeck Institute, New York.

August Sapandowski

Ilse Totzke

Ilse Schöneberg

Ludwig Schöneberg

Jean Friedrich

Felicitas Pauselius and son, 1943

Ulla von Hielmcrone, who helped
smuggle the author's papers to
Switzerland

Josef Höfler

Ref.II I.

Nürnberg 1, Abholfach 210
Fernsprecher Nr. 2951
Postscheckkonto Nürnberg Nr. 35696

Nürnberg, den 6.März 1942.

An die

Karteikarte: vorhanden
nicht vorhanden

Geheime Staatspolizei
Staatspolizeistelle Nürnberg-Fürth
Aussendienststelle Würzburg

in W ü r z b u r g .

==========================

Betrifft: Schutzhaft des Juden S t r a u s s Benno.Israel,
geb.20.7.76 in Heilbronn.

Vorgang: Dort.Schreiben vom 27.9.41 II D - 3711/40.

Da eine Auswanderung des Juden S t r a u s s im Hinblick
auf die allgemeine Auswanderungssperre in absehbarer Zeit nicht
in Betracht kommt, hat das Reichssicherheitshauptamt Berlin
mit FS-Erlass vom 5.3.42 IV C 2 H.Nr.St.1261 den Schutzhaftbefehl vom 1.11.38 gegen S t r a u s s wieder in Kraft gesetzt
und die neuerliche Festnahme des St. und seine Überstellung in
das Konzentrationslager Sachsenhausen angeordnet.

Im Auftrage des SS-Brigadeführers und Generalmajors der
Polizei bitte ich, St. festnehmen und mit dem nächsten Sammel-
transport in das KL.Sachsenhausen überstellen zu lassen.

Über den Vollzug bitte ich unter Vorlage der dortigen
Schutzhaftakte alobald zu berichten.

I.V.

Gestapo order to arrest the author's father,
Benno Strauss, and to transfer him to the
concentration camp at Sachsenhausen. In actual
fact, he had already been transferred to the
Warsaw Ghetto. Inset: this photo, mailed from
Warsaw to his wife, is the last memento of
Benno Strauss.

Above: Lotte and Herbert Strauss, 1960s. Below: their son-in-law and daughter, Robert E. Jones and Jane Helen Jones.

lum. The actual number of *refoulés* (those returned) was probably considerably higher than those registered by the police, not counting those who despaired of reaching safety or were turned back by Swiss consulates abroad or at the borders without ever appearing in police reports. Ilse Totzke and Ruth Basinski fell victims precisely to a turn in *Asylpolitik* (rules governing asylum) that belied the well-established Swiss policy of liberality, while humanitarian activists in politics, churches, the trade unions, and the Jewish community had erupted in protest and public opinion began to return to its senses. Such currents, of course, ran parallel to opinion and policies in other countries in the 1930s and in wartime. As in other free democracies, decency and common sense prevailed in the end, but too late for victims like Ruth and Ilse whose lives would have been saved.

Thus, when the Schönebergs and Jean Friedrich began to plan Lotte's escape, they had to minimize the risk of Lotte's being sent back. Once again, coincidence created opportunities. The Schönebergs found an émigré physician, Dr. Nathan Wolff, who was practicing medicine in Stein-am-Rhein, the picturesque border town. One of his women patients had married a German citizen, Josef Höfler, who lived in a village across the river on German territory. He worked for the largest factory in the area, Fahr Agricultural Machines Manufacture. The Höflers were practicing Christians; their first child, a daughter, was born in 1938. Dr. Wolff persuaded Josef Höfler to guide Lotte across the way.

Meanwhile, Jean Friedrich had made contact with a German woman living in Berlin, Luise Meier. She knew three Jewish women who waded to freedom in Switzerland across a shallow spot at the end of the western part of Lake Constance (Bodensee). One of these women was a former secretary of Ludwig Schöneberg's—Mrs. Franken—another of those unlikely coincidences. They approached Jean Friedrich through the Schönebergs in Lausanne with the request that their identity papers be turned over to Luise Meier in Berlin for use by other fugitives. Informed of Lotte's hope of crossing into Switzerland, she declared herself ready to accompany her to the border, to Lotte's enormous relief.

Then, a date was agreed upon with the helper and his assistant: May 1, 1943. They would meet at the corner of the post office in the district town of Singen at 5:00 P.M. Friedrich took a picture of

Lotte and passed it on to Dr. Wolff, who would hand it to the two helpers to identify Lotte.

At her last meeting with Friedrich in Berlin, Lotte was told that the two young men who would serve as her guides had agreed to do so on condition that they would not have to take me across the border and that they would not meet with anyone but Lotte. Their agreement with Dr. Wolff included Lotte only. Anything else they considered far too risky. In the first place I would not be able to pass through all the controls between Berlin and the border, this being the new "total war" Goebbels had proclaimed in February 1943, and they would not be able to get me across, because any young man of military age would be stopped. I was present at this last meeting with Friedrich in his office at Ballenstetter Strasse and heard Lotte say that in this case she would refuse their offer. As she explained later, she felt deep, nagging guilt about spoiling my chances of being spared deportation because she had enmeshed me in the turbulent events of October 24–25.

Guilt, of course, knows no reason. Only an incident like this would ever have propelled me into action and forced me to take the risks that would save me from my misplaced confidence in my ability to survive an extremity I was able to imagine only from past experience. A rabbinical student who had studied at the Hochschule and had worked for the Jüdische Gemeinde was close to the top of the Nazis' hate list, no matter who his mother might have been. My mother, of course, had been impulsive and irrational in her angst back in November. I joined Jean Friedrich in persuading Lotte to leave and lived through a half-hour of heartbreak and melancholy I thought I had been inured to by the losses and good-byes that had become my life. It might well have been the final separation. No brave "women and children first" thoughts, shades of adolescent readings, could repress the admission that we were in mortal danger whatever we did. True, she left under the best plan we would ever find. True, I had the sleepwalker's confidence in my luck and ability: I "knew" I would be getting through as well. In the end she had to yield to the argument that her going now increased my own chances of survival. Instead of sitting in Berlin, she would throw herself fully into the task of getting me out.

I saw Lotte and Luise Meier off at Berlin Anhalter Railroad Station in the evening of April 30, 1943. I believe it was a Friday. The day seemed well chosen: May 1 was the Nazi "Day of National Labor," the date replacing socialist May Day celebrations, and trains would be severely overcrowded, even if rolling stock had not been cut by war shortages. Nobody asked for identity papers right up to the border. The last part of the journey they were invited to travel in the train conductor's service compartment with some other passengers. Luise Meier held out the promise that she would see to it that I would follow soon, and said she would burn a candle and pray for our success.

Luise Meier has left a description of her involvement in this underground "railway."[2] She recalled assisting twenty-eight Jewish victims to reach the border and cross it with Josef Höfler's help. In a German-language interview conducted for the Wiener Library, London, in November 1955, she dated her initial contact with persecuted Jews in Berlin to a boardinghouse apartment directed by a Jewish woman for Jews waiting to emigrate and located in her own apartment building in Berlin-Grunewald. Her husband, a civil servant who had died earlier, had been transferred from Cologne to Berlin in 1936, two of her sons served in the SS and were ultimately killed in action, and a third son became a British prisoner of war. Several Jewish women living in this "pension" had fled to Switzerland across a shallow spot in the Rhine River near Lake Constance. Luise Meier on her own initiative had traced the "railway" chain to "helpers" living close to the Swiss border, as local guides across the border. A transcript of her interview states:

> A few weeks following the successful escape of Mrs. Franken, a delegate of the Geneva Red Cross visited me and gave me . . . identity papers sent to me by Mrs. Franken to serve other refugees in similar circumstances. . . . Mrs. Franken hoped, he told me, that I would accompany a young woman to Singen [a town at the Swiss border] who should be helped to enter Switzerland. Her parents had already died [*umgekommen*]; her uncle, a Jew who had emigrated to Argentina, had employed Mrs. Franken as his secretary in Berlin. . . . Jean Friedrich—the name of the delegate—later reimbursed me for the expenses I incurred for this trip to the border. The lady later married

---

[2] Luise Meier, "Assistance to Jews Escaping from Germany," a report based on the transcript of a German-language interview conducted by Ruth Koerner in November 1955, Wiener Library, III, f. 6 (the transcript is in the Library Archives, in London or Jerusalem).

Mr. Herbert Strauss, whom Mr. Höfler also brought to Switzerland, along with another young man, without my help. Höfler and Strauss met each other in my house, but that was the extent of my participation.

I now got in touch with the lady. We traveled to Singen, and I accompanied her through the turnstile at the railroad station, left her on the square in front of the station, and returned to the train platform to take the next train for Berlin. From the platform I kept an eye on the turnstile and saw the young woman suddenly standing at it, her face white as chalk. Shaking all over, she said to me when I went to her that all was lost now, a young man had approached her on the square; all she wanted now was to return with me to Berlin. To me, this appeared dangerous, because it would be noticed. I asked her to accompany me to the square and show me the young man. . . . I asked him why he had approached the lady. After some hemming and hawing, he said that it had been in order, that he had been waiting for this lady, there could have been no mistake, he had a photograph of her. Asked to show it to me, he claimed not to have it on him but offered to fetch it from a friend of his who, he stressed, "had come over from Switzerland." All this convinced me that this young man was one of the helpers and I told my companion to trust him, and we went on our way in the direction of Gottmadingen, the last small [German] hamlet before the border. On our way, the young man asked me to turn back to Singen, for safety's sake. I should wait there until he let me know how the matter had turned out. Lotte would stay overnight in Josef Höfler's house. At noon the next day, he came and reported that the crossing had been accomplished successfully. In this way I made the acquaintance of Josef Höfler quite by coincidence. Höfler, assisted by other Germans, in part by himself, had helped numerous people to take flight. By himself, he brought sixteen people across the Swiss border.

When Luise Meier made this deposition for a German interviewer, Ruth Koerner, in 1955, she had been through harrowing experiences. The Gestapo had arrested her in mid-1944, shifting her from prison to prison in Singen and environs. She believed afterward that the court calendar was too crowded at the time with trials of the conspirators of July 20, 1944, to leave room for her minor case. During her absence, she lost all her belongings through confiscation and theft by Gestapo, police, or civilians. She met Josef Höfler and one of his helpers in 1945 after being set free by Moroccan units who had conquered that area of southwest Germany. They were caught after a woman they had tried to help behaved recklessly and gave them away in a police interrogation. The interview also speaks of problems she herself had been having with the behavior of other people she had been helping. Some, she claimed, arrived with several suitcases or provoked police attention by failing to camouflage their appearance, behavior, or language, used local commuter trains in tourist clothing, or failed to obey instructions she or Josef Höfler had given. Several conflicts centered in money and property. Gestapo and postwar German opinion defamed persons who helped Jews if or when they suspected them of having been reimbursed for expenses or more. Such aspersions expressed hostility for the standing of these good samaritans—as if there had not been easier and safer ways of earning money, and as if money could tip the balance against a human life saved.

For some reason, I cannot call up in my mind what Josef Höfler and Luise Meier looked like, but I retain gratitude and respect for them and their work. Yizchak Schwersenz, who led a Jewish boy scout troop in Berlin and chaperoned their escape when they were forced underground, probably had it right, in line with Ludwig Schöneberg's experiences and my observations: Luise had been a believing Westphalian Catholic atoning for the burden her family had placed on her conscience. Höfler may have been part of a larger group of frontiersmen engaged in trading or trafficking across the border, and expected to be paid for his labor.[3] Can you balance their "unlawful" acts against the law-and-order middle and upper classes who had heaved the Nazis into power and been paid in exchange with careers, profits, and promotions? Lotte made the Höflers promise to help me across, too. To paraphrase: Whoever destroys a life destroys a world. Whoever saves a life preserves a world.

And their enterprise had, in fact, entailed considerable risks.

That Sunday morning in May 1943 the Höflers and their helper and his wife intended to place Lotte on a road or path where she

---

[3] Yitzchak Schwersenz, *Makhteret Halutzim be-Germania ha-nazit* (Eyn Charod: Hakibutz Hame'uchad Publishing House, 1965). An abridged German edition: *Jüdische Jugend im Untergrund: Eine zionistische Gruppe in Deutschland während des zweiten Weltkriegs* (Tel Aviv: Verlag Bitaon, 1965; 2nd ed., 1992), originally appeared in the *Bulletin of the Leo Baeck Institute*.

would not be stopped too close to the border and be returned to Germany forthwith. They set out as if on a Sunday walk. Lotte wore a gay straw hat decorated with primulas that disguised her cosmopolitan hair cut and dark color, and wore her old coat, the one she had saved in Berlin. Unexpectedly, the party met two German customs police officials who stepped into the road from under the trees and requested identification. The men walking in front complied without difficulties. The police did not bother with the women: workers' wives, a child, and a friend who passed by with a customary "Heil Hitler." Deeper in the forest Lotte left them and entered a path they expected to be relatively unsupervised by Swiss officials, but they had miscalculated. A Swiss border guard soon stopped her and took her to his post. Lotte explained her situation to him, he telephoned the cantonal police station nearby. An officer took her into custody, asked about her history, wrote a protocol, and invited her to take the customary *café complêt* (a solid snack, with croissants or rolls, butter, jam, and café au lait) with him and his wife, apparently not considering her enough of a danger to Swiss law and order to lock her up in the single-cell jail, as per regulations. Obviously, by May 1943 panic had subsided enough to again perceive Jewish refugees as individual human beings in need, not a horde of not quite desirable aliens. He took Lotte by train to Schaffhausen, the cantonal capital, and deposited her in the women's section of the jail. Policeman and prisoner were observed on the train by a traveler who informed Dr. Wolff in Stein-am-Rhein. He in turn alerted Ludwig and Ilse in Lausanne and relieved their anxiety. The much-worried-over operation had gone as planned in amazing simplicity and within a few hours of one day.

After five days in Schaffhausen prison, Lotte was released and interned in the (usual) military "reception camp" (*Auffanglager*), fortunately and probably not accidentally in La Ramée, a former girls' boarding school in La Rosiaz sur Lausanne, up the hill from the Schöneberg's residence. The Schaffhausen cantonal police officer, Mr. Brütsch-Mäder, who was detailed to take her to La Rosiaz, agreed to a detour to the Schoeneberg's residence. In the train, Brütsch-Mäder used his professional cunning to interview Lotte about one of her cell mates, a local peasant woman he had taken into custody on the suspicion that she had illegally slaughtered one of her pigs and sold the meat on the black market: "I hen nur a saeuli g'schlachtet," if the transcription conveys the inimitable flavor. Lotte, in turn, told him about Berlin, which confirmed what they had learned from their interrogation in prison. While he ate breakfast at the Schönebergs, he volunteered to draw up a precise description for two escape routes through German customs, one across an arm of Lake Constance, the second over the "green frontier." He suggested a disguise as an agricultural laborer, and gave information on the farmer in whose employ I would be working, on the disposition of the German customs men, on landmarks to be guided by, on what to watch out for in the service routine of the guards, and so on. Only the intimate knowledge he had acquired over many years of service could have made his precise and thoughtful "order of battle" possible.

His proposal never reached me. I found the typewritten original taken down by Ilse Schöneberg in files Ilse passed on to me in the 1980s. He was one of the unacknowledged heroes among Swiss citizens, of whatever stripe and in whatever position, who bent their rules and acted on their humanity. We celebrated a cheerful reunion with Officer Brütsch-Mäder, retired, when we visited Schaffhausen in 1958 to acquaint daughter Jane (then twelve years old) with "our" prison.

When Lotte left Berlin, on April 30, 1943, I had already taken some steps preparing the escape to Switzerland on which Lutz and I were now focused. Ludwig's plan had been based on my proficiency as a swimmer. I held a certificate as a lifeguard from the rescue society Deutsche Lebensrettungsgesellschaft (literally, the German Lifesavers Society) which I had earned through fairly stiff tests in 1935. Ludwig and Ilse sent the somewhat utopian suggestion via Jean Friedrich that I swim the Rhine near Stein-am-Rhein where it formed the border between Germany and Switzerland. Another suggestion was to swim Lake Constance where it divided into smaller arms at its western end. They knew that several women had waded across where the lake was shallow. All this presupposed topographical knowledge, or assistance by a knowledgeable local guide. The banks were guarded by police and customs officers arranged, no doubt, in a sophisticated and tested observation system; guards patrolled on bicycle or foot and passed at regular intervals.

Lotte knew nothing of these possibilities when we had said goodbye on Anhalter Bahnhof. To my great relief, I learned only three days later that she had arrived safely and had not been sent back at the border. She also had been given a promise by her host in Gottmadingen that he would show me the way if I managed to pass through controls and met him or his associate exactly where Lotte had been expected to meet him, in front of the Singen post office across the way from the station. Höfler was told by Luise Meier that I did "not look Jewish" and would not draw attention to myself by unusual or uncontrolled behavior, a remark taking account of Nazi racism.

I was convinced at the time that without local guides an attempt to break through the police cordon watching the German borders was doomed to failure. Among the examples constantly before my eyes at the time was the fate of Anneliese Levy's parents, a Berlin gynecologist and his wife. They had tried to cross into Switzerland across mountain paths in the Alps from a vacation spot they knew intimately, and got caught.

Whatever plan I would follow, I needed identity papers, since trains, especially long-distance trains, were rigorously controlled. Police, SS, and military constabularies looked for politically wanted persons, German deserters, couriers to resistance groups from German exile parties abroad, escaped prisoners of war, or Allied fliers shot down over German territory. In 1943, Jews in flight from deportation were a new and rare occurrence, and Jews traveling in D (express) trains, second class in Germany in 1943 even rarer. (The Reichsbahn still ran third-class cars at that time.) We would be caught in somebody else's dragnet if we had no authentic-looking papers.

For at least three or four months I had moved around Berlin without any papers except an obviously fake company letter which I lost when the Gestapo almost cornered me in Leibnizstrasse 48. My first lucky break came when Ossi, who knew of my plans, came home soon afterward on some February or March late afternoon after his shift, and presented me with an authentic German *Wehrpass* (military service book), the passport-like booklet each German of military age was issued even if he did not serve. It had belonged to one of his co-workers, he said, and he needed RM 1,000 to cover his expenses. It was a matter-of-fact business transaction. Neither Ossi nor I had been captivated by the moralism with which the respectable *bourgeois*, the good German *gentilhomme*, would have viewed this probably not quite unobjectionable deal: their morality had hidden their abysmal political immorality from view. Ossi and I, from very different starting points, had arrived at similar attitudes, the proletarian super-realist and the middle-town middle-class fugitive from deportation whose probable end—being murdered—I still did not fully accept at that time. I never inquired how Ossi got this precious document.

I knew nothing of the original owner of this passport. This might have presented dangers, but Ossi proved to be as trustworthy as I expected: he would not pass on the papers of a deserter or a criminal who would land on the guillotine following a sham trial by the "jurists" of one of the People's Courts, whose judges were never brought to trial after 1945. I soon set out to practice my new signature. Age and physical characteristics did not clash too obviously with mine. The passport photo, however, needed to be replaced. At the time, the photos, about 2½ x 1½ inches in black and white, were pasted into the left upper corner of page 2 and affixed to the paper with an eye-style fastener on the upper-right and the lower-left corner of the picture. It would then be stamped on the upper-left corner by the issuing agency.

We needed the right kind of fasteners and a stapler, and a graphic artist who could duplicate the stamp. Stapling the photo to the page was easy enough: our old friend Wanda Dombrowski could not hide her mirth—nor could I—when we put to use the stapler and the round open fasteners she employed in her work: she had been a lady's fashion tailor and now made her living by sewing corsets for a lingerie store where foundations of a sturdy kind—I knew them from my mother's wardrobe—were needed to subdue sturdy ladies' flesh into the forms of the day. The stamp was affixed by a graphic artist I never met. I believe we owe the connection with him to Lutz Ehrlich and Dr. Schürholz, a Catholic resistance conduit whose home was in Wangen, near Lake Constance.

The military paper would be vital for my protection if I would be stopped by civil or military police, or by the S.D. or SS, but would be fatal as the only identification. The trust I had in my luck by traveling around Berlin for months without any identification paper would have been suicidal in long-distance travel in trains, the only means available. I knew that I would have to pass two or three such police controls in a through-train to the Swiss border. Avoiding it by taking local trains and switching frequently would probably have aroused suspicion and denunciation, one of the dangers I was quite conscious of, not only since my father was sent to prison, to camp, and to his death in response to such a denunciation in Würzburg. I looked for such a paper for quite some time. At one point, I went to lunch with one of the more unusual friends of ours, K. "Klix," and had been offered his military and civilian papers to try crossing the mountains to Switzerland. "Klix" was a romantic nationalist and expansionist on the conservative-revolutionary right, and had joined a Nazi Party intelligence unit before 1933. He became disillusioned soon after, but stayed on and played that morally untenable role of wanting to avoid the worst while hoping for the fulfillment of his foreign policy dreams. Not unlike some of the unsuccessful conservative conspirators of July 20, 1944, he had liberal opinions on every other subject and was hiding a Jewish woman disguised as his secretary all through the war. He represented the second-generation right-radical nationalist dreamers of the 1920s: his father had been a professional staff officer of bourgeois lineage, an engineer by training, which set him apart from the *Junker*-gentry kind of sentimental loyalty to the vanished monarchies and their glamorous culture.

As soon as "Klix" had offered me his papers I had turned him down, with regrets. The risk was too high, with torture and decapitation as the predictable result of being discovered. I also thought it was too high for "Klix," who had seen enough combat to appear fatalistic about the possibility of his being caught, or who may have trusted his connections with conservative nationalists or military intelligence. He was wounded at the Eastern front before we escaped Berlin, and we visited him several times in the Berlin military hospital where he was recovering.

I owe it to pure chance, and to Lotte, that I did find a source that would provide me with an authentic and near-foolproof identity card in the spring of 1943. Lotte's uncle and aunt Bildesheim had a circle of friends and acquaintances in their apartment with whom they regularly played bridge, then fashionable in Berlin society. Lotte, at some point before the war, had been helping them with refreshments while their household aide was on vacation. Among the people she met and befriended then were a physician, Dr. Walter Blank, and a former Prussian state attorney, Dr. Rudolf Caspary.

They became good friends; Dr. Blank became the family physician. She consulted him several times, most recently for a severe bronchitis after going into hiding. Dr. Caspary promised her that he would assist her if she would find an opportunity to flee abroad. She remembered this conversation, and showed Dr. Blank the letter in which Ludwig outlined his ideas about ways across the border. Blank found it realistic enough to act. Dr. Caspary turned out to be an intelligent and educated conversationalist and a man of great compassion and spiritual reserve, well aware of the melancholy precariousness of our situation. He offered to help with a valid identity document and agreed to give me a second one for Lutz Ehrlich. A week or two later, he handed Lotte two authentic blank identity cards issued by the Armament and Procurement Authority, Heeresund Bewaffnungsamt in Berlin, Albert Speer's super production ministry. It was a singular and uniquely humane act, the turning point in our lives underground. The risks for all involved were unimaginable.

It was the ultimate good turn in our condition. Dr. Caspary never told me how and from whom he had obtained the identity cards. In the 1990s, I was able to reconstruct only bare outlines of his life from printed reference works and from documents in the Landesarchiv Berlin.[4] He was about fifty years old when I met him on two short occasions in 1943, a born Berliner and most likely the son of Eugen Caspary, a Jewish sculptor prominent at the time as one of the founder-directors of German Jewish professional social agencies. (A register of "Greater Berlin" Jews published in 1931 lists the

---

4 *Jüdisches Adressbuch für Grossberlin, Ausgabe 1931*, s. 56, NW 87, Lessingstrasse 12 (address identical with Eugen Caspary's [1853–1931], sculptor and founder-director of major Jewish welfare organizations like Zentralwohlfahrtsstelle der deutschen Juden, 1917); Thesis dr. jur. Würzburg 1921, entitled "Der Rechtsschutz der vom Arbeitnehmer in die Betriebsräume eingebrachten Sachen, zugleich ein Beitrag zur Lehre von dem Auslegungsformen des bürgerlichen Rechts"; Friedrich Karl Kaul, *Pitaval* (Berlin: Akademie Verlag, 1947[?]), pp. 19, 20, 21, 28, 29, 41 (attacks on Rudolf Caspary for his activities in the Kutisker-Barmat pretrial investigation by Soviet Occupied Zone chief prosecutor; *Handbuch des Preussischen Staates, 1931*, p. 145; Landesarchiv Berlin, Oberfinanzpräsident: Rudolf Caspary's Gestapo questionaire filled out after his arrest. Death notice in *Gedenkbuch* (see above, chap. 7, note 3), s.v. "Caspary, Rudolf" (I am grateful to the late Ludwig von Hammerstein, Berlin, for connecting me with Dipl. Pol. Klaus Mayer, who traced the basic data, and Rechtsanwalt Dr. Tillman Krach, Mainz, for drawing my attention to F. K. Kaul's pamphlet on Rudolf Caspary).

addresses for both as Lessingstrasse 12, NW 89.) He had studied law and received a doctorate from the University of Würzburg in 1921; his dissertation topic, on a labor-law problem, suggests that he may have shared his father's social concerns. (On November 22, 1994, the University Library Würzburg [Amtsrätin G. Sprenger] informed me that the dissertation copy in its files does not include the customary autobiographical sketch.) In about 1924, he gained considerable newspaper attention when he was appointed to a team of Prussian state attorneys prosecuting a politically explosive corruption case against two (Jewish) businessmen-bankers, Barmat and Kutisker, accused of bribing prominent figures of the Social Democratic Party and the Berlin city government. Lurid boulevard-press reports were skillfully exploited in the Goebbels press in the later 1920s, and turned into antisemitic and anti-left propaganda. As late as 1945–47, Caspary and his prosecutorial colleagues would be singled out in a political pamphlet issued in the Soviet Occupied Zone of Germany as "lackeys of the capitalistic system and of right-wing reaction."

Following this public concern with Dr. Caspary, the sources permit only the barest reconstruction of his professional life. The 1931 Prussian State Handbook listed him at midpoint in his judicial career as "*Amtsgerichtsrat*" (Prussian district court judge), a position he lost under Nazi laws in 1933 or 1935 with a small pension. He listed it as RM 250.00 in the questionnaire the Gestapo made him fill out in the Gestapo detention center, Grosse Hamburger Strasse, in January 1944. They had arrested him on September 30, 1943, and they deported him and thirty-one other prisoners with the "50th Osttranport" to Auschwitz. The files of the German Federal Archives list him as "*verschollen*" (presumed dead). I did not find anything else about him or his family, but would assume that the virulent hostility from the political left he earned for his judicial work would not have been conducive to a socialist orientation that might have influenced his interest in labor law. I hope he found some satisfaction from our successful escape in May–June about which he must have heard before they caught him in September.

I also never met the person from whom Rudolf Caspary received our identity blanks. I learned in the spring of 1993 that he probably was Werner Keller, a German writer, whose book *The Bible as History* (*Und die Bibel hat doch recht*) I read in the 1950s in New York after it had become an international bestseller translated into several languages. I do not remember clearly who told me his name. His Oxford and Düsseldorf publishers referred me to his daughter, Dr. Christiane Balogh-Keller, a Berlin gynecologist. She had given his papers to an associate of the Stauffenberg-Gedenkstätte (the Stauffenberg Memorial Authority), Dr. Norbert Haase, who attended a seminar with me at the Zentrum für Antisemitismus-forschung in the 1980s.[5] In the summer of 1994, Lotte and I met Dr. Balogh-Keller for several personal talks, and I went to see Dr. Haase in his office. He and a group of young German scholars had published several books and articles on the harsh and abusive military justice meted out by Nazi military courts under Hitler's directive Hitler never forgot that the revolution of 1918 had started

---

[5] The Stauffenberg Memorial Authority aims at preserving the memory of the men and women who resisted Nazism and the Third Reich, often losing their lives while fighting Hitler's evil government. The authority is located in the former headquarters of the Germany army supreme command in Berlin's Bendler Strasse where military leaders and leading civil servants had planned to assassinate Hitler and bring World War II to a conclusion in the latter years of the war. When their coup d'état failed on July 20, 1944, the Nazi military and judicial machines retaliated with barbaric vengeance against the conspirators led by Colonel Claus von Stauffenberg. They executed Stauffenberg and five other leading general staff officers immediately in the courtyard of these headquarters, and subsequently sentenced 200 officers and civilians to death in rigged "people's courts" and executed them in a Berlin prison (Plotzensee). Many were strung up on piano wires and choked to death while exposing their private parts. Another 7,000 persons were incarcerated because they were related to the *Sippe* (extended families) of the men accused of sharing in the conspiracy. After the war, annual memorial meetings, exhibitions, archives and information efforts helped to give these headquarters symbolic significance as exemplars of the courageous if futile dissent unto death of anti-Nazi Germans of all political persuasion or religious affiliation.

The Zentrum für Antisemitismusforschung was established as a graduate research and teaching institute at the Technical University of Berlin in the late 1970s. In 1982 I was appointed as its "founder-director" to assemble an interdisciplinary team of historians, sociologists, literary scholars, and political scientists and to develop its program of teaching, research, publications, and international conferences. When I left Berlin once more for New York in 1990 under very different circumstances from those in 1943, faculty and students not only had placed the study of antisemitism on the map of respectable academic subjects in Germany but had contributed innovative work to related fields such as the social and psychological theory of prejudice, antisemitism in German (and comparative) literature, the emigration and resettlement of refugees during the Nazi period, the transfer of scholarship through emigration, and the study of acculturation among Jewish immigrants from Central Europe. I plan to reflect on the first ten years of this Zentrum in a subsequent volume of this biography.

with a "mutiny" of sailors in Kiel and was carried through by soldiers and workers.[6] Werner Keller had been enmeshed in the web of the Gestapo which had turned him over to military courts. Dr. Haase gave me free use of the relevant documentation in the Stauffenberg Memorial Authority files and kindly handed me a copy of a short biographical summary he had prepared (for the occasion?) on Dr. Keller.

For me, and maybe for Christiane Keller, our encounters carried a special poignancy. Fourteen years after her father's death, Lotte and I were flesh-and-blood evidence of what she had known only in general terms from her father's papers. He never shared his memories with his children. Dr. Norbert Haase, who had known me previously only in the classroom, worked to bring to light a somber chapter of the Third Reich's use of the military courts endeavoring to stamp out all dissent and protest in the armed forces, all individual acts of resistance to military orders and discipline through an utterly cruel and murderous application of the law. Werner Keller fully expected to be murdered or executed before the Allies arrived at his prison.[7]

It was one of those encouraging moments that encircled the eight years I spent in Berlin in the 1980s: I was encountering another member of a growing group of German scholars, by no means all as young as Norbert, who were at one with us in not flinching in the face of the inhumanity spilling over into postwar respectability from the universal taint of the Third Reich in important segments of a society struggling back to sanity.

The history of Werner Keller (born 1909) was that of a young German in whose character personal integrity and public service for the Third Reich kept clashing, at first uneasily, ultimately to the brink of his destruction.[8] He had been a youth leader in the

---

[6] Norbert Haase, *Das Reichskriegsgericht und der Widerstand gegen die nationalsozialistische Herrschaft* (Berlin: Gedenkstätte deutscher Widerstand, 1993). Norbert Haase and Brigitte Oleschinski, *Das Torgau Tabu: Wehrmachtstrafsystem, NKWD Speciallager, DDR Strafvollzug* (Leipzig: Forum Verlag, 1993); Norbert Haase, "Aus der Praxis des Reichskriegsgerichts," *Vierteljahrshefte für Zeitgeschichte*, 39 (1931), 379ff.

[7] The following is based on Werner Keller's papers in the Archives of the Stauffenberg-Gedenkstätte Berlin and on Dr. Norbert Haase's biographical sketch.

[8] Dietrich Güstrow (that is, Dietrich Wilde), *Tödlicher Alltag: Strafverteidiger im Dritten Reich* (Munich: Deutscher Taschenbuchverlag, 1984), p. 209.

conservative and nationally oriented *Ringpfadfinder* (boy scouts) (Haase) which, I conclude from my own youth-movement experience without being able to document it, may have shaped his personal and public values for life. Precise information on their history is hard to come by. One of their leaders, it seems, Hans Fritzsche, had refused to amalgamate his groups with Hitler's youth organization: he was sentenced to three years of hard labor in 1940, and died two years later. Werner Keller studied law but dropped out of a promising career in 1937 during the last stages of post-graduate studies (the *Referendariate*, qualifying for the German equivalent of the bar). He had been "advised" by the president of the Berlin court he worked for, the Kammergericht, to join the Nazi Party, and did so in 1933. In 1939, he canceled his membership in protest against the pogroms of November 1938. Similar motives also had moved him to abandon his career in a law system corrupted by Nazi brutality and interference. Still, short of total withdrawal or emigration, his professional life after the law enmeshed him again in the state's business: he was drafted for military service in 1939 and attached to Supreme Command headquarters as a communications specialist; he took up journalism and writing, possibly as most distant from Nazism. Such army services as public relations, war reporting, or censorship were considered nonpolitical escapes by many intellectuals and dissenters during the war. The Luftwaffe Ministry gave him major responsibilities for publicity on airplane production and procurement, and decorated him for going on flying missions in several combat zones. An affidavit in his papers asserts that witnessing the destruction of Coventry in 1940 shocked him into a deepening moral conflict about the meaninglessness of war. In October 1943, he was transferred to the Armaments and War Production Ministry, headed by Albert Speer, and assigned significant responsibilities for public relations, technical publications, liaison with airplane production centers, and so forth. The documents Dr. Haase collected from his various sources, if I read them correctly, do not reveal when Werner Keller began to project the internal Protestant dialogue between his private moral conscience and his service for the Nazi war machine—even if that involved only words and plans—into moral action, resistance through compassionate acts and personal risks for the victims. In 1940, he married a nineteen-year-old woman, the daughter of a Berlin patent lawyer. She shared

Werner Keller's attitudes and reinforced his strong sympathies for the United States: a five-week exchange study at a Cleveland, Ohio, high school under the "Carl Schurz Exchange Program" had anchored her anti-Nazism and her enthusiasm for American popular culture in a cherished experience.

At first Werner Keller helped individuals persecuted for political reasons or hiding from Nazi deportation: Keller's social circle included many Berlin Jews. He may have known Rudolf Caspary from his service at the same Berlin Court, Kammergericht, that had employed Caspary as an *Amtsgerichtsrat*. He hid Jews in his apartment and helped to direct them to the "underground railway" operated by the Swedish or other Scandinavian churches in Berlin. And he supplied authentic identity cards of the Speer Ministry to an apparently larger number of enemies of the regime, political persecutees, Jews, draft evaders, fugitives from the Gestapo, among them Hans Hirschel and the circle assisted by Maria von Malzan, Hirschel's later wife. His papers date the escalation of his resistance activities into the end of 1943, when he "saw clearly that further meaningless sacrifice of men and materiél could be stopped only if Hitler and his hangers-on could be removed" (paraphrase of affidavit, October 20, 1947, Haase biography). Since several groups of ministerial civil servants and high Nazi Party functionaries pursued peace initiatives with Western allies or with Moscow in open conflict with Hitler's death-wish for the German people, Werner Keller's place in these schemes during the last year or years of the war, if any, is hard to establish in the face of his self-imposed silence about his activities. With anti-Nazi friends and fellow officers, he drew up several plans to assassinate Hitler and Himmler, some as late as November 1944. In Berlin, he became the center of oppositionists of varied backgrounds. He also made contact with parallel groups. Keller's goal was to persuade Allied (U.S.) policy makers to cooperate with German resistance groups and join in a common defense against the threatening Russian conquest of Central Europe.[9] Keller identified these peace feelers and his far-reaching activities for opponents and victims of the regime as *"Amerika-Bewegung"* (Movement America) and moved to a new level of resistance to achieve these goals: they printed leaflets and operated two short-wave transmitters for con-

---

[9] See Norbert Haase's biographical sketch.

tacts with U.S. units. In the end, Keller was denounced to the Gestapo by several of the ubiquitous informers: household aides, neighbors, the landlady. His radio transmissions were located by an SS radio-detection car. They bored small holes through one of his walls and tapped his emissions, and the cleaning woman found paper shreds of his broadcast manuscripts in his wastepaper basket and turned them over "to the authorities." Finally they arrested him on February 1 or 2, 1945. An attempt to escape was foiled by bystanders on a subway platform in Berlin. Walter Reichert, who had constructed the transmitters, was arrested at the same time in his workplace and shot by the Gestapo when he tried to escape in the Siemens factory in Berlin-Spandau. Werner Keller survived considerable mental and physical suffering in the central prison for military personnel in Torgau (Elbe). He was liberated by American troops reaching the Elbe River and joining up with Russian forces advancing from the East, or he may have taken advantage of the confusion within the prison when the Allies approached and escaped, walking in the direction of the Americans. It would seem logical, because he expected a mass slaughter of prisoners before the liberation.

For reasons not entirely clear, Werner Keller was not executed outright by the Gestapo but turned over to the military courts who had formal jurisdiction over military defendants. According to one published account from a somewhat self-serving source, a Third Reich establishment lawyer telling his side of the story,[10] Keller's trial and the mandatory death sentence could be entangled long enough in procedural wrangles until mooted by the end of the war.

It was apparently not his helping *me* with identity papers that brought about his arrest and near-destruction in the torture and execution prison run by the military court system. I regretted that I had not known the identity of my benefactor, and had begun searching for sources only ten years after he had died. He might have been willing to answer my questions born of gratitude, not curiosity. Had his humanitarian very-youth-movement impulses, in fact, matured into public action only when defeat began to drive home the meaninglessness of further sacrifice in 1943? Did he have contact with conservative politicians whose unrealistic perception

---

[10] See Güstrow's *Tödlicher Alltag* (see note 8, above).

of Allied policy he seemed to have shared? Did he actually have contact with American agencies in the military or the O.S.S.? Were his activities financed from his own private resources? Did he owe his survival to intra-government protection in high places against SS and Gestapo murder squads? Why did he state in an affidavit in 1947 that he would "not entrust the specifics of his activities and of the goals of his resistance work to paper . . . lest . . . unauthorized third parties [NKVD?] . . . gain access to them. . . . By the way I did everything in my power to mitigate the harsh Nazi crimes by helping Jews, and by frustrating attempts to send children into combat"? Does this defensive posture point to more than his tedium—I have long shared such feelings—with busybodies raiding the curiosity shops of contemporary history? Keller's resistance work, his lifesaving work for many, may have been taboo for German establishment historians, constructing a tradition for the new Federal Republic of Germany. We will remember him and our other helpers, of whatever religion, as towers of integrity and encouragement in a hellish world.[11]

At the time, of course, the peculiar twists of fate that made me a beneficiary of Werner Keller's largesse—in fact, his very existence—disappeared behind the naturally self-absorbed singlemindedness that concentrated energies on the goal of survival. Even if it had been a matter of protecting Keller's security and thus rational not to know who Caspary and Keller were, Caspary's murder silenced the one voice that might have let me know. I trust, though, that Rudolf Caspary had learned of our successful escape and shared the good news with Werner Keller.

Once I had been given the blank, turning it into a foolproof identity card was almost routine. My new name had to be the one entered on Ossi's military pass. The signature was being practiced. Once again, Wanda's corset stapler was put to use for the passport photo, and the authentic stamp affixed by the (unknown) expert. To top the deception, Lutz expected to receive military travel or-

---

[11] The illustrated edition of Werner Keller's *Und die Bibel hat doch recht* (Düsseldorf: Econ Verlag, 1989) that we received from Dr. Christiane Balogh-Keller in July 1994 bears the following dedication: "In celebration [*Erinnerung*] of the unusual meeting I had with you, Lotte and Herbert Strauss, I wish you much joy with this third illustrated edition of my father's book. Yours, Christiane Balogh-Keller. Berlin, July 2, 1994."

ders—a *Marschbefehl*—directing the bearer to inspect a heavy agricultural equipment factory near the Swiss border. It would be typed on authentic stationery of the Supreme Command of the Armed Forces—Oberkommando der Wehrmacht. The cover story as to where the stationery had come from—Lutz Ehrlich pretended to have taken it from the Supreme Army Headquarters building in Berlin—was unbelievable. I presumed that Dr. Schürholz, a Catholic lawyer said to be active in Catholic resistance groups near Singen, at the Swiss border, had written the letter for us and supplied the stationery from his own resources.

To assemble this set of documents had taken some weeks, maybe months. I received the military passport in March 1943. Dr. Schürholz took the initiative of helping with the travel orders at about the same time, after he heard of our plans to escape across the border and judged them realistic. In May, after Lotte had left, I met Höfler, the border guide, in Mrs. Meier's Berlin apartment to agree on the time and place of meeting him in Singen. Beyond this I was entirely on my own, presumably because everybody considered the risks for a young man or men of getting caught much higher than for women, and took cover.

A letter written soon after my arrival in Switzerland describes the fragility of survival and the complex landscape of sympathy and friendship that carried me through these last weeks:

> Mrs. Pauselius reported that the entire building at Schulenburgring 5 had begun to speculate murkily who I might be. The funniest version was that they thought me an illegitimate son of Felicia's whom she had taken in again after having banned him from her presence. . . . She and I had developed a rare and precious feeling for each other. Our farewell dinner five days before I left Berlin [June 1943] turned into an exquisite feast of conversation—and then she, the sixty (?)-year-old woman[12] saw me, the mere youngster, to the subway station, remained on the platform, and kept waving until the train had disappeared.
>
> The next two nights I spent with Dr. Steinitz's family—they never failed if they were needed. Then a week in Friedeberg's small house, the husband being kept ignorant of the arrangement.[13] The last week

---

[12] Felicia Pauselius was probably ten to fifteen years younger than I had thought at the time.

[13] I retain no recollection of this family.

with Strindbergs was filled with tensions between Friedrich and Utje.
. . . When the week was over, I moved in with Wanda, who was
sincerely glad to see me. She was convinced that I belonged to the
"charmed ones" and would come through, and when a minor error
of hers in giving me her house and apartment keys almost led to a
catastrophe—"*Abholers*" entered the house and took a neighbor, Mrs.
Kanarek, to the deportation center—she saw herself in her imagination crossing the Swiss border with me to freedom. . . . We continued
to make light of the situation and of our relationship, celebrated my
birthday together, and went out to reasonably good restaurants to
avoid cooking.

The nights from Monday to Tuesday I spent regularly at Ossi's.
We had a hearty men's-style meal, listened to the BBC, and discussed
the state of affairs, *die Weltlage*. The first time I returned to Wanda
from being with Ossi, I found her unconscious on the floor of the
Berliner Zimmer in a deep faint. I carried her to her bed and applied
vinegar compresses, she came to, but then slept for nearly 24 hours,
complaining intermittently of strong headaches—she had probably
hit her head—a solid Hessian peasant skull—against a chair. . . . Two
evenings later Lutz had procured tickets for Shaw's *Saint Joan* [*Hei-
lige Johanna* in translation], with Käthe Gold moving and superior as
Joan.

A new crisis appeared at this time when Willie turned up and reported that three battalions of Bavarian Riflemen had been ordered
to the Swiss border: sixty British officers had escaped from their
POW camp near Nuremberg and were expected to head for the
nearest—the Swiss—border.[14] I was ready to heed this omen, but
Wanda, to my surprise, urged me to go through with the plan. The
next day Dr. Caspary was told by his contacts in the Security Service
(SD) that the officers had moved north, and that the border rein-
forcements had been recalled to barracks. Had they remained, it
would have been nearly impossible to reach the Swiss border across
the no-man's-land.

News about our friends are pretty bad. The Flatow couple has
only money for four more months and will be evicted by the land-
lord, who as yet knows nothing about their being Jews in hiding. . . .
I tried to pass on all our connections to them. . . . August [Sapandow-
ski] is in jail; his companion Else was arrested on the street. . . . Georg
Israel [a classmate and friend of Ehrlich's] has been sentenced to one

---

[14] Willie Jankowiak, then a courier with the German Foreign Office, was in close
contact with Ludwig Schöneberg, for whose company he had worked before 1933.

year at hard labor because he had picked up a few candies from the floor of his (candy?) factory. Father Israel, a lawyer, kept him from going underground because he believed in the German judicial system!! [Georg] will end up in a concentration camp. Even Caspary's connections failed to effect his release. I felt great pity for his mother and visited them; they bore up under this calamity with outward calm ["*mit Fassung, aber es ist unfasslich*"]. Georg's school friends meanwhile are leading comfortable lives with their girlfriends, going to theater and movie performances and thinking that trying to reach Switzerland was a form of suicide . . . [July 24, 1943] [author's translation].

The date for crossing the border was set for June 13. Lutz and I agreed that I would leave Berlin a day early with the evening express (D) Train to Stuttgart, and telephone him after my arrival to let him know of possible problems I encountered on the way. Before I boarded the train at Anhalter Bahnhof as Lotte had, Lutz gave me a folded, letter-size paper: "Put this in your pocket; these are your marching orders." Without looking at it I placed it in the breast pocket of my jacket.

The train to Stuttgart was quite crowded, but I had a reserved seat—courtesy of Luise Meier's janitor, who had "connections with" the Deutsche Reichsbahn. I carried nothing but a briefcase, the obligatory status symbol of the German professional at the time. It contained a book of drawings by the nineteenth-century German painter Adolf Menzel (1815–1905), whom I knew Lotte liked for the spontaneity of his stroke and gift of observation. The Swiss cantonal police officer at the border later listed the property he took from me as RM 350.13, a briefcase containing underwear, a fountain pen, a mechanical pencil, a wristwatch, and a wallet. I don't understand why he failed to list the Menzel, which I delivered to Lotte at the first possible occasion. The protocol taken down, still at the police post of Ramsen (to which I was given access by the Swiss Federal Archives in the summer of 1993), fixes the proper dates I had forgotten later. I left Berlin on the 9th of June. The trip, like Lotte's, was timed to coincide with the peak travel time of Whitsuntide, a long holiday weekend in Germany and a traditional day for family visits, spring outings, the first outdoor picnics.

In the train, after some time, I felt restless being hemmed in by two substantial neighbors on the bench of the compartment, and went out to the corridor which, in this (old-style) type of express railroad car, was separated by a door from each compartment. I traveled second class, not wishing to risk exposure to inquisitive bigwigs in brown uniforms traveling first.

The conversation in the crowded corridor concerned the war, about whose uncertain course the group of men appeared to agree, albeit with the kind of dissimulation that had become customary in any public exchange of opinion among strangers. At one point, the conversation turned to Jews. One enlisted man in uniform announced quite loud and clear that "the Jews, in the East, we kill them all" (bringen wir alle um). He repeated it twice.[15] Nobody volunteered a comment. The talk veered off to another war-related subject. Behavior like this was absolutely standard. One noted such information in a matter-of-fact way; one kept silent and accepted things one could not change; nobody expressed or, presumably, felt a collective sense of guilt. I did not think the footslogger felt that he said anything sensational. I am of the opinion that Germans in mid-1943 or earlier "knew" about the Holocaust as a fact, if not in all its murderous detail, but "knowing" was part of many other things one "knew," took cognizance of, in an abstract detached way, a universe that had no relationship to one's life or well-being and its increasingly urgent needs.

After a while I went back to my compartment and fell asleep, tired out by the events, the heat, the overcrowded compartment. I woke up only when the compartment door was opened with a bang "Your papers please, Geheime Staatspolizei." I reached for my Speer Ministry paper, and held it out when my turn came; the policeman, in civies, returned it with a salute, finished his round, and closed the door. Nobody was asked a question, it seemed routine, and I had fallen in with it. After a while, when it was safe, I did

---

[15] On July 17, 1943, I included in a report a Swiss journalist had requested of me for transmission to Swiss and Allied intelligence agencies: "A Bavarian soldier told me in the train [to the border] that 'the Gestapo was now killing the Jews in all larger towns as they had done previously in Warsaw. . . . All Jews. We are forced to do this or else they would murder us.' This soldier belonged to a mountain unit, came from the Kuban salient, a member of the Heeresgruppe List; he traveled to Greece; I trust that he did not see any Jew there." (I knew nothing then of the destruction of Greek Jewry in the Holocaust and the cooperation of German and Austrian army personnel [Waldheim affair] in their war crime.)

yield once again to my need for some fresh air on the corridor, still crowded with standing-room-only passengers.

After I arrived uneventfully in Stuttgart on the morning of the 10th, I first phoned Lutz in Berlin and conveyed the facts in veiled allusions. Then I turned to a Stuttgart policeman who stood guard somewhere in the station, and asked for his help in finding a good middle-class but not too expensive hotel, I was traveling on official business ("*eine Dienstreise*"). He responded quite positively, probably bored stiff by having to stand around the station in the morning, and I put up in the hotel and went to sleep. On the 11th, in the morning, with the same train, Lutz Ehrlich arrived, and I met him as planned. With his first words, he asked, with some urgency, whether I had used my travel orders. "No," I said; "I had forgotten all about them," and reached into my breast pocket where the paper had remained since Lutz had handed it to me in Anhalter Bahnhof two days earlier. "I gave you the paper with my false name instead of yours." We were buoyed by our success so far. I experienced a physical high, like a boy clearing the first hurdle on a dangerous course.

One June 12, Whitsuntide Saturday, we took a local train from Stuttgart to Singen. It also was quite crowded, and we had to stand. After a while, a police officer and an SS man carrying a carbine at the ready entered the (large) compartment one found in local trains, and asked for our papers. I gave him mine, and quickly got quite panicky. He looked at it far too long, so it seemed to me, and asked about my destination. I identified it as the Fahr Agricultural Machine Works in Gottmadingen, as we had planned, and then pointed to Lutz and said, "There, by the way, is my *Regierungs-rat*"—I had assumed a preposterously high civil service rank which even then, with young Nazis jumping the career ladder against seniority, might have been unusual and could have aroused suspicion. To my relief, the ploy worked. The officer was convinced by two identical identity card-forms, and did not notice that a man of my (assumed) standing would never have identified himself by pointing to an inferior. They left with the proper salutation, which I returned, and our fellow travelers kept whatever they may have noticed to themselves. They were all on their way to or from work on the Saturday before the holiday.

The train arrived at Singen station, and we had to pass through a gate in an iron fence to leave the platform. There was a customs man on duty, but he was distracted by a boy pushing his bicycle whom he wanted to check, probably for food acquired without stamps or in excess amounts. I slipped by, Lutz with me, and across the street we saw a man with a bicycle waiting before the post office. It turned out to be Höfler. He moved ahead, and we followed him. When we reached a wooded area, he turned off and guided us to a steep, overgrown knoll in the woods. It overlooked a street, some fields planted with grain, and a triangle of dense forest, a few hundred meters across, that jutted into the field. Höfler warned us about the road: it was traveled in close intervals by custom guards on bicycles. They had orders to guard the border more closely, because, a few days earlier, some Royal Air Force officers interned in an *Oflag* (prisoner-of-war officers' camp) had finished digging a tunnel and managed to escape. They would try to reach the Swiss border, the only international border close to southern Germany. Obviously, his information was dated. Thus, we had to cross between patrols, traverse the fields, and reach the forest triangle. He warned us that the street and the fields were under field-glass observation from the fixed posts that dotted the border a few hundred meters apart. We thanked him, gave him all our valuable false papers for use by other fugitives like us, and he departed with good wishes. We in turn had to wait until it got dark enough to risk the breakout. We had used all our remaining meat ration coupons to buy cold cuts and rolls, and had a solid meal. We felt awed enough for gallows humor.

The night turned out to be only half-friendly. Fast-flying clouds passed before a nearly full moon but never long enough to cover its light. Between 10:00 and 11:00 we started to move down, crossed the street in crouching positions, and then I hit the ground after we had entered the field, and pushed Lutz down beside me. In front against the half-light I saw something upright and immobile close to the street. We waited what seemed to me a very long time, and it still did not move. Then we ran through the field, the last distance upright to reach the trees that would be Swiss territory. We had barely entered when I saw a guard, carbine at the ready, wearing a steel helmet that was definitely not German. I embraced him. "Dies ist die Schweiz? We are fugitives from the Nazis; if you want to send us back, shoot us first" ("Koennen Sie uns doch gleich erschiessen"). It was the formula we had been instructed by Friedrich to use. It would have been more in line with the Swiss rules of the time if we had identified ourselves as "political persecutees seeking asylum to escape danger to our lives."

"So schnell schiessen die Schweizer nicht!" ("That fast the Swiss don't shoot!") came the answer in slow local tempo, cadence, and characteristic pronunciation. It was 11:30 P.M., June 12, 1943. The guard, a young man, walked us to the next customhouse; from there we were transferred to the local Kantonspolizisten (Officer Mösle) who put us into his cell. Only a few hours later, he took us by train to the cantonal prison in the city of Schaffhausen. The train left at 7:30 A.M. I am afraid we must have spoiled his Whitsuntide Sunday. I do not know who informed Ludwig, Ilse, and Lotte of our arrival. I sent my first postcard on June 17, when a prison guard, Polizei-wachtmeister Sturzenegger, was transferring us to a detention camp in the Jura, and we had to wait for a local train in Basel Station, SBB (Swiss Railroad).

We were saved! The overwhelming feeling of having been tested in this high drama and having stood the test with incredible luck against so many odds penetrated me to such an extent that for weeks I was quite unable to think critically and rationally about what had happened. I knew that my feelings for Lotte had changed. Being in love, doing many things in common, being playful, physical, vital, and mutually supportive, feeling good in each other's company, had turned into the profound wish to stay together. Now I knew that we had grown into each other, that I had reached a new seriousness, that I understood while I had been confined to the Swiss military reception camp ("*Auffanglager*")—certainly not a bad experience, or in any way oppressive in spite of its military routine—that I needed Lotte to be complete. After I was transferred from prison to the camp, I proposed to Lotte by Swiss mail, and I did not mind that the military censors in this camp would share our intimacies.

The euphoria had affected prison behavior, too—we were about fourteen days in prison, in a cell we shared with two Russian escapees from German forced labor. They had walked through half of Germany at night and had lived on what they could find or steal. It was hard to talk with them, but then the prison warden was asked if he had anything to read in the Russian language. He brought a Russian Bible. It allowed us to be present at the creation of what I romanticized as a new religious experience. They had never seen or read a Bible. I'll never forget their earnest disputations about their texts, even if we did not understand them. We were being interrogated by the police, who wanted to extract information on our lives and conditions in Berlin and possible resistance groups we had had contact with. When we were reunited in our cell, we tried to ease our boredom by singing all the arias and choral pieces we could remember from operas or operettas. I at least had no time perspective but the present, release of tensions, and shutting out the need to weigh decisions.

The loose, military discipline imposed on us by the men (and some women) who ran the military detention camp to which we were transferred after Schaffhausen prison did not faze me as, by their confessions, it did other internees. I was safe at last, free, the burden of subconscious vigilance slowly receded; everything Swiss was wonderful, the picture-postcard railroad stations, the posters, the food—the Suchard milk chocolate tasted deliciously like the one father had brought home to Edelstrasse from his Swiss business trips.

We were allowed a daily recreational walk around the village of Büsserach, a stretch of houses between hills that did not give much room to the valley. That middle-aged guards with carbines walked ahead and behind us may have disturbed some fellow internees; it did not disturb me. They were elderly reserve types from our camp contingent, and not the least bit threatening. We had straw mats and blankets, and culture was represented by a small collection of novels and art books, provenance unknown. When they made me the caretaker of the camp library, I gained a good deal of time to read, a first tentative return to continuity. All the great issues of my former life and study seemed to be wiped off the center, separated from the emotional involvement I had had with them. It was as if the old intellectual compulsions had been drained away by the adventures just behind me. I slept my usual eight to nine hours, apparently undisturbed by the tense situations I had just been through. It felt like vacations from duty during the five weeks I was detained in this military reception camp, but I have absolutely no recollection of any of my fellow refugees, and don't remember one face or the name of one guard.

The return to the bitter memory of our personal losses, the emotional labor to accept their absolute finality, the destruction of our civilization, the emotional demands made on me by the Holocaust, the radical rethinking of my perspectives on German history and civilization—all this was ahead of me. Ever since I took part in an interview study of concentration camp survivors at the New School for Social Research in New York between 1948 and 1951, I have become acquainted with the course this de-construction and re-construction takes, as the survivor copes with the demands of his new normality. This first phase was still determined by the over-whelming sense of having been freed from what lay behind me, exuberant joy, the freshness of a cool Jura morning, the sun raying between the trees reflecting the dew and the mists of night. Noth-ing was repressed in my awareness of the past, but it was made "light" by the "high" that suffused me. The difficult part would be to be *free for* the challenges to self-understanding and the breaks in continuity, the hard labor of learning to live with people who did not share the memory of ten years of growing up in a multitiered culture of persecution. I had just passed my twenty-fifth birthday.

INDEX